Betty Crocker's
GOOD AND EASY
COOKBOOK

Photography Directors:
LEN WEISS / STEPHEN MANVILLE

GOLDEN PRESS NEW YORK
WESTERN PUBLISHING COMPANY, INC.

First Printing, 1971

Library of Congress Catalog Card Number: 76-150742

To Busy Women Everywhere—

Good and easy. It's an unbeatable combination of the best of both worlds. And with this cookbook in hand, you can prepare 365 breakfasts, lunches and dinners every year, in a hurry—without skimping on quality or any of the nice little touches that make mealtime a pleasure.

Consider this latest edition of *Good and Easy* your ultra-modern shortcut to this kind of mealtime pleasure. We show you how to use the latest convenience foods in new and unusual ways; how to serve nourishing food without being ho-hum; how to plan menus that will make your family sit up and take notice. We offer ingredient substitutions to help you use what you have on hand. We suggest splendid revivals for leftovers. And for instant decision-making, we have main-meal meats at the beginning—because they're the starting point for most of your meal planning.

We hope you'll use these recipes as guides to branch out and create ideas of your own—that's part of the fun of cooking. And we'd like to think that our *Good and Easy Cookbook* will give you extra time for the many other good things in your life.

Cordially,

Betty Crocker

P.S. Each and every recipe has been tested, of course—in our Kitchens and in the kitchens of busy women across the country.

Contents

Pictured at right:

TOP

Orange-glazed Baked Ham
Skillet-glazed Sweet Potatoes
Herbed Salmon Steaks
Golden Parmesan Chicken

CENTER

Polish Sausage Boil
Country Cassoulet
Mixed Grill

BOTTOM

Meatball Stew
Breaded Veal Cutlets
Braised Short Ribs

Meats and Main Dishes

Stop! Here's where the road to good and easy mealtimes begins. You probably start thinking about the meat you're going to serve for dinner first. Right? Well, we do too. Why? Because until that decision has been made, you can't even begin to think intelligently about side dishes and desserts. And besides, you'll have a much better idea of what you can do with the rest of the food budget. It only stands to reason, then, that the main-meal meat becomes the natural starting point for your over-all menu plot, be it daily or weekly.

So choose your entree from this chapter—depending on the week's best buys, or what you have in the freezer. Then move on to the following chapters and round out the three daily meals —remembering snacktime, of course. You'll find some interesting menu clues with many of these main dish recipes. (And if you feel you need to brush up on the basics of meal planning, take our refresher course on pages 152 and 153.)

Be Choosey

Eye those meat cuts like a pro. Look for flecks of fat within the lean; it's called marbling, and it increases juiciness, flavor and tenderness. Take note of the U.S. stamp of approval, too, which tells you all is well. And where grading is concerned, remember this: U.S. Prime and Choice offer deluxe quality but the less expensive grades, if properly cooked, give you the same good nutrition.

Be bright about bargains. Ask questions about the day's best buys. If your meat retailer has a special on a new cut, go ahead and try it—for variety and for savings. When you spot a particularly good buy on roast lamb, for example, think ahead: Sunday's dinner, Tuesday's casserole. Then buy for two meals at a time and plan to combine the leftovers with speedy, easy convenience foods. Take a clue from Shepherds'

Pie (page 32). If you're not looking to "planned overs," buy in exact amounts. Meat that you don't need or won't eat is an expensive loss.

How Much Is Enough?

As a rule of thumb, figure on 3 ounces of *cooked* meat or 4 ounces of *uncooked* meat for each serving. Here are some guidelines to follow:

Meats with large bone	1 or 1½ servings per pound
Meats with medium bone (pot-roast, ham, chicken, rib roast, dressed fish)	2 or 3 servings per pound
Meats with small or no bone (ground meat, fish fillets, boneless roast)	3 or 4 servings per pound

With main dish combinations like Dried Beef Casserole (page 14), however, the meat protein is supplemented by that of other foods; so you can get by with less meat.

Storing Meat

Store fresh meat uncovered or loosely covered in the coldest part of the refrigerator. Keep the temperature as low as possible without actually freezing the meat. Plan on using fresh meats within 2 or 3 days, ground meats and variety meats within 24 hours. Cured or smoked meats can be stored 1 to 2 weeks.

Take special care with cooked meats and casseroles. Cool *quickly,* then cover or wrap tightly; they, too, go in coldest part of the refrigerator. You can speed the cooling of a main dish casserole by placing it in a pan of ice and water.

And lucky you, if you own a freezer. You can really shop and cook for the good and easy life. See pages 154-155 for specific information for freezing and thawing meats and main dishes.

Beef

TO ROAST BEEF

Select roast from those listed in chart below. Allow about ½ pound per person—less for boneless roasts, more for roasts with a bone. If desired, season with salt and pepper before, during or after roasting.

Place meat fat side up on rack in open shallow roasting pan. The rack keeps the meat out of the drippings. (In roasts such as standing rib, the ribs form a natural rack.) It is not necessary to baste.

Insert meat thermometer so tip is in center of thickest part of meat and does not touch bone or rest in fat. Do not add water. Do not cover.

Roast meat in 325° oven. (It is not necessary to preheat oven.) Roast to desired degree of doneness (see Timetable), using thermometer reading as final guide.

Roasts are easier to carve if allowed to set 15 to 20 minutes after removing from oven. Since meat continues to cook after removal from oven, if roast is to "set," it should be removed from oven when thermometer registers 5 to 10° lower than the desired doneness.

You'll find some guidelines for carving a standing rib roast on page 156.

HORSERADISH SAUCE

In chilled bowl, beat ½ cup chilled whipping cream until stiff; stir in 3 tablespoons horseradish and ½ teaspoon salt. Refrigerate until serving time.

1 cup.

TIMETABLE

Cut	Approximate Weight	Meat Thermometer Reading	Approximate Cooking Time (Minutes per Pound)
Standing Rib	6 to 8 pounds	140° (rare)	23 to 25
		160° (medium)	27 to 30
		170° (well)	32 to 35
	4 to 6 pounds	140° (rare)	26 to 32
		160° (medium)	34 to 38
		170° (well)	40 to 42
Rolled Rib	5 to 7 pounds	140° (rare)	32
		160° (medium)	38
		170° (well)	48
Delmonico (rib eye)*	4 to 6 pounds	140° (rare)	18 to 20
		160° (medium)	20 to 22
		170° (well)	22 to 24
Rolled Rump (high quality)	4 to 6 pounds	150 to 170°	25 to 30
Sirloin Tip (high quality)	3½ to 4 pounds	150 to 170°	35 to 40
Tenderloin (whole)**	4 to 6 pounds	140° (rare)	¾ to 1 hour (total)
Tenderloin (half)**	2 to 3 pounds	140° (rare)	¾ to 1 hour (total)

*Roast at 350°   **Roast at 425°

CALIFORNIA ROAST

4-pound beef rolled rump roast
1 cup orange juice
1 cup tomato juice
¼ cup salad oil
2 teaspoons salt
½ teaspoon allspice
¼ teaspoon chili powder
⅛ teaspoon instant minced garlic
  Tangy California Gravy (below)

Place meat in deep glass bowl or plastic bag. Mix remaining ingredients except Tangy California Gravy; pour on meat. Cover; refrigerate at least 4 hours, turning meat occasionally. Remove meat from marinade; reserve 2 cups of the marinade for the gravy.

Place meat fat side up on rack in open shallow roasting pan. Insert meat thermometer so tip is in center of thickest part of meat and does not rest in fat. Roast in 325° oven to desired degree of doneness, about 2 hours. (Meat thermometer should register 150° for rare, 160° for medium, 170° for well.) Place meat on warm platter; keep warm while making gravy.

8 to 10 servings.

TANGY CALIFORNIA GRAVY

Heat reserved marinade to boiling. In tightly covered jar, shake ¼ cup water, 2 tablespoons vinegar and 3 tablespoons flour; stir into hot marinade. (If you prefer a less tangy gravy, omit vinegar and shake flour with ⅓ cup water.) Heat to boiling, stirring constantly. Boil and stir 1 minute. If necessary, season with salt and pepper.

To Cook on a Rotisserie: Insert spit rod lengthwise through center of roast; secure with holding forks. Check balance by rotating spit in palms of hands. Insert meat thermometer in center of thickest part of meat, making sure it does not touch fat or spit. Set oven control to rotisserie. Cook roast until thermometer registers 5 to 10° below desired doneness, about 2 hours.

Substitutions

For rolled rump roast: 4-pound beef sirloin tip roast.

For instant garlic: 1 clove garlic, minced.

CRANBERRY-PEPPER ROAST

4-pound beef sirloin tip roast
2 tablespoons cracked pepper
3 tablespoons salad oil
2⅔ cups cranberry cocktail
  Cranberry Gravy (below)

Score meat (cut lightly in a crisscross pattern). Rub all sides but not ends with pepper. Brown meat in oil over medium heat, about 15 minutes.

Reduce heat; pour cranberry cocktail on meat. Cover tightly; simmer on top of range or in 325° oven 2½ hours or until tender. Place meat on warm platter; keep warm while making gravy.

8 servings.

CRANBERRY GRAVY

Strain hot broth; measure 3 cups and heat to boiling. In tightly covered jar, shake ¾ cup cranberry cocktail and ⅓ cup Gold Medal Flour; stir into hot liquid. Heat to boiling, stirring constantly. Boil and stir 1 minute. Season with salt.

Substitutions

For sirloin tip roast: 4-pound beef rolled rump roast.

For cranberry cocktail: 2⅔ cups water with the roast and ¾ cup water in the gravy.

POT-ROAST IN FOIL

4-pound beef chuck pot-roast
½ envelope (about 1½-ounce size)
  onion soup mix
1 can of our mushroom sauce (1 cup)

Place 30 × 18-inch piece of heavy-duty aluminum foil in baking pan, 13 × 9 × 2 inches; place meat on foil. Sprinkle soup mix on meat and spread with cream of mushroom soup. Fold foil over meat and seal securely. Cook in 450° oven 1½ hours.

Perfect menu-mates: baked potatoes, broccoli and Orange-Cauliflower Salad (page 60).

8 to 10 servings.

Substitution

For chuck pot-roast: 4-pound beef rump, top round or bottom round roast.

TO BROIL BEEF

For each serving, allow about 1 pound of any steak with a bone, about ½ pound for boneless cuts.

Diagonally slash outer edge of fat on steak at 1-inch intervals to prevent curling (do not cut into lean). Set oven control at broil and/or 550°. Place meat on rack in broiler pan so tops of ¾- to 1-inch steaks are 2 to 3 inches from heat, 1- to 2-inch steaks are 3 to 5 inches from heat. Broil until brown. The meat should be about half done (see Timetable).

If desired, season brown side with salt and pepper. (Always season after browning as salt tends to draw moisture to surface and delay browning.) Turn meat; broil until brown.

TIMETABLE

Cut	Approximate Cooking Time per Side	
	Rare	Medium
Rib, Rib Eye or Club Steak		
1 inch	8 minutes	10 minutes
1½ inches	12 minutes	15 minutes
2 inches	17 minutes	22 minutes
Sirloin, Porterhouse or T-bone Steak		
1 inch	10 minutes	12 minutes
2 inches	20 minutes	22 minutes
Tenderloin Filet Mignon		
(4 to 8 ounces)	5 to 7 minutes	8 to 10 minutes
Chuck Steak (high quality)		
1 inch	12 minutes	15 minutes
1½ inches	20 minutes	22 minutes
Ground Beef Patties		
(1 inch)	7 minutes	12 minutes

TERIYAKI STEAK

  2-pound beef sirloin steak,
    1 to 1¼ inches thick
  ½ cup soy sauce
  ½ cup water
  1 tablespoon brown sugar
  1½ teaspoons ginger

Diagonally slash outer edge of fat on steak at 1-inch intervals to prevent curling (do not cut into lean). Score meat (cut lightly in a crisscross pattern) and place in shallow glass dish. Heat remaining ingredients to boiling, stirring occasionally; pour on meat. Cover; refrigerate at least 2 hours, turning meat occasionally.

Set oven control at broil and/or 550°. Remove meat from marinade. Broil 3 to 4 inches from heat about 10 minutes on each side for rare, about 12 minutes for medium. Cut meat across grain at a slanted angle into ¼-inch slices.

Play up the Oriental origin and serve with Snow Peas and Carrot Nuggets (page 66), buttered rice and, as dessert, lemon sherbet and Polynesian Cookies (page 93).

8 servings.

Substitution

  For sirloin steak: 2 pounds beef round steak, ¾ inch thick; broil 8 minutes for medium, 10 minutes for well.

Charcoal-grilled Steak

Whether you're splurging with sirloin or going the way of a family steak and meat tenderizer, you'll want to do it right. So choose steaks 1 to 2 inches thick. Trim off excess fat (to cut down on flare-ups). Slash rest of fat every 2 inches; this keeps steak from curling. Check timetable below; check coals to be sure they're hot. (If you can hold your hand near the grid 3 seconds, they're *not!*) When you're ready to go, grill steaks 4 inches from coals; use tongs to turn. Season after turning and after grilling. To test for doneness, make a knife slit along the bone.

	1 Inch Thick Minutes per Side	2 Inches Thick Minutes per Side
Rare	4 to 5	12 to 13
Medium	7 to 8	15 to 17
Well	10 to 11	22 to 25

PEPPER STEAK BORDELAISE

1½ pounds sirloin steak, ½ inch thick
2 tablespoons salad oil
½ teaspoon salt
½ teaspoon freshly ground pepper
1 clove garlic, minced
1 green pepper, cut into 1-inch pieces
(about 1 cup)
1 can of our Bordelaise sauce (1 cup)
2 tomatoes, peeled and cut into eighths
3 to 4 cups hot cooked rice

Trim fat and bone from meat; cut into 4 to 6 serving pieces. In large skillet, brown meat on one side in oil over medium-high heat. Turn meat; season with ¼ teaspoon salt and ¼ teaspoon pepper. Brown other side of meat; turn. Season with remaining salt and pepper. Remove meat from skillet.

In same skillet, cook and stir garlic and green pepper until tender. Stir in Bordelaise sauce. Add meat; cook uncovered 10 minutes. Add tomatoes; heat through. Serve on rice.

Orange and Onion Salad (page 58) is a colorful companion.

4 to 6 servings.

BARBECUED ROUND STEAK

2-pound beef round steak, ¾ inch thick
2 tablespoons salad oil
3 tablespoons instant chopped onion
1 cup barbecue sauce
½ cup water

Cut meat into 6 serving pieces. In large skillet or Dutch oven, brown meat in oil over medium heat. Stir in remaining ingredients. Cover tightly; cook on top of range or in 325° oven 1½ hours or until meat is tender.

Suggested accompaniments: green beans, Carrots Bouillon (page 64) and Macaroni Fruit Salad (page 60).

6 servings.

Substitutions

For round steak: 2-pound beef sirloin tip steak.
For instant onion: ½ cup chopped onion.

STEAK SUPPER IN FOIL

1½-pound chuck steak, 1 inch thick
1 can (10½ ounces) condensed
cream of mushroom soup
1 envelope (about 1½ ounces)
onion soup mix
3 medium carrots, quartered
2 stalks celery, cut into 2-inch pieces
3 medium potatoes, pared and quartered
2 tablespoons water

Heat oven to 450°. Place 24 × 18-inch piece of heavy-duty aluminum foil in baking pan; place meat on foil. Stir together mushroom soup and onion soup mix (dry); spread on meat. Top meat with vegetables; sprinkle water on vegetables. Fold foil over and seal securely. Cook 1½ hours or until tender.

All this meal needs is the zing of Country-style Waldorf Salad (page 58). For dessert, serve ice cream and Sour Cream Brownies (page 89).

4 servings.

CUBE STEAK STROGANOFF

1 package (about 17½ ounces)
beef cubed steaks
1 package of our noodles stroganoff
¼ teaspoon garlic salt
⅛ teaspoon pepper
Sliced pitted ripe olives
Pimiento strips

Cut meat into ½-inch strips. Brown meat over medium-high heat. Drain off fat; set meat aside.

Cook noodles and prepare sauce as directed on package except—omit ground beef and stir garlic salt and pepper into sauce. Stir meat into sauce; heat through. Serve on noodles and garnish with olive slices and pimiento strips.

Company fare with Asparagus à la Polonaise (page 61), Sweet and Sour Beets (page 63) and Orange-Cherry Pie (page 106).

4 servings.

Pictured at right:
Steak Supper in Foil—a one-dish dinner
that's tailor-made for today.

SWISS STEAK

¼ cup Gold Medal Flour
½ teaspoon salt
¼ teaspoon pepper
2-pound beef round steak, 1 inch thick
2 tablespoons shortening
1 can (8 ounces) tomatoes
½ cup minced onion
¼ cup minced green pepper
½ teaspoon salt
⅛ teaspoon pepper

Mix flour, salt and pepper. Sprinkle one side of meat with half the flour mixture; pound in. Turn meat; pound in remaining flour mixture. Cut meat into 6 serving pieces. Melt shortening in large skillet; brown meat over medium heat, about 15 minutes.

Cover tightly; simmer 1 hour. Add small amount of water if necessary. Mix remaining ingredients; pour on meat. Cover tightly; simmer 30 minutes or until tender.

Broccoli 'n Chips (page 63), combining two family favorites, is a good choice for the vegetable.

6 servings.

Substitutions

For round steak: 2-pound beef sirloin tip steak.
For fresh onion: 3 tablespoons instant minced onion.
For fresh green pepper: 2 tablespoons dried green pepper.

LONDON BROIL
WITH MUSHROOM SAUCE

Season 1½- to 2-pound flank steak with salt; place in shallow glass dish. Pour 1 can of our mushroom sauce (1 cup) on steak. Cover; refrigerate at least 8 hours, turning meat occasionally.

Set oven control at broil and/or 550°. Remove steak from sauce; reserve sauce. Broil steak 3 to 4 inches from heat about 5 minutes on each side. Heat reserved sauce. Cut meat across grain at a slanted angle into thin slices. Pour mushroom sauce on steak.

4 to 6 servings.

BRAISED SHORT RIBS

Pictured on page 5.

2 pounds beef short ribs, cut into pieces
2 teaspoons salt
½ teaspoon pepper
2 tablespoons shortening
½ cup water
2 tablespoons horseradish
8 small carrots
4 medium onions
3 stalks celery, cut into eighths

Season meat with salt and pepper. Melt shortening in Dutch oven; brown meat over medium-high heat. Drain off fat. Pour water and horseradish on meat.

Cover tightly; simmer on top of range or in 325° oven about 2½ hours or until meat is tender. Add small amount of water if necessary. About 1 hour before end of cooking time, add vegetables.

Nice with fluffy mashed potatoes and Tossed Salad with Classic Dressing (page 55).

4 servings.

BEEF MUSHROOM

1 pound beef stew meat, cut into
    1-inch cubes
½ teaspoon seasoned instant meat tenderizer
2 tablespoons salad oil
1 can of our mushroom sauce (1 cup)
5 ounces uncooked medium noodles

Sprinkle meat with tenderizer; pierce each piece with fork. Cover; refrigerate 2 to 24 hours.

In large skillet, brown meat in oil over medium heat. Reduce heat; stir in sauce. Cover tightly; simmer about 45 minutes, stirring occasionally. (Meat will not be fork-tender but it will be tender to eat.)

Cook noodles as directed on package; drain. Serve beef and sauce on noddles.

Complete the meal with Green and Gold Salad (page 56) and Biscuit Fan-tans (page 78). And for dessert, offer Caramel Peach Crisps (page 84).

3 or 4 servings.

GOOD BROWN STEW

2 pounds beef stew meat, cut into
   1-inch cubes
1 to 2 tablespoons salad oil
¼ cup instant chopped onion
1 small bay leaf
2 teaspoons salt
1 teaspoon sugar
¼ teaspoon allspice
⅛ teaspoon instant minced garlic
1 teaspoon lemon juice
1 teaspoon Worcestershire sauce
1 can (16 ounces) whole carrots, drained
   (reserve liquid)
1 can (15 ounces) whole potatoes, drained
   (reserve liquid)
1 can (8 ounces) whole onions, drained
   (reserve liquid)

In Dutch oven, brown meat in oil over medium heat. Sprinkle seasonings on meat. Add enough water to reserved vegetable liquids to measure 4 cups; pour on meat. Heat to boiling.

Reduce heat; simmer 2 hours or until meat is tender. Add small amount of water if necessary. Add vegetables; simmer 15 minutes longer or until vegetables are heated through.

Serve with a simple salad of lettuce wedges and a typical U.S.A. dessert—strawberry shortcake.

6 servings.

Substitutions

For instant onion: 1 large onion, chopped.
For instant garlic: 1 clove garlic, minced.
For canned vegetables: 6 carrots, quartered, 3 medium potatoes, pared and cut into eighths, 8 small onions; add 30 minutes before end of cooking time.

Stew-pendous Substitutes

You're proud of your beef stew and you always buy foreshank or brisket beef. But why not branch out? Especially if you find a special on beef. From the chuck, use blade pot-roast or the English (Boston) cut. From the round, use rump or round roast; the steaks, too. For a lighter stew, switch off to veal or lamb—just forego the browning.

OVEN STEW

2 pounds beef round steak, cut into
   1-inch cubes
2 cups sliced carrots
1 cup sliced celery
2 medium onions, sliced
1 can (5 ounces) water chestnuts,
   drained and sliced
1 can (6 ounces) sliced mushrooms, drained
3 tablespoons flour
1 tablespoon sugar
1 tablespoon salt
1 can (16 ounces) tomatoes
1 cup red Burgundy

Mix meat, carrots, celery, onions, water chestnuts and mushrooms in Dutch oven. Mix flour, sugar and salt; stir into meat mixture. Stir in tomatoes and wine. Cover tightly; cook in 325° oven or on top of range 4 hours.

Bread in the Round (page 80) goes well with this easy but elegant stew.

6 servings.

Substitution

For Burgundy: 1 cup water and 1 teaspoon instant beef bouillon.

PICCALILLI STEW

1 can (24 ounces) beef stew
½ cup pickle relish

Stir together stew and pickle relish in saucepan. Simmer about 10 minutes or until heated through.

Quick meal plan: sliced tomatoes, bread sticks and a fixed-up frozen apple pie (page 105).

4 servings.

VARIATION

■ *Stroganoff Stew:* Stir ½ cup dairy sour cream into heated stew, or serve sour cream as a garnish. Nice to serve on toast.

SAVORY BEEF PIE

 2 tablespoons shortening
 ¼ cup chopped onion
 2 tablespoons chopped green pepper
 2 cups cut-up cooked beef
 2 cups cooked vegetables
 1¼ cups gravy
   Drop Biscuits

Melt shortening in large skillet; cook and stir onion and green pepper until tender. Stir in meat, vegetables and gravy; heat about 5 minutes.

Heat oven to 450°. Prepare 10 to 12 Drop Biscuits as directed on Bisquick package except—drop dough by spoonfuls onto hot meat mixture. Bake uncovered 15 to 20 minutes or until biscuits are brown.

Serve with individual tossed green salads and, for the finale, Triple Fudge Cake (page 98).

4 to 6 servings.

Substitutions

For gravy: 1 can (10¾ ounces) gravy or 1 envelope (⅞ ounce) gravy mix prepared as directed.

For cooked vegetables: 1 package (10 ounces) frozen mixed vegetables, broken apart.

VARIATIONS

■ *Savory Lamb or Veal Pie:* Substitute 2 cups cut-up cooked lamb or veal for the beef.

Spicing Up Yesterday's Beef

Sunday dinner's gone, but the pot-roast lingers on. Lucky you, you're a meal ahead. And here's your chance to experiment with spices. Accompany the second go-round with fluffy mashed potatoes and whip in a taste of horseradish and a pinch of dill weed. Delicious! Or how about beefing up the leftover gravy with a dash of allspice or nutmeg?

If cold beef sandwiches are a specialty of the house, spice up the spread for the bread—just a sprinkling of chili powder or ginger mixed into the butter.

For a salad supper, try this: diced cold beef and rice, mixed with mayonnaise and spiced with dill weed, mace or soy sauce.

However and whatever you spice, sprinkle softly. You know what they say about too much of a good thing.

DRIED BEEF CASSEROLE

 1 cup uncooked elbow macaroni
   (about 4 ounces)
 1 can (10½ ounces) condensed cream
   of mushroom soup
 ½ cup milk
 1 cup shredded Cheddar cheese
   (about 4 ounces)
 3 tablespoons finely chopped onion
 ¼ pound dried beef,* cut into
   bite-size pieces
 2 hard-cooked eggs, sliced

Heat oven to 350°. Cook macaroni as directed on package; drain. Blend soup and milk in large bowl. Stir in cheese, onion, macaroni and dried beef; fold in eggs.

Pour mixture into ungreased 1½-quart casserole. Cover tightly; bake 30 minutes or until heated through.

4 to 6 servings.

°If dried beef is very salty, pour boiling water over it and drain.

Substitution

For fresh onion: 1 tablespoon instant minced onion.

CORNED BEEF STEW

 1 can (12 ounces) corned beef
 1 can (15 ounces) sliced white potatoes,
   drained
 1 can (16 ounces) tomatoes, cut up
 1 can (16 ounces) whole onions
 1 package (10 ounces) frozen peas and
   carrots
 1 teaspoon salt
 ½ teaspoon marjoram
 ½ teaspoon thyme
 2 cups shredded Cheddar cheese
   (8 ounces)

Break apart corned beef in Dutch oven. Stir in potatoes, tomatoes (with liquid), onions (with liquid), frozen peas and carrots, salt, marjoram and thyme. Heat to boiling, stirring occasionally. Reduce heat. Cover tightly; simmer 30 minutes. Serve topped with cheese.

6 servings.

LIVER

To Panfry: Have liver sliced ½ to ¾ inch thick. Coat with flour. Melt ¼ cup shortening in skillet; brown liver over medium-high heat, 2 to 3 minutes on each side. Season to taste.

To Broil: Have baby beef, veal (calf) or lamb liver sliced ½ to ¾ inch thick. Dip into melted bacon drippings, butter or margarine. Set oven control at broil and/or 550°. Broil liver 3 to 5 inches from heat just long enough for meat to change color and become light brown, about 3 minutes on each side.

To Braise: Have beef or pork liver sliced ½ to ¾ inch thick. Coat with flour. Brown in small amount of fat. Add ¼ cup liquid. Cover tightly; cook on top of range or in 350° oven 20 to 30 minutes. For a large piece, increase liquid to ½ cup; cook about 30 minutes per pound.

LIVER AND ONIONS

Have 1 pound liver sliced ½ to ¾ inch thick. In large skillet, cook and stir 2 cups thinly sliced onion in 3 tablespoons butter or margarine until tender. Remove from skillet; keep warm. Panfry liver as directed above. Add onions for the last minute of cooking.

4 servings.

LIVER CREOLE

    4 slices bacon
    1 pound sliced beef liver
    3 tablespoons flour
    ⅓ cup chopped green pepper
    1 can (16 ounces) tomatoes
 1½ teaspoons salt
    ½ teaspoon chili powder
    ⅛ teaspoon cayenne red pepper

Fry bacon until crisp; remove bacon and drain. Drain off all but 3 tablespoons fat. Coat liver with flour; brown in bacon fat. Stir in remaining ingredients except bacon. Cover tightly; simmer 20 minutes. Garnish with bacon.

4 servings.

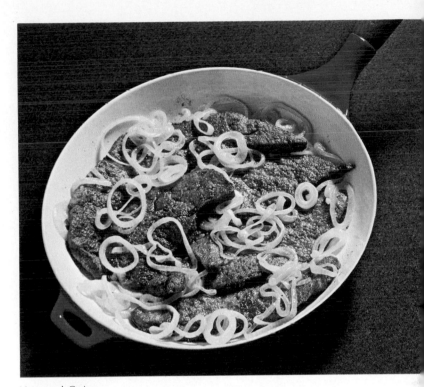
Liver and Onions

Liver Creole

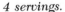

BAKED MEATBALLS

2 pounds ground beef
1 cup dry bread crumbs
½ cup milk
2 eggs
¼ cup instant minced onion
2 teaspoons salt
¼ teaspoon pepper

Mix all ingredients. Shape mixture by ¼ cupfuls into balls (do not pack). Place in ungreased jelly roll pan, 15½×10½×1 inch. Bake uncovered in 350° oven 30 to 40 minutes or until brown.

6 servings (18 meatballs).

Substitutions

For dry bread crumbs: 3 slices bread, cubed.
For instant onion: ¾ cup minced onion.

MEATBALL STEW

Pictured on page 5.

1 pound ground beef
1 egg
½ cup dry bread crumbs
¼ cup milk
2 tablespoons instant minced onion
1 teaspoon salt
⅛ teaspoon pepper
1 can (16 ounces) stewed tomatoes
1 package (24 ounces) frozen vegetables
  for stew
2 teaspoons salt

Mix ground beef, egg, bread crumbs, milk, onion, 1 teaspoon salt and the pepper. Shape mixture by ¼ cupfuls into balls (do not pack); brown in Dutch oven over medium-high heat. Drain off fat.

Stir in stewed tomatoes, frozen vegetables and 2 teaspoons salt; heat to boiling. Reduce heat. Cover tightly; simmer on top of range or in 325° oven until vegetables are tender, 1¼ to 1½ hours.

Serve with Garlic French Bread Sticks (page 77) and, for dessert, Spice Cake with Browned Butter Icing (page 101).

4 or 5 servings.

Substitution

For instant onion: ⅓ cup minced onion.

BAKED MEAT LOAF

2 pounds ground beef
1 cup seasoned bread crumbs
¾ cup milk
2 eggs
2 tablespoons instant minced onion
2 teaspoons salt
¼ teaspoon pepper

Mix all ingredients. Spread mixture in ungreased loaf pan, 9×5×3 inches. Bake uncovered in 350° oven about 1½ hours or until done.

8 to 10 servings.

Substitution

For instant onion: ¼ cup minced onion.

CORN HAMBURGER BAKE

1 pound ground beef
1 large onion, sliced
¼ cup sliced celery
2 cans (16 ounces each) cream-style corn
1 teaspoon salt
¼ teaspoon pepper
1 teaspoon instant beef bouillon
1 cup Bisquick
2 tablespoons butter or margarine, melted
¼ teaspoon garlic salt

Heat oven to 450°. Cook and stir ground beef, onion and celery in large skillet until meat is brown. Drain off fat.

Reserve ½ cup of the corn. Stir remaining corn, the salt, pepper and bouillon into meat mixture; heat to boiling. Pour into ungreased 2½-quart casserole.

Stir Bisquick and reserved corn with fork to a soft dough. Drop dough by tablespoonfuls onto hot meat mixture. Mix butter and garlic salt; drizzle half the butter on biscuit dough. Bake 20 to 25 minutes. Brush biscuits with remaining butter.

For the salad, offer lettuce with a simple dressing of mayonnaise laced with chili sauce or turn to your favorite combination of mixed greens.

6 servings.

Substitution

For instant bouillon: 1 beef bouillon cube.

COMPLETE HAMBURGER CASSEROLE

1 pound ground beef
1 tablespoon instant minced onion
½ teaspoon salt
½ teaspoon pepper
1 package (10 ounces) frozen mixed
    vegetables, broken apart
1 can of our cheese sauce (1 cup)
1 package (16 ounces) frozen fried
    shredded potato rounds

Heat oven to 375°. Mix beef, onion, salt and pepper in ungreased 2-quart casserole. Arrange vegetables on meat; pour cheese sauce on vegetables. Cover with frozen potato rounds. Bake uncovered 1 hour or until potatoes are golden brown.

Add crunch to this dinner in a dish with celery and carrot sticks. Try Raspberry-Raspberry (page 87) and Almond Shortbreads (page 91) for dessert.

4 or 5 servings.

Substitutions

For instant onion: 3 tablespoons minced onion.
For frozen mixed vegetables: 1 package (10 ounces) frozen peas and carrots, corn or chopped broccoli.
For cheese sauce: 1 can (10¾ ounces) condensed Cheddar cheese soup.

HEARTY HAMBURGER BAKE

1 pound ground beef
1 small onion, chopped (about ⅓ cup)
1 teaspoon salt
¼ teaspoon pepper
1 can (16 ounces) cut green beans,
    drained
1 can (10¾ ounces) condensed tomato soup
    Potato Buds (enough for 4 servings)

Heat oven to 350°. Cook and stir meat and onion in large skillet until meat is brown. Drain off fat. Stir in seasonings, beans and soup. Pour into ungreased 2-quart casserole.

Prepare Potato Buds as directed on package. Spoon potatoes onto meat mixture in 4 mounds. Bake uncovered 30 minutes or until bubbly.

Serve with a simple but zesty fruit salad.

4 servings.

COUNTRY-STYLE HOMINY

1 pound ground beef
¼ cup instant chopped onion
⅛ teaspoon instant minced garlic
⅓ cup chopped ripe or pimiento-stuffed
    olives
1 can (28 ounces) tomatoes
1 teaspoon salt
1 teaspoon oregano
⅛ teaspoon Tabasco
¼ cup butter or margarine
2 cans (20 ounces each) hominy, drained

Cook and stir ground beef, onion and garlic until meat is brown. Drain off fat. Stir in remaining ingredients except butter and hominy. Simmer uncovered 1 hour.

Melt butter in medium saucepan. Stir hominy into butter; heat through. Serve sauce on hominy.

4 to 6 servings.

Substitutions

For instant onion: 1 large onion, chopped.
For instant garlic: 1 clove garlic, minced.
For hominy: 3 to 4 cups hot cooked rice, macaroni or noodles.

HAMBURGER STROGANOFF

1 pound ground beef
½ cup minced onion
1 clove garlic, minced
1 can of our mushroom sauce (1 cup)
1 cup dairy sour cream
2 to 3 cups hot cooked noodles

Cook and stir ground beef, onion and garlic until meat is brown. Stir in mushroom sauce; simmer uncovered 10 minutes. Mix in sour cream; heat through. Serve on noodles.

Nice with any green vegetable and Ambrosia Salad (page 60).

4 servings.

Substitutions

For fresh onion: 3 tablespoons instant minced onion.
For garlic clove: ⅛ teaspoon instant minced garlic.

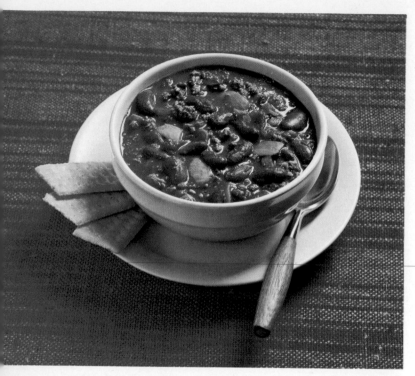

Chili Con Carne

Giant Burger

CHILI CON CARNE

1 pound ground beef
½ pound bulk pork sausage
1 can (16 ounces) tomatoes
1 can (15½ ounces) chili beans
4 medium onions, chopped (about 2 cups)

In large skillet, cook and stir ground beef and pork sausage until brown. Drain off fat. Stir in remaining ingredients; simmer uncovered 1 hour.

Nice with Molded Waldorf Salad (page 57) and crackers or quick-from-a-mix corn muffins.

4 servings.

Substitution

For chili beans: 1 can (15½ ounces) kidney beans and 1 to 2 tablespoons chili powder.

GIANT BURGER

1½ pounds ground beef
1½ teaspoons salt
1 package (3 ounces) cream cheese, softened
1 tablespoon prepared mustard
1 tablespoon horseradish, drained
1 can (3½ ounces) French fried onion rings, if desired

Heat oven to 350°. Mix ground beef and salt; divide in half. Pat one half evenly in 8-inch pie pan. Mix cream cheese, mustard and horseradish; spread to within 1 inch of edge of meat in pan.

Shape remaining meat into 8-inch circle. Place on cheese mixture; pinch edge to seal securely. Bake uncovered 45 minutes for medium, 55 minutes for well.

Heat onion rings in oven 5 minutes. Remove meat to large serving plate; arrange onion rings around meat. Cut into wedges.

Complete menu plan: Mushroom Italian Green Beans (page 62), Cucumber Relish Mold (page 57), potatoes and Caramel Peach Crisps (page 84).

4 to 6 servings.

VARIATION

■ *Gourmet Burger:* Add 2 tablespoons crumbled blue cheese to cream cheese mixture.

Pork

TO ROAST FRESH PORK

Select roast from those listed in chart below. Allow about ½ pound per person—less for boneless roasts, more for roasts with a bone. If desired, season with salt and pepper.

Place meat fat side up on rack in open shallow roasting pan. The rack keeps the meat out of the drippings. (In some roasts, the ribs form a natural rack.) It is not necessary to baste.

Insert meat thermometer so tip is in center of thickest part of meat and does not touch bone or rest in fat. Do not add water. Do not cover.

Roast meat in 325° oven. (It is not necessary to preheat oven.) Roast to desired degree of doneness (see Timetable), using thermometer reading as final guide. Roasts are easier to carve if allowed to set 15 to 20 minutes after removing from oven. Since meat continues to cook after removal from oven, if roast is to "set," it should be removed from oven when thermometer registers 5° lower than the desired doneness.

You'll find some guidelines for carving a pork loin roast on page 156.

MUSTARD-TOMATO SAUCE

2 egg yolks
½ cup sugar
½ cup undiluted condensed tomato soup
½ cup prepared mustard
½ cup butter or margarine
¼ cup vinegar

Mix all ingredients in saucepan. Cook over low heat, stirring constantly, until sauce thickens. This is one of our favorite accompaniments for pork roasts.

2 cups.

TIMETABLE

Cut	Approximate Weight	Meat Thermometer Reading	Approximate Cooking Time (Minutes per Pound)
Loin			
Center	3 to 5 pounds	170°	30 to 35
Half	5 to 7 pounds	170°	35 to 40
End	3 to 4 pounds	170°	40 to 45
Roll	3 to 5 pounds	170°	35 to 45
Boneless Top	2 to 4 pounds	170°	30 to 35
Crown	4 to 6 pounds	170°	35 to 40
Picnic Shoulder			
Bone in	5 to 8 pounds	185°	30 to 35
Rolled	3 to 5 pounds	170°	35 to 40
Boston Shoulder	4 to 6 pounds	185°	45 to 50
Leg (fresh ham)			
Whole (bone in)	10 to 14 pounds	185°	30 to 35
Whole (boneless)	7 to 10 pounds	170°	30 to 35
Half (bone in)	5 to 7 pounds	170°	35 to 40
Tenderloin	½ to 1 pound		¾ to 1 hour (total)
Spareribs, Back Ribs, Country-style Backbones*			1½ to 2½ hours (total)

All three are always cooked until well done.

TO BROIL FRESH PORK

For each serving, allow about ½ to ¾ pound of chops and steaks with bone in, about ⅓ pound for boneless cuts.

Diagonally slash outer edge of fat on chops or steaks at 1-inch intervals to prevent curling (do not cut into lean). Set oven control at broil and/or 550°. Place meat on rack in broiler so top of meat is 3 to 5 inches from heat. Broil until light brown. The meat should be about half done by this time (see Timetable).

If desired, season brown side with salt and pepper. (Always season after browning as salt tends to draw moisture to surface and delay browning.) Turn meat; broil until brown.

TIMETABLE

Cut	Approximate Cooking Time per Side
Chops (¾ to 1 inch)	10 to 12 minutes
Shoulder Steaks (½ to ¾ inch)	10 to 12 minutes
Patties (1 inch)	10 to 12 minutes
Kabobs (1½ × 1½ × ¾ inch)	11 to 12 minutes

PORK CHOP DINNER

    4 pork loin or rib chops, 1 inch thick
    ¼ cup water
    4 medium potatoes, pared
    4 small carrots
    4 medium onions
    1 teaspoon salt
    ¼ teaspoon pepper

Brown meat in large skillet over medium heat. Drain off fat. Add water and vegetables. Season with salt and pepper. Cover tightly; simmer 1 hour or until done.

Try this skillet meal with Pineapple-Marshmallow Slaw (page 55) and Herb-topped Rolls (page 77).

4 servings.

MEXICAN PORK CHOPS

    4 pork loin or rib chops, 1 inch thick
    1 teaspoon salt
    ⅛ teaspoon pepper
    1 medium green pepper, cut into 4 rings
    4 tablespoons uncooked instant rice
    1 can (about 16 ounces) stewed tomatoes

Brown meat over medium heat. Season with salt and pepper. Top each chop with a green pepper ring; fill each ring with 1 tablespoon rice. Carefully pour ¼ cup stewed tomatoes on rice in each ring. Pour remaining tomatoes into skillet. Cover tightly; simmer 1 hour or until done. Add a small amount of water if necessary.

Menu mates: lettuce wedges, Perky Lima Beans (page 62) and Graham Cracker Torte (page 100).

4 servings.

STUFFING-TOPPED PORK CHOPS

    6 pork loin or rib chops, 1 inch thick
    ½ cup water
    ¼ cup chopped celery
    2 tablespoons finely chopped onion
    2 tablespoons butter or margarine
    2 cups herb-seasoned stuffing
    1 can (8 ounces) cream-style corn

Heat oven to 350°. Arrange meat in ungreased baking dish, 13½ × 9 × 2 inches. Add the water and bake uncovered 45 minutes.

Cook and stir celery and onion in butter until tender; stir in stuffing and corn. Spoon ⅓ cup stuffing onto each chop. Bake uncovered 30 minutes longer.

Accompany with buttered spinach and Okra and Tomato Salad (page 56).

6 servings.

BRAISED PORK CHOPS

4 pork loin or rib chops, ½ to
  1 inch thick
1 teaspoon salt
¼ teaspoon pepper
¼ cup pineapple juice
  Pan Gravy (below)

Brown meat over medium heat. Season with salt and pepper. Reduce heat; pour pineapple juice on meat. Cover tightly; simmer ½-inch chops 20 to 25 minutes, 1-inch chops 30 to 35 minutes or until done. Serve with Pan Gravy.

Sprouts Sauté (page 63), an apple salad and mashed potatoes are nice serve-alongs for the braised chops. For dessert try Coconut Pudding (page 85).

4 servings.

PAN GRAVY

Place meat on warm platter; keep warm while making gravy. Pour drippings (fat and juices) into bowl, leaving brown particles in pan. Let fat rise to top of drippings; skim off fat, reserving ¼ cup. Place the ¼ cup reserved fat in pan. Blend in ¼ cup Gold Medal Flour. Cook over low heat, stirring until mixture is smooth and bubbly. Remove from heat. Stir in 2 cups water. Heat to boiling, stirring constantly. Boil and stir 1 minute. Season with salt and pepper.

2 cups.

Substitution

  For pineapple juice: ¼ cup apple juice or ¼ cup water.

For Perfect Pan Gravy

Pan gravy is really very simple. Just follow the instructions carefully and rely on three little secrets to success:

☐ Be exact with the fat—too little makes the gravy lumpy.
☐ Be just as exact with the flour—too little makes the gravy greasy. And when you blend it into the fat, scrape the pan often as you go.
☐ Then boil for just a minute, stirring until smooth. You can even deepen the color with a few drops of bottled brown bouquet sauce.

BARBECUED RIBS

4½ pounds pork back ribs, cut into pieces
 ¼ cup soy sauce
  1 tablespoon plus 2 teaspoons cornstarch
  1 bottle (18 ounces) barbecue sauce

Arrange ribs meaty side up in open shallow roasting pan. Do not add water. Do not cover. Roast in 325° oven 1¾ hours.

Mix remaining ingredients; pour on meat. Bake uncovered about 45 minutes longer or until meat is done.

Team up with Best Tossed Salad (page 55) and Hopping John (page 76), a zesty combo of black-eye peas and rice.

5 or 6 servings.

Substitution

  For back ribs: 4½ pounds spareribs.

BAKED SPARERIBS

Arrange 3 to 4 pounds spareribs meaty side up in open shallow roasting pan. Do not add water. Do not cover. Roast in 325° oven 1½ to 2½ hours or until meat is done.

4 servings.

GLAZED BARBECUED SPARERIBS

4 servings ready-to-eat barbecued spareribs
¼ cup orange marmalade, melted
2 tablespoons lemon juice

Heat oven to 300°. Arrange spareribs meaty side up in ungreased baking pan, 13×9×2 inches. Mix marmalade and lemon juice; spoon onto ribs. Heat uncovered 25 minutes or until heated through.

While you're at the deli, pick up some coleslaw and potato salad. Garnish them prettily and no one will guess you didn't do it *all* yourself.

4 servings.

Substitution

  For orange marmalade: ¼ cup lime marmalade.

PINEAPPLE-STUFFED SPARERIBS

1 rack spareribs (about 3 pounds)
¼ cup chopped celery
2 tablespoons chopped onion
2 tablespoons butter or margarine
1 can (13¼ ounces) pineapple tidbits,
   drained (reserve syrup)
½ teaspoon cloves
2 cups packaged seasoned stuffing

Tie spareribs in circle; place bone tips up on rack in open shallow roasting pan. Do not add water. Do not cover. Roast in 325° oven 2 hours.

Cook and stir celery and onion in butter until tender. Mix with pineapple, cloves, stuffing and enough reserved pineapple syrup to moisten. Spoon dressing into circle of ribs; bake uncovered 30 minutes longer or until meat is done.

4 servings.

GLAZED RIBS

4 pounds spareribs
1 can (15 ounces) tomato sauce
1 envelope (.7 ounce) onion salad
   dressing mix
¼ cup vinegar
¼ cup light molasses
2 tablespoons salad oil
1 teaspoon dry mustard
1 cup water

Heat oven to 350°. Arrange spareribs meaty side up in open shallow roasting pan. Heat remaining ingredients to boiling, stirring constantly. Boil and stir 3 minutes. Pour sauce on meat. Bake uncovered about 1½ hours, basting 4 or 5 times.

Buttered Brussels sprouts and Green Rice (page 75) are nice accompaniments.

4 servings.

Substitution

For spareribs: 4 pounds pork back ribs or country-style ribs.

Pictured at left:
Pineapple-stuffed Spareribs—a new twist to a proven family favorite.

TENDERLOIN PATTIES SUPREME

6 pork tenderloin patties, 1 inch thick
Salt
6 onion slices, ¼ inch thick
¼ cup catsup
⅓ cup lemon-lime carbonated beverage
1 teaspoon Worcestershire sauce
⅛ teaspoon chili powder

Season patties with salt; arrange in ungreased baking pan, 9×9×2 inches. Top each patty with an onion slice. Bake patties uncovered in 325° oven 30 minutes.

Mix remaining ingredients; pour on patties. Bake uncovered 30 minutes longer. Serve patties with sauce.

Pork patties for a party? Sure! Dress them up with Green Beans and Bacon (page 62) and Poppy Seed Noodles (page 72). For dessert, Lemon Pudding Shells (page 85).

4 servings.

PORK AND FRUIT SKILLET

Uncooked instant rice (enough for
   6 servings)
1 can (13¼ ounces) pineapple chunks,
   drained (reserve syrup)
1 package (about 17½ ounces) frozen
   breaded pork patties (10)
1 can of our sweet and sour sauce
   (1 cup)
½ cup dried or canned apricot halves
½ cup water

Cook rice as directed on package except—substitute reserved pineapple syrup for part of the water. Cook pork patties as directed on package.

While meat cooks, heat pineapple chunks, sweet and sour sauce, apricot halves and water to boiling. Reduce heat; simmer uncovered 10 minutes. Spoon sauce on pork patties. Serve with rice.

For a quick-as-can-be meal, serve with buttered peas and Pudding-Pie Dessert (page 85), a speedy but smashingly attractive combination of canned pudding and pie filling.

5 or 6 servings.

CHEESE-TOPPED PORK CUTLETS

Pound 1½ pounds pork cutlets to flatten. Season with salt and pepper. Dip into beaten egg, then coat with dry bread crumbs. Melt shortening in large skillet; brown meat over medium heat. Pour in small amount of water. Cover tightly; simmer 30 minutes.

Arrange cutlets in lightly oiled baking pan; spoon 1 can of our cheese sauce (1 cup) on meat. Set oven control at broil and/or 550°. Broil until sauce is bubbly.

6 servings.

CHINESE PORK AND RICE

⅔ cup uncooked regular rice
1 medium onion, chopped
2 stalks celery, cut into diagonal slices
2 tablespoons salad oil
1½ cups boiling water
1 teaspoon instant chicken or beef bouillon
2 tablespoons soy sauce
2 cups cut-up cooked pork (¾- to 1-inch pieces)
1 medium green pepper, chopped

In large skillet, cook and stir rice, onion and celery in oil over medium heat until rice is golden brown and onion is tender. Stir in remaining ingredients except green pepper and heat to boiling. Reduce heat.

Cover tightly; simmer 18 to 20 minutes or until rice is tender and liquid absorbed. Stir in green pepper. Cover tightly; simmer 10 minutes longer.

Serve with a salad of tossed greens sparked with watermelon pickles.

4 servings.

Note: Be sure to use regular rice—not converted or instant.

Substitution

For instant bouillon: 1 chicken or beef bouillon cube.

SUBGUM

1 can (4 ounces) sliced mushrooms
2 cups diced cooked pork
4 stalks celery, sliced (about 2 cups)
1 tablespoon butter or margarine
1½ cups gravy
1 can (20 ounces) bean sprouts, drained
Chow mein noodles

Cook and stir mushrooms (with liquid), pork and celery in butter until celery is tender, about 10 minutes. Stir in gravy; reduce heat. Cover tightly; simmer 15 minutes. Stir in bean sprouts; heat through. Serve on chow mein noodles.

4 servings.

Substitution

For chow mein noodles: Hot cooked rice.

BAKED MEAT SANDWICH

1 pound ground lean pork
½ cup chopped onion
½ cup shredded Swiss cheese
¼ cup grated Parmesan cheese
1 egg, slightly beaten
2 tablespoons snipped parsley
1½ teaspoons salt
¼ teaspoon Tabasco
Rolled Biscuit dough
2 tablespoons mayonnaise or salad dressing

Heat oven to 400°. Grease baking pan, 8×8×2 inches, or 4 individual casseroles. In large skillet, cook and stir pork and onion until pork is light brown. Drain off fat. Stir in cheeses, egg, parsley, salt and Tabasco. Remove from heat.

Prepare Biscuit dough for 10 to 12 biscuits as directed on Bisquick package except—add mayonnaise with the water. With floured fingers, pat half the dough into pan. Spread meat mixture on dough. Turn remaining dough onto meat mixture; with floured fingers, pat on meat. Bake uncovered 25 to 30 minutes. Especially delicious with cheese or mushroom sauce.

4 to 6 servings.

Substitution

For pork: 1 pound ground beef.

BAKED HAM

Select ham or other cut from those listed in chart below. Allow about ½ pound per person—less for boneless roasts, more for a roast with a bone. Place ham fat side up on rack in open shallow roasting pan. The rack keeps the meat out of the drippings. It is not necessary to baste.

Insert meat thermometer so tip is in center of thickest part of meat and does not touch bone or rest in fat. Do not add water. Do not cover.

Roast meat in 325° oven. (It is not necessary to preheat oven.) Roast to desired degree of doneness (see Timetable), using thermometer reading as final guide.

Ham is easier to carve if allowed to set 15 to 20 minutes after removing from oven. Since meat continues to cook after removal from oven, if ham is to "set," it should be removed when thermometer registers 5° lower than desired doneness.

You'll find some guidelines for carving a whole ham on page 156.

GLAZED BAKED HAM

Pictured on page 5.

For a glazed ham, remove ham 30 minutes before it is done. Pour drippings from pan. Score fat surface of ham lightly, cutting uniform diamond shapes. A whole clove can be inserted in each. Pour on Orange Glaze (below); continue baking 30 minutes, basting as directed. Or use any of the commercial glazes now available in supermarkets, but be sure to follow the directions on the label.

ORANGE GLAZE

1 can (6 ounces) frozen orange
   juice concentrate (thawed)
¼ cup brown sugar (packed)
¼ teaspoon cloves
¼ teaspoon cinnamon

Mix all ingredients. Pour half the glaze on ham. Baste ham occasionally with remaining glaze during the last 30 minutes of baking time.

Enough for a 4-pound ham.

TIMETABLE

Cut	Approximate Weight	Meat Thermometer Reading	Approximate Cooking Time (Minutes per Pound)
Ham (cook before eating)			
Whole	10 to 14 pounds	160°	18 to 20
Half	5 to 7 pounds	160°	22 to 25
Shank Portion	3 to 4 pounds	160°	35 to 40
Butt Portion	3 to 4 pounds	160°	35 to 40
Ham (fully cooked)			
Whole	10 to 15 pounds	130°	10 to 15
Half	5 to 7 pounds	130°	18 to 24
Loin	3 to 5 pounds	160°	25 to 30
Picnic Shoulder (cook before eating)	5 to 8 pounds	170°	35
Picnic Shoulder (fully cooked)	5 to 8 pounds	130°	25 to 30
Shoulder Roll (butt)	2 to 4 pounds	170°	35
Canadian-style Bacon	2 to 4 pounds	160°	35 to 40
Ham Loaf	2 pounds	160°	1½ hours (total)
Ham Patties	1 inch thick		¾ to 1 hour (total)

SMOKED HAM SLICE

Allow about ½ to ¾ pound for each serving. Diagonally slash outer edge of fat at 1-inch intervals to prevent curling. Then proceed with your favorite method of cooking.

To Bake: Place 1-inch-thick ham slice in ungreased baking dish. If desired, spread with ¼ cup favorite jelly, slightly beaten, or Brown Sugar Glaze: Mix ½ cup brown sugar (packed), ¼ teaspoon dry mustard and 1½ teaspoons vinegar. Bake uncovered in 325° oven 30 minutes.

To Panfry: Rub skillet with small piece of fat cut from slice. Cook ½-inch-thick ham slice over medium heat about 3 minutes or until light brown. Turn ham slice; cook about 3 minutes longer.

To Broil: Set oven control at broil and/or 550°. Place 1-inch-thick ham slice on rack in broiler pan so top of ham slice is 3 inches from heat. Broil about 10 minutes or until light brown. Turn ham slice; broil about 6 minutes longer. If desired, after turning and during last 2 minutes of broiling, brush with 3 tablespoons jelly, slightly beaten.

HAM 'N LIMAS

1 package (10 ounces) frozen baby
  lima beans
1 fully cooked smoked ham slice,
  1 inch thick
1 cup shredded Cheddar cheese (4 ounces)

Cook lima beans as directed on package; drain. Diagonally slash outer edge of fat on ham slice at 1-inch intervals to prevent curling.

Set oven control at broil and/or 550°. Broil ham 3 inches from heat about 10 minutes or until light brown. Turn meat; broil 6 minutes longer. Top with lima beans and sprinkle with cheese. Broil about 2 minutes or until cheese is melted and bubbly.

For family or company, serve with Cinnamon-Applesauce Salad (page 58), Tangy Noodles (page 72) and Perfect Pineapple Pie (page 106).

4 to 6 servings.

Substitution

For frozen lima beans: 1 can (8 ounces) lima beans, drained.

TAHITIAN HAM DINNER

1 fully cooked smoked ham slice,
  ¾ inch thick (about 1½ pounds)
2 packages (10 ounces each) frozen
  Brussels sprouts
2 tablespoons water
1 or 2 bananas
  Sauce (below)

Place 30×18-inch piece of heavy-duty aluminum foil in jelly roll pan, 15½×10½×1 inch. Place ham slice on foil; arrange Brussels sprouts around ham. Sprinkle water on Brussels sprouts. Fold foil over meat and seal securely. Cook in 400° oven 40 minutes.

Open foil packet; fold edges back, keeping Brussels sprouts covered. Diagonally slice bananas onto meat. Pour Sauce on bananas.

Set oven control at broil and/or 550°. Broil 4 to 5 inches from heat 5 minutes or until Sauce is bubbly and brown.

6 or 7 servings.

SAUCE

Heat 12 large marshmallows (or 1 cup miniature marshmallows), 3 tablespoons milk and 2 tablespoons butter or margarine over medium heat, stirring constantly, just until marshmallows are melted.

SCALLOPED POTATOES "AND"

Prepare 1 package of our scalloped potatoes as directed on package except—try one of the additions below:

■ *Canadian-style Bacon:* Before baking, top with four ½-inch-thick slices Canadian-style bacon. Bake 30 to 35 minutes.

■ *Ham Cubes:* Omit butter; stir in 1½ cups cubed cooked ham. Bake 35 to 40 minutes.

■ *Sausage:* Omit butter; top with 1 package (8 ounces) fully cooked brown and serve link sausage. Bake 35 to 40 minutes.

4 servings.

HAM CASSEROLE

1 cup shredded sharp Cheddar cheese
(4 ounces)
½ cup light cream
2 cups diced cooked potatoes
1½ to 2 cups cubed cooked ham
2 tablespoons chopped pimiento

Heat oven to 350°. In medium saucepan, heat cheese and cream, stirring constantly, until cheese melts and sauce is creamy. Remove from heat. Stir in remaining ingredients. Pour into ungreased 1½-quart casserole. Cover tightly; bake 45 minutes.

Brussels and Carrots Salad (page 56) is a colorful salad that's perfect with this family favorite.

4 servings.

Substitution

For ham: 1½ to 2 cups cubed pork luncheon meat.

RAVIOLI-SAUSAGE CASSEROLE

1 can (4 ounces) mushroom stems
and pieces, drained
1 can (15½ ounces) ravioli in tomato sauce
¼ cup catsup
1 green pepper, finely chopped
1 cup shredded mozzarella cheese
(4 ounces)
1 package (8 ounces) fully cooked brown and
serve link sausage

Heat oven to 350°. Mix mushrooms, ravioli in tomato sauce and catsup.

In ungreased 1-quart casserole, alternate layers of ⅓ of the ravioli mixture and ½ each green pepper and cheese. Arrange sausage spoke-fashion on top. Bake uncovered 45 minutes or until bubbly.

Best Tossed Salad (page 55) and hot French bread are the simple but perfect asides for this double-quick casserole.

6 to 8 servings.

LAYERED HAM DINNER

1 package (9 ounces) frozen
cut green beans
1 can (10½ ounces) condensed
cream of celery soup
¼ cup mayonnaise
1 tablespoon prepared mustard
2 packages (3 or 4 ounces each)
thinly sliced cooked ham
1 cup shredded Cheddar cheese (4 ounces)
¼ cup dry bread crumbs

Heat oven to 350°. Rinse beans with small amount of running cold water to separate and remove ice crystals; drain. Place beans in ungreased 1½-quart casserole.

Mix soup, mayonnaise and mustard; spoon half the mixture on beans. Top with ham and spoon remaining soup mixture on meat. Sprinkle with cheese and bread crumbs. Bake uncovered 20 minutes.

To accompany this hearty casserole, we suggest Pineapple-Banana Salad (page 60) and parsley buttered potatoes.

4 to 6 servings.

Substitution

For packaged ham: ½ pound fully cooked ham, cut into julienne strips.

SAUSAGE AND KRAUT ROMANOFF

1 package (8 ounces) fully cooked
brown and serve link sausage
1 package (5.5 ounces) of our noodles
Romanoff
½ teaspoon caraway seed
1 can (8 ounces) sauerkraut, drained

Heat oven to 350°. Brown meat as directed on package. Drain off fat. Prepare noodles Romanoff as directed on package except—increase milk to ½ cup and stir in caraway seed and sauerkraut.

Pour into ungreased 1½-quart casserole; arrange sausage spoke-fashion on top. Cover tightly; bake 25 minutes.

Accent with Bright Bean Salad (page 56).

4 servings.

Pineapple-Cherry Bologna

Chili Dogs

PINEAPPLE-CHERRY BOLOGNA

1- pound ring bologna
   Pineapple-Cherry Glaze (below)
   Potato Buds (enough for 4 servings)

If necessary, remove casing from bologna; arrange bologna in ungreased 9-inch pie pan. Cut ring diagonally at 2-inch intervals, being careful not to cut completely through. Carefully separate cuts and spoon in part of the glaze. Spread remaining glaze on top of bologna.

Heat oven to 400°. Prepare Potato Buds as directed on package. Mound potatoes in center of ring. Bake 20 minutes or until potatoes are light brown.

4 servings.

PINEAPPLE-CHERRY GLAZE

½ cup crushed pineapple
¼ cup coarsely chopped maraschino
   cherries
¼ cup light corn syrup
 2 tablespoons white vinegar
¼ teaspoon cloves
 2 drops red food color
1½ teaspoons water
1½ teaspoons cornstarch

Heat pineapple, cherries, corn syrup, vinegar, cloves and food color to boiling, stirring occasionally. Reduce heat; simmer 15 minutes. Blend water and cornstarch; stir into fruit. Cook, stirring constantly, until mixture thickens and boils. Boil and stir 1 minute.

POLISH SAUSAGE BOIL

Pictured on page 5.

1 pound fully cooked Polish sausage
½ to ¾ cup beer

In covered skillet, simmer Polish sausage in beer 10 minutes. (If using uncooked Polish sausage, increase cooking time to 20 minutes.)

Sauerkraut or Scalloped Potato Salad (page 71) and dark pumpernickel buns are perfect go-withs.

4 servings.

Substitution

For beer: ½ to ¾ cup water.

PEASANTS' FEAST

1 can (16 ounces) sauerkraut
1 can (16 ounces) tomatoes
1 medium onion, thinly sliced
2 tablespoons brown sugar, if desired
½ teaspoon salt
4 medium baking potatoes
1 package (12 ounces) smoked small
    sausage links
    Butter
    Snipped parsley

Heat oven to 350°. Mix sauerkraut, tomatoes, onion, sugar and salt in ungreased baking dish, 11½ × 7½ × 1½ inches. Rub potatoes with shortening and prick with fork; arrange on sauerkraut mixture. Bake uncovered 1 hour.

Add sausages, covering each with sauerkraut mixture. Bake uncovered 30 minutes longer or until potatoes are done. Make crosswise slits on potatoes; squeeze until some potato pops up through opening. Slip butter into opening and sprinkle with parsley.

All this meal-in-one needs is a simple green salad.

4 servings.

Substitution

For sausage links: About 1 pound Polish sausage or 2-pound piece large bologna (if necessary, remove casing; score top of piece and place on sauerkraut mixture).

FRANKFURTER CASSEROLE

6 frankfurters, cut into 1-inch pieces
1 package (9 ounces) frozen cut green
    beans, broken apart
1 can of our cheese sauce (1 cup)
1 cup unseasoned croutons

Heat oven to 375°. Mix frankfurters, green beans and sauce. Pour into greased 1½-quart casserole. Sprinkle with croutons. Bake uncovered 30 minutes or until sauce is bubbly.

6 servings.

Substitution

For cheese sauce: 1 can (10¾ ounces) condensed Cheddar cheese soup.

CREOLE WIENERS

8 slices bacon, diced
3 cups minced onion
1 can (16 ounces) tomatoes
¾ teaspoon salt
⅛ teaspoon pepper
1 pound frankfurters

Fry bacon and onion in large skillet until bacon is crisp and onion is tender. Drain off all but 2 tablespoons fat. Stir in tomatoes, salt and pepper.

Heat to boiling. Reduce heat; simmer 15 minutes, stirring occasionally. Stir in frankfurters. Cover tightly; simmer 15 minutes.

Menu plan: rice, green beans, Perfection Salad (page 57) and Chocolate-Cherry Parfait (page 85).

5 or 6 servings.

CHILI DOGS

12 frankfurters
1 slice American cheese, 3½ × 3½ inches
2 cans (15 ounces each) chili hot beans
1 can (8 ounces) tomato sauce
¼ teaspoon chili powder
¼ teaspoon cumin
⅛ teaspoon cayenne red pepper, if desired

Heat oven to 400°. Make three ½-inch-deep diagonal cuts at regular intervals in each frankfurter. Cut cheese slice into 36 strips, about 1 × ¼ inch. Insert cheese strip in each frankfurter cut.

Mix beans, tomato sauce and seasonings in ungreased baking dish, 11½ × 7½ × 1½ inches. Arrange franks on beans. Bake 20 to 25 minutes.

Superstar supper plan for a teenage bash: Fresh Vegetable Relishes (page 150) and Bun Sticks (page 77) for the crunch; Chocolate Fondue (page 84) for sweet swirling.

4 or 5 servings.

Substitutions

For frankfurters: 1 package (12 ounces) smoked small sausage links.

For chili hot beans: 2 cans (15½ ounces each) kidney beans.

For seasonings: 1 envelope (1¼ ounces) chili seasoning mix.

Lamb

TO ROAST LAMB

Select roast, allowing about ½ to ¾ pound per person. Do not remove "fell" (the paperlike covering). Roasts keep their shape better, cook in less time and are juicier when the "fell" is left on.

If desired, season meat with salt and pepper. For a quick seasoning, 4 or 5 slivers of garlic can be inserted in roast. Remove garlic before serving.

Place meat fat side up on rack in open shallow roasting pan. It is not necessary to baste; the meat does its own basting.

Insert meat thermometer so tip is in center of thickest part of meat and does not touch bone or rest in fat. Do not add water. Do not cover.

Roast meat in 325° oven. Roast to desired degree of doneness (see Timetable), using thermometer reading as final guide. Lamb is done when meat thermometer registers 175 to 180°.

Roasts are easier to carve if allowed to set 15 minutes. If roast is to "set," it should be removed from oven when thermometer registers 5 to 10° lower than the desired doneness.

See page 156 for carving tips.

TIMETABLE

Cut	Approximate Weight	Approximate Cooking Time (Minutes per Pound)
Shoulder		
Bone in	4 to 6 pounds	30 to 35
Rolled	3 to 5 pounds	40 to 45
Cushion	3 to 5 pounds	30 to 35
Crown Roast or Rib (Rack)	4 to 5 pounds	40 to 45
Leg	5 to 8 pounds	30 to 35
Boneless Leg	3 to 5 pounds	35 to 40

CUCUMBER SAUCE

1 cup finely chopped unpared cucumber (about 1 medium cucumber)
½ teaspoon finely chopped onion
1 tablespoon prepared mustard
½ cup mayonnaise or salad dressing
½ teaspoon salt
¼ teaspoon pepper

Mix all ingredients. Cover and refrigerate. A delicious sauce for lamb—try it with veal and fish, too.

1¼ cups.

SWEDISH LEG OF LAMB

5-pound leg of lamb roast
1 tablespoon salt
1 teaspoon pepper
5 carrots, sliced
3 onions, sliced
1 teaspoon instant beef bouillon
1 cup hot water
1½ cups hot strong coffee
½ cup milk
1 tablespoon sugar

Place meat fat side up on rack in open shallow roasting pan. Season with salt and pepper. Insert meat thermometer so tip is in center of thickest part of meat and does not touch bone or rest in fat. Do not add water. Do not cover. Roast in 325° oven 1½ hours. Drain off fat.

Mix remaining ingredients; pour on meat. Continue baking about 1 hour, basting meat every 15 minutes with liquid. Meat thermometer should register 175°. If desired, prepare gravy using liquid.

Need menu help? Serve the roast with a spinach salad, boiled potatoes, Minted Grapefruit (page 82) and Creamy Vanilla Fondant (page 95).

8 to 10 servings.

Substitution

For instant bouillon and water: 1 cup canned condensed beef broth (bouillon).

TO BROIL LAMB CHOPS

Remove "fell" (the paperlike covering) if it is on chops. Diagonally slash outer edge of fat on meat at 1-inch intervals to prevent curling. Set oven control at broil and/or 550°. Place chops on rack in broiler pan so tops of ¾- to 1-inch chops are 2 to 3 inches from heat, 1- to 2-inch chops are 3 to 5 inches from heat. Broil until brown. The chops should be about half done (see Timetable).

If desired, season *brown* side with salt and pepper. Turn chops; broil until brown.

TIMETABLE

Thickness	Approximate Cooking Time per Side*
1 inch	6 to 7 minutes
1½ inches	9 to 10 minutes
2 inches	10 to 11 minutes

Time given is for medium doneness; lamb chops are not usually served rare.

PRINCESS LAMB CHOPS

  4 lamb shoulder chops, 1 inch thick
  ½ cup red wine
  ½ cup salad oil
  1 tablespoon vinegar
  2 tablespoons chopped green onion
  1 teaspoon grated lemon peel
1½ teaspoons salt
  ½ teaspoon pepper
  ¼ teaspoon dry mustard
  ⅛ teaspoon thyme
  ⅛ teaspoon basil
  ⅛ teaspoon instant minced garlic

Place meat in shallow glass dish. Mix remaining ingredients; pour on meat. Cover; refrigerate at least 2 hours, turning meat occasionally.

Set oven control at broil and/or 550°. Brush some of the marinade on meat. Broil 3 inches from heat 7 minutes. Brush meat with marinade; turn and brush again. Broil 5 minutes longer.

4 servings.

Substitutions

  For wine: ½ cup apple juice.
  For instant garlic: 1 clove garlic, minced.

MIXED GRILL

Pictured on page 5.

6 lamb kidneys
6 lamb loin or rib chops, 1 inch thick
6 pork sausage links
1 teaspoon salt
6 tomato slices, ½ inch thick
½ teaspoon salt
¼ teaspoon pepper
¼ teaspoon basil leaves
6 large fresh mushroom caps,
    washed and trimmed
1 tablespoon butter or margarine, melted

Wash kidneys; split each in half. Remove membrane, hard parts and white veins. Arrange kidneys, lamb chops and sausages on rack in broiler pan. Set oven control at broil and/or 550°. Broil 3 inches from heat 7 minutes. Season chops and kidneys with 1 teaspoon salt; turn meats.

Place tomato slices on rack. Mix ½ teaspoon salt, the pepper and basil leaves; sprinkle on tomatoes. Place mushroom caps rounded side up on rack; brush with butter.

Broil 5 minutes, brushing mushrooms with butter once during broiling. Season chops and kidneys with salt. To serve, arrange a chop, kidney, sausage link, mushroom cap and tomato slice on each plate.

Carrots Bouillon (page 64) and Best Tossed Salad (page 55) add just the right color accents.

6 servings.

Substitutions

  For kidneys: 6 chicken livers or 6 small pieces of calf liver.
  For sausage: 6 slices bacon.

Charcoal-grilled Lamb Chops

Beautifully juicy and slightly pink—that's how charcoal-grilled lamb chops should be. And are, with a little know-how. Choose loin, rib or shoulder chops, one or two to a person. Trim off the excess fat and place the chops on grill 4 inches from medium coals. Grill ¾-inch chops 10 to 12 minutes on each side; for 1-inch chops, make it 14 to 16 minutes. Test for doneness by making a knife slit along the bone. Perfect!

LAMB OSSOBUCO

¼ cup Gold Medal Flour
1 teaspoon salt
¼ teaspoon pepper
4 lamb shanks (about ¾ pound each)
⅓ cup shortening
½ cup tomato sauce
½ cup white wine
½ cup water
½ teaspoon instant beef bouillon
2 carrots, chopped
3 stalks celery, chopped
⅛ teaspoon each oregano, thyme, rosemary
    and basil

Mix flour, salt and pepper; coat meat with flour mixture. Melt shortening in large skillet or Dutch oven; brown meat over medium heat, turning occasionally. Drain off fat.

Reduce heat; stir in remaining ingredients. Cover tightly; simmer 2 hours or until meat is tender. If you like, thicken broth.

Nice with lettuce wedges, Bulgur Pilaf (page 76) and French bread.

4 to 6 servings.

BEST BROILED LAMB PATTIES

1 pound ground lamb
2 tablespoons dry bread crumbs
1 tablespoon parsley flakes
½ teaspoon salt
¼ teaspoon dill weed
1 egg
⅛ teaspoon instant minced garlic
4 slices bacon

Mix meat, bread crumbs, parsley, salt, dill weed, egg and garlic. Shape mixture into 4 patties, 1 inch thick and about 3 inches in diameter. Wrap slice of bacon around edge of each patty and secure with wooden picks.

Set oven control at broil and/or 550°. Broil patties 3 inches from heat about 15 minutes, turning once.

4 servings.

Substitutions

For parsley flakes: 1 tablespoon snipped parsley.
For instant garlic: 1 clove garlic, minced.

CURRIED LAMB AND BARLEY CASSEROLE

1 pound boneless lamb, cut into 1-inch cubes
¾ cup uncooked barley
2 cups water
1 can (16 ounces) whole tomatoes
1 tablespoon plus 1 teaspoon instant
    chopped onion
1 tablespoon parsley flakes
2 teaspoons salt
½ teaspoon curry powder

Heat oven to 350°. Mix all ingredients in ungreased 2½-quart casserole. Cover tightly; bake 2 hours or until barley is tender and liquid is absorbed.

Perfect with Brussels and Carrots Salad (page 56).

4 servings.

Substitutions

For instant onion: 4 tablespoons chopped onion.
For parsley flakes: 1 tablespoon snipped parsley.

SHEPHERDS' PIE

Potato Buds (enough for 8 servings)
2 tablespoons parsley flakes
2 cups cubed cooked lamb
¼ cup chopped onion
2 cups cooked vegetables (peas, carrots,
    corn)
2 cups gravy
½ teaspoon salt

Heat oven to 350°. Prepare Potato Buds as directed on package except—stir in parsley flakes; set potatoes aside.

Mix remaining ingredients in ungreased 2½-quart casserole. Mound potatoes on meat mixture. Bake uncovered 30 minutes or until potatoes brown slightly.

4 to 6 servings.

Substitutions

For parsley flakes: 2 tablespoons snipped parsley.
For lamb: 2 cups cubed cooked beef or veal.
For cooked vegetables: 1 package (10 ounces) frozen mixed vegetables, broken apart.
For gravy: 2 cans (10¾ ounces each) gravy or 2 envelopes (⅞ ounce each) gravy mix prepared as directed.

Veal

TO ROAST VEAL

Select roast, allowing about ½ pound per person —less for boneless roasts, more for roasts with a bone. If desired, season with salt and pepper before, during or after roasting.

Place meat fat side up on rack in open shallow roasting pan. The rack keeps the meat out of the drippings. (In roasts such as rib roasts or racks, the ribs form a natural rack.) If roast has little or no fat, place 2 or 3 slices bacon or salt pork on top.

Insert meat thermometer so tip is in center of thickest part of meat and does not touch bone or rest in fat. Do not add water. Do not cover.

Roast meat in 325° oven. (It is not necessary to preheat oven.) Roast to desired degree of doneness (see Timetable), using thermometer reading as final guide. Veal is done when meat thermometer registers 170°.

Roasts are easier to carve if allowed to set 15 to 20 minutes after removing from oven. If roast is to "set," remove from oven when thermometer registers 5 to 10° lower than the desired doneness.

TIMETABLE

Cut	Approximate Weight	Approximate Cooking Time (Minutes per Pound)
Leg	5 to 8 pounds	25 to 35
Loin	4 to 6 pounds	30 to 35
Rib (Rack)	3 to 5 pounds	35 to 40
Rolled Rump	3 to 5 pounds	40 to 45
Rolled Shoulder	4 to 6 pounds	40 to 45

SAVORY VEAL ROAST

4-pound veal rolled rump or leg roast
1 teaspoon salt
¼ teaspoon pepper
¼ cup soy sauce
¼ teaspoon garlic powder

Place meat fat side up on rack in open shallow roasting pan. Season with salt and pepper. If roast has little or no fat, place 2 or 3 slices bacon on top. Insert meat thermometer so tip is in center of thickest part of meat. Do not add water. Do not cover.

Roast in 325° oven 2½ to 3 hours or until thermometer registers 170°. During last hour of baking, baste often with mixture of soy sauce and garlic powder.

Wondering what to serve with the roast? We like Green Rice (page 75) and Perfection Salad (page 57).

6 to 8 servings.

VEAL PAPRIKA

⅓ cup Gold Medal Flour
3 teaspoons salt
2 teaspoons paprika
⅛ teaspoon pepper
2 pounds boneless veal, cut into 1-inch cubes
3 tablespoons shortening
⅛ teaspoon instant minced garlic
2 cups dairy sour cream
Poppy Seed Noodles (page 72)

Heat oven to 350°. Mix flour, salt, paprika and pepper; coat meat with flour mixture. Melt shortening in large skillet. Add garlic and meat; brown meat thoroughly. Remove from heat; stir in sour cream. Cover tightly; bake 1 hour. Serve on Poppy Seed Noodles.

Marinated Cucumber Salad (page 56) adds just the right degree of contrast—in flavor and texture.

6 servings.

Substitution

For instant garlic: 1 clove garlic, minced.

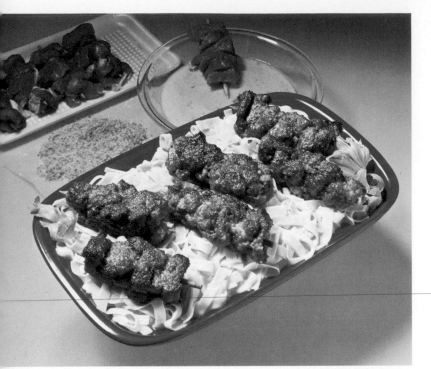

Seasoned City Chicken

SEASONED CITY CHICKEN

1 egg
¼ cup water
1 envelope (about .6 ounce)
   blue cheese salad dressing mix
6 city chicken legs* (about 1½ pounds)
¼ cup shortening
½ to ¾ cup dry bread crumbs
¼ cup shortening
1 teaspoon salt

Beat egg and water slightly; stir in salad dressing mix. Dip meat into egg, then coat with bread crumbs. Melt shortening in large skillet; brown meat quickly. Season with salt and pepper. Reduce heat.

Cover tightly; simmer 1 hour or until meat is done. Add small amount of water if necessary.

Turn city chicken into company fare with broiled tomatoes, French-style green beans and our noodles Romanoff.

4 servings.

*Equal parts pork and veal cubes placed on skewers.

Schnitzel Surprise

SCHNITZEL SURPRISE

5 thin slices Swiss cheese (each
   about 3¾ × 2½ inches)
5 thin slices boiled ham (each about
   3¾ × 2½ inches)
1 package (about 20 ounces)
   frozen breaded veal patties (10)
½ teaspoon salt

Heat oven to 450°. Place Swiss cheese and ham on 5 frozen veal patties; top with remaining patties. Season with ¼ teaspoon salt.

Bake on ungreased baking sheet 10 minutes. Turn patties; season with ¼ teaspoon salt. Bake 10 minutes longer.

4 or 5 servings.

Substitution

For frozen breaded veal patties: 1 pound veal steak, cut into 8 serving pieces and pounded until ¼ inch thick. Dip into beaten egg, then coat with 1 cup dry bread crumbs.

VEAL WITH TOMATO SAUCE

6 boneless veal cutlets
 (about 4 ounces each)
¼ cup salad oil
2 cloves garlic, crushed
1 cup thinly sliced onion
1 jar (3 ounces) sliced mushrooms, drained
2 tablespoons flour
1 teaspoon salt
¼ teaspoon pepper
1 can (8 ounces) tomato sauce
⅔ cup water

Pound meat until ¼ inch thick. In large skillet, heat oil and garlic over medium-high heat. Brown meat quickly, about 5 minutes. Remove meat from skillet.

Reduce heat to medium. Add onion and mushrooms; cook and stir until onion is tender. Stir in flour, salt and pepper; pour in tomato sauce and water. Heat to boiling, stirring constantly. Boil and stir 1 minute. Return meat to skillet. Cover tightly; simmer about 30 minutes or until tender.

Theme your whole menu Italian with Green and White Salad (page 55), buttered spaghetti and Parmesan Supper Bread (page 80). Fruit Dessert Freeze (page 87) is a refreshing finish.

6 servings.

Substitution

For canned mushrooms: 2 cups sliced fresh mushrooms (¼ pound).

Coping with Cutlets

Most veal cutlet recipes call for meat that's ¼ inch thick. Sometimes you can buy the cutlets that way; sometimes you have to do the pounding yourself. You can even buy veal round steak and do both the cutting *and* the pounding. It's up to you—and your budget.

If you're a do-it-yourselfer, start with ½-inch-thick cutlets or steaks. To pound down to ¼ inch, use a metal or wooden mallet—or even the dull edge of a knife or cleaver. Or do as grandma did and use the edge of a saucer. However you get them pounded, do make sure they're ¼ inch thick so you'll have no problem with the cooking time in the recipes.

BREADED VEAL CUTLETS

Pictured on page 5.

½ cup Gold Medal Flour*
1 teaspoon salt
½ teaspoon paprika
¼ teaspoon pepper
4 boneless veal cutlets (about 4 ounces each)
1 egg
2 tablespoons water
1 cup dry bread crumbs
¼ cup shortening
1 lemon, cut into wedges

Mix flour, salt, paprika and pepper; coat meat with flour mixture. Pound until ¼ inch thick. Beat egg and water slightly. Dip meat into egg, then coat with bread crumbs.

Melt shortening in large skillet; brown meat quickly. Reduce heat. Cover tightly; cook about 45 minutes or until done. Serve with lemon wedges.

4 servings.

*If using Self-Rising Flour, decrease salt to ⅛ teaspoon.

VEAL MUSTARD

4 veal rib or loin chops, ¾ inch thick
1 teaspoon salt
½ teaspoon pepper
3 tablespoons prepared mustard
½ cup diced bacon
¾ cup light cream (20%)
2 tablespoons drained capers

Heat oven to 350°. Season meat with salt and pepper; spread mustard on both sides. Arrange meat in ungreased baking pan, 9×9×2 inches. Sprinkle bacon on and around meat. Bake uncovered 1 hour 15 minutes. Place meat on warm platter; keep warm while making sauce.

Drain off all but 1 tablespoon fat, leaving bacon and mustard in pan. Stir in cream and capers. Heat to boiling, stirring constantly. Reduce heat; simmer about 10 minutes or until sauce is consistency of thin white sauce. Pour sauce on chops.

4 servings.

Substitution

For veal chops: 2 veal sirloin steaks, cut in half.

Chicken

ROAST CHICKEN

Young chickens of any weight can be roasted, stuffed or unstuffed. A plump chicken, at least 2½ pounds, is particularly desirable. Allow about ¾ pound per serving. If desired, season cavity of chicken lightly with salt. Do not salt cavity if bird is to be stuffed.

Stuff chicken just before roasting—not ahead of time. (See Sausage Stuffing, right.) Fill wishbone area with stuffing first. Fasten neck skin to back with skewer. Fold wings across back with tips touching. Fill body cavity lightly. (Do not pack—stuffing will expand while cooking.) Tie drumsticks to tail.

Heat oven (see Timetable). Brush chicken with melted butter or margarine. Place breast side up on rack in open shallow roasting pan. Do not add water. Do not cover.

Follow Timetable for approximate total cooking time. Chicken is done when drumstick meat feels very soft when pressed between fingers.

You'll find some guidelines for carving a roast chicken on page 156.

TIMETABLE

Ready-to-Cook Weight	Oven Temperature	Approximate Total Cooking Time
Broiler-fryer		
1½ to 2 pounds	400°	¾ to 1 hour
2 to 2½ pounds	400°	1 to 1¼ hours
2½ to 3 pounds	375°	1¼ to 1¾ hours
3 to 4 pounds	375°	1¾ to 2¼ hours
Capon (stuffed)		
5 to 8 pounds	325°	2½ to 3½ hours

GIBLETS

Wash gizzard, heart, liver and neck. Cover all except liver with water; season with ½ teaspoon salt, 2 peppercorns, 2 cloves, a small bay leaf and a little onion. Heat to boiling. Reduce heat; cover and simmer 1 to 2 hours or until gizzard is tender. Liver is very tender and can be fried, broiled or simmered in water, 5 to 10 minutes.

Giblet broth can be used in stuffing, gravy and recipes where chicken broth is specified. Cooked giblets can be cut up and added to gravy or stuffing. Refrigerate giblets and broth separately.

SAUSAGE STUFFING

Prepare 1 package (7 ounces) dry herbed stuffing mix as directed on package except—add ½ pound bulk pork sausage, crumbled and browned.

About 5 cups (enough for 5- to 8-pound chicken).

VARIATIONS

- *Apple-Raisin Stuffing:* Omit sausage; add 1 medium apple, finely chopped, and ⅓ cup raisins.
- *Pecan Stuffing:* Omit sausage; add 1 cup coarsely chopped pecans.

CHICKEN IN A POT

Pictured on page 38.

  1 apple, quartered
2½- to 3-pound broiler-fryer chicken
  2 tablespoons lemon juice
  2 teaspoons onion salt
  ½ teaspoon rosemary
  ⅛ teaspoon instant minced garlic

Heat oven to 375°. Place apple in cavity of chicken. Fold wings across back with tips touching. Place chicken breast side up in small Dutch oven or clay pot. (If using clay pot, line with parchment.) Brush chicken with lemon juice; season with remaining ingredients. Cover and bake about 1½ hours or until done.

4 servings.

Substitution

For instant garlic: 1 clove garlic, minced.

BROILED CHICKEN

Pictured on page 38.

Young chickens, weighing 2½ pounds or less, can be broiled. They should be halved, quartered or cut into pieces. If using chicken halves or quarters, turn wing tips onto back side.

Set oven control at broil and/or 550°. Brush chicken with melted butter or margarine. Place skin side down on rack in broiler pan; place broiler pan so top of chicken is 7 to 9 inches from heat. (If it is not possible to place the broiler pan this far from heat, reduce temperature to 450°.)

Broil chicken 30 minutes. Season brown side with salt and pepper. Turn chicken; if desired, brush again with butter or margarine. Broil 20 to 30 minutes longer or until brown, crisp and done.

FRIED CHICKEN

½ cup Gold Medal Flour*
1 teaspoon salt
½ teaspoon paprika
¼ teaspoon pepper
  Salad oil
2- to 3-pound broiler-fryer chicken, cut up

Mix flour, salt, paprika and pepper. Heat salad oil (¼ inch) in large skillet. Coat chicken with flour mixture. Brown chicken lightly in oil over medium heat, 15 to 20 minutes.

Reduce heat. Cover tightly; simmer 30 to 40 minutes or until done. (If skillet cannot be covered tightly, add 1 to 2 tablespoons water.) Turn chicken once or twice to assure even browning. Uncover for the last 5 minutes of cooking to crisp chicken.

Team this traditional favorite with something unexpected—perhaps Okra and Tomato Salad (page 56) and Curried Rice (page 75).

4 servings.

If using Self-Rising Flour, decrease salt to ½ teaspoon.

VARIATION

■ *Maryland Fried Chicken:* Beat 2 eggs and 2 tablespoons water. After coating chicken with flour, dip into egg, then coat with 2 cups cracker crumbs or dry bread crumbs.

OVEN-FRIED CHICKEN

¼ cup shortening
¼ cup butter or margarine
½ cup Gold Medal Flour*
1 teaspoon salt
1 teaspoon paprika
¼ teaspoon pepper
2½- to 3-pound broiler-fryer chicken,
  cut up

Heat oven to 425°. In oven, melt shortening and butter in baking pan, 13×9×2 inches. Mix flour, salt, paprika and pepper; coat chicken with flour mixture.

Arrange chicken skin side down in shortening. Bake uncovered 30 minutes. Turn chicken; bake uncovered 30 minutes longer or until done.

For an easy, everything-in-the-oven meal, accompany with baked squash, Oven-fried Eggplant (page 65) and even Raspberry Pie (page 105).

4 servings.

If using Self-Rising Flour, omit salt.

VARIATIONS

■ *Crusty-Curried Chicken:* Omit flour mixture; coat chicken with mixture of 1 cup Bisquick, 2 tablespoons curry powder, 1½ teaspoons salt and ¼ teaspoon pepper.

■ *Garlic Chip Chicken:* Omit flour mixture for coating chicken. In large skillet, melt ¼ cup butter or margarine with 1 teaspoon garlic salt, 1 teaspoon salt and ⅛ teaspoon pepper. Remove from heat. Finely crush 1 bag (5½ ounces) potato chips. Dip chicken into garlic butter, then coat with crushed chips.

■ *Saucy Oven-fried Chicken:* After baking chicken, drain off fat. Pour 1 can of our mushroom sauce (1 cup) on chicken; return to oven to heat through.

GOLDEN PARMESAN CHICKEN

Pictured on page 5.

1¼ cups grated Parmesan cheese
 1 teaspoon salt
 ¼ teaspoon pepper
 3-pound broiler-fryer chicken, cut up
 ⅓ cup butter or margarine, melted

Heat oven to 425°. Grease baking pan, 13×9×2 inches. Mix cheese, salt and pepper. Dip chicken into butter, then coat with cheese mixture.

Arrange chicken skin side down in pan. Pour remaining butter on chicken. Bake uncovered 30 minutes. Turn chicken; bake uncovered 20 minutes longer or until done.

Chilled Asparagus (page 61) and potato salad play up to the Parmesan.

4 servings.

Note: This is delicious served cold. After baking, cool, cover and refrigerate.

BARBECUED CHICKEN

 ¼ cup butter or margarine
2½- to 3-pound broiler-fryer chicken, cut up
 ½ cup barbecue sauce
 ¼ cup frozen lemonade concentrate (thawed)
 ¼ cup water
 2 tablespoons instant minced onion

Heat oven to 425°. In oven, melt butter in baking pan, 13×9×2 inches. Place chicken in butter, turning to coat. Arrange skin side down in pan. Bake uncovered 30 minutes. Drain off fat; turn chicken.

Mix remaining ingredients; pour on chicken. Bake uncovered 30 minutes longer or until done, basting occasionally with sauce.

4 servings.

Substitution

For instant onion: ⅓ cup minced onion.

Pictured at left:
Broiled Chicken, Islander Chicken, Chicken in a Pot

ISLANDER CHICKEN

Pictured at left.

4 servings ready-to-eat fried chicken (about 12 pieces)
1 can of our sweet and sour sauce (1 cup)
8 large twist pretzels, if desired

Heat oven to 300°. Brush chicken with sauce. Arrange in ungreased baking pan, 13×9×2 inches. Bake uncovered 30 minutes or until heated through. Heat pretzels during the last 5 minutes.

With Snow Peas and Carrot Nuggets (page 66) and Mashed Potatoes flecked with green pepper (page 69), who would guess this meal started at the deli?

4 servings.

BARBECUED CHICKEN FIX-UP

1 ready-to-eat barbecued chicken, split in half
¼ cup honey
¼ cup lemon juice
¼ teaspoon tarragon

Heat oven to 300°. Place chicken skin side up in ungreased baking pan, 13×9×2 inches. Mix remaining ingredients; pour on chicken. Bake uncovered about 25 minutes or until heated through.

Pick up a three-bean salad at the deli.

2 servings.

CHICKEN BAKE

2½- to 3-pound broiler-fryer chicken, cut up
 1 can of our mushroom sauce (1 cup)
 ½ envelope (about 1½-ounce size) onion soup mix

Heat oven to 375°. Arrange chicken skin side up in ungreased baking pan, 13×9×2 inches. Mix mushroom sauce and onion soup mix (dry); pour on chicken. Cover tightly; bake 30 minutes. Uncover; bake 30 minutes longer or until done.

Need some menu help? We suggest Celery Seed Mashed Potatoes (page 69), Peas and Almonds (page 66), and Chocolate Chip Bars (page 92) with ice cream.

4 to 6 servings.

STEWED CHICKEN

3- to 4-pound broiler-fryer chicken, cut up
1 sprig parsley
1 celery stalk with leaves, cut up
1 carrot, sliced
1 small onion, sliced
2 teaspoons salt
½ teaspoon pepper

Place chicken with giblets and neck in kettle or Dutch oven. Add water to cover chicken. Add remaining ingredients; heat to boiling. Reduce heat. Cover tightly; simmer about 45 minutes or until done. Allow chicken to cool slightly in broth; refrigerate just until cool.

When cool, remove meat from bones and skin in pieces as large as possible. Skim fat from broth. Refrigerate broth and chicken pieces separately in covered containers; use within several days. For longer storage, package chicken and broth together and freeze.

3 to 4 cups cubed cooked chicken and 2 to 3½ cups broth.

Note: To cook a stewing chicken, select 4- to 5-pound stewing chicken. Simmer 2½ to 3½ hours or until tender.

About 5 cups cubed cooked chicken and 5 to 6 cups broth.

━━━━━━━━━━━━━━

Concocting a Casserole?

Improvising, stretching or changing just for the sake of change? Whatever your reason for wanting to ad lib a bit, you can do so if you know how to figure.

To Equal:	Use:
2 cups cooked chicken or turkey	half of a 3- to 4-pound broiler-fryer or stewing chicken or 1½ to 2 pounds turkey pieces
1 cup cleaned cooked shrimp	¾ pound raw shrimp in the shell or 1 package (7 ounces) frozen peeled shrimp or 1 can (4½ to 5 ounces) shrimp
1 cup cooked rice	⅓ cup regular rice or ¼ cup converted rice or ½ cup instant (precooked) rice
2 cups cooked macaroni, spaghetti or noodles	3½ ounces macaroni or spaghetti or 4 ounces noodles

CAN-OPENER COMBO

1 can (16 ounces) French-style green beans, drained
1 can (10½ ounces) condensed cream of mushroom soup
2 jars (5½ ounces each) boned chicken
½ teaspoon sage
Chow mein noodles

Heat green beans, soup, chicken and sage, stirring occasionally. Serve on noodles.

A simple salad of lettuce wedges and your favorite dressing is just enough.

4 servings.

Substitution

For chicken: 1½ cups cubed cooked chicken or turkey.

CHICKEN AND MACARONI CASSEROLE

1½ cups uncooked elbow macaroni (about 5 ounces)
1 cup shredded Cheddar cheese (4 ounces)
1½ cups cut-up cooked chicken
1 can (4 ounces) mushroom stems and pieces, drained
¼ cup chopped pimiento
1 can (10½ ounces) condensed cream of chicken soup
1 cup milk
½ teaspoon salt
½ teaspoon curry powder

Heat oven to 350°. Mix all ingredients in ungreased 1½-quart casserole. Cover tightly; bake 1 hour.

Complete the menu with broccoli, Cucumber Relish Mold (page 57) and Date or Mocha Brownies (page 89).

4 to 6 servings.

VARIATIONS

■ *Ham or Turkey and Macaroni Casserole:* Substitute 1½ cups cubed cooked ham or 1½ cups cubed cooked turkey for the chicken.

Turkey

ROAST TURKEY

Allow ¾ to 1 pound per serving when roasting turkeys under 12 pounds. For heavier birds, 12 pounds and over, allow ½ to ¾ pound per serving. If desired, season cavity of turkey lightly with salt. Do not salt cavity if turkey is to be stuffed.

Stuff turkey just before roasting. Fill wishbone area with stuffing first. Fasten neck skin to back with skewer. Fold wings across back with tips touching. Fill body cavity lightly. (Stuffing will expand.) Tuck drumsticks under band of skin or tie together with heavy string, then tie to tail.

Heat oven to 325°. Place turkey breast side up on rack in open shallow roasting pan. Brush with shortening, oil or butter. Insert meat thermometer so tip is in thickest part of inside thigh muscle or thickest part of breast meat and does not touch bone. Do not add water. Do not cover.

Follow Timetable. Place a tent of aluminum foil loosely over turkey when it starts to turn golden. When ⅔ done, cut band or string holding legs.

There is no substitute for a meat thermometer. It should register 185°. If the bird is stuffed, the point of the thermometer can be placed in the center of the stuffing and will register 165°. If a thermometer is not used, test for doneness about 30 minutes before Timetable so indicates. Move drumstick up and down—if done, the joint should give readily.

When turkey is done, remove from oven and allow to stand about 20 minutes for easiest carving. As soon as possible after serving, remove every bit of stuffing from turkey. Cool stuffing, meat and any gravy promptly; refrigerate separately. Use gravy or stuffing within 1 or 2 days; heat them thoroughly before serving. Serve cooked turkey meat within 2 or 3 days after roasting. If frozen, it can be kept up to 1 month.

See page 156 for carving tips.

TIMETABLE

Ready-to-Cook Weight	Approximate Total Cooking Time	Internal Temperature
6 to 8 pounds	3 to 3½ hours	185°
8 to 12 pounds	3½ to 4½ hours	185°
12 to 16 pounds	4½ to 5½ hours	185°
16 to 20 pounds	5½ to 6½ hours	185°
20 to 24 pounds	6½ to 7 hours	185°

This timetable is based on chilled or completely thawed turkeys at a temperature of about 40° and placed in preheated ovens. Time will be slightly less for unstuffed turkeys. Differences in the shape and tenderness of individual turkeys can also necessitate increasing or decreasing the cooking time slightly. For best results, use a meat thermometer. For prestuffed turkeys, follow package directions carefully; do not use timetable.

COOKING TURKEY IN FOIL

Prepare turkey as directed for Roast Turkey (at left). To wrap, place turkey breast side up in middle of large sheet of heavy-duty aluminum foil. (For larger birds, join two widths of foil.)

Brush with shortening, oil or butter. Place small pieces of aluminum foil over the ends of legs, tail and wing tips to prevent puncturing. Bring long ends of aluminum foil up over the breast of turkey and overlap 3 inches. Close open ends by folding up foil so drippings will not run into pan. Wrap loosely and do not seal airtight.

Heat oven to 450°. Place wrapped turkey, breast up, in open shallow roasting pan. Follow Timetable for approximate cooking time. Open foil once or twice during cooking to judge doneness. When thigh joint and breast meat begin to soften, fold back foil completely to brown turkey and crisp skin. Insert meat thermometer at this time.

TIMETABLE

Ready-to-Cook Weight	Approximate Total Cooking Time	Internal Temperature
7 to 9 pounds	2¼ to 2½ hours	185°
10 to 13 pounds	2¾ to 3 hours	185°
14 to 17 pounds	3½ to 4 hours	185°
18 to 21 pounds	4½ to 5 hours	185°
22 to 24 pounds	5½ to 6 hours	185°

HERBED TURKEY ROAST

3½- to 4-pound turkey roast
1 cup white wine
2 tablespoons butter or margarine, melted
½ teaspoon salt
⅛ teaspoon pepper
⅛ teaspoon sage
⅛ teaspoon thyme
¼ cup water
2 tablespoons flour

Bake turkey roast as directed on package except —before roasting, mix wine, butter, salt, pepper, sage and thyme and pour on roast.

Remove roast from pan; keep warm. Skim fat from broth. Measure broth; return 1 cup to roasting pan. In tightly covered jar, shake water and flour; stir slowly into broth in pan. Heat to boiling, stirring constantly. Boil and stir 1 minute. Serve gravy with turkey.

Serve this elegant roast with elegant accompaniments: Honey-Chili Squash (page 67), Creamed Onions and Broccoli (page 66), Molded Waldorf Salad (page 57) and Hot Fruit Compote (page 83).

6 to 8 servings.

Note: If turkey roast is in cello-bag and directions call for cooking in bag, do not remove. With kitchen scissors, snip a small X in top of bag; pour wine mixture through funnel into bag.

Substitution

For wine: 1 cup apple juice.

TURKEY ROAST BORDELAISE

Bake 2-pound frozen turkey roast as directed on package except—30 minutes before end of roasting time, drain meat drippings from pan. Pour 1 can of our Bordelaise sauce (1 cup) on turkey; bake uncovered 30 minutes longer.

We like this with Green and White Salad (page 55) and Frozen Rice in Combination (page 74).

6 servings.

PINEAPPLE BRAISED DRUMSTICKS

1 package (about 2½ pounds) frozen
  turkey drumsticks, thawed
2 tablespoons shortening
  Salt and pepper
1 cup pineapple juice
½ cup pineapple juice
2 tablespoons flour

In large skillet, brown drumsticks slowly in shortening. Drain off fat. Season with salt and pepper and pour on 1 cup pineapple juice. Cover tightly; simmer 2 to 2½ hours or until tender, turning occasionally. Remove drumsticks and keep warm.

In tightly covered jar, shake ½ cup pineapple juice and flour; stir slowly into hot liquid. Heat to boiling, stirring constantly. Boil and stir 1 minute. Serve gravy with drumsticks.

Menu suggestions: spinach, Cucumber Relish Mold (page 57) and Coconut Rice (page 74).

4 servings.

VARIATION

■ *Deluxe Turkey Drumsticks:* Stir in 1 can (13½ ounces) pineapple chunks, drained, and 1 green pepper, thinly sliced, 15 minutes before end of cooking time.

SAUCY TURKEY CUTLETS

1 package (12 ounces) frozen turkey cutlets
1 can of our Bordelaise sauce (1 cup)

Cook turkey cutlets as directed on package except—5 minutes before end of cooking time, pour sauce on cutlets.

Team up with Green Beans and Bacon (page 62), a fruit salad (perhaps grapefruit and avocado) and Chive Mashed Potatoes (page 69).

4 servings.

Pictured at right:
Herbed Turkey Roast and Deluxe Turkey
Drumsticks—turkey treatments for today.

SLICED TURKEY AND DRESSING BAKE

1 package (7 ounces) dry herbed
    stuffing mix
1 package (28 ounces) frozen turkey slices
    in gravy

Heat oven to 400°. Prepare stuffing as directed on package; pat into greased baking dish, 11½ × 7½ × 1½ inches. Remove frozen turkey and gravy from foil; place on stuffing. Bake uncovered 1 hour.

A green vegetable and a salad such as Seedless Grape Salad (page 60) round out the menu.

6 servings.

VARIATION

■ *Sliced Beef and Dressing Bake:* Substitute 1 package (24 ounces) frozen beef slices in gravy for the turkey slices in gravy.

TURKEY DIVAN

2 packages (10 ounces each) frozen
    broccoli spears
6 slices turkey, about ¼ inch thick
1 can of our cheese sauce (1 cup)
1 can (3½ ounces) French fried onion rings

Heat oven to 350°. Rinse broccoli with small amount of running cold water to separate and remove ice crystals; drain. Arrange broccoli in ungreased baking dish, 11½ × 7½ × 1½ inches. (If broccoli stems are more than ½ inch in diameter, cut lengthwise in half.)

Top with turkey slices and spoon on cheese sauce. Bake uncovered 25 minutes. Sprinkle with onion rings; bake 5 minutes longer.

4 to 6 servings.

Substitutions

    For broccoli: 2 packages (10 ounces each) frozen asparagus spears.
    For sliced turkey: 1½ to 2 cups cut-up cooked turkey.

VARIATION

■ *Chicken Divan:* Substitute 1½ to 2 cups cut-up cooked chicken for the turkey slices.

WILD RICE AND TURKEY CASSEROLE

2 cups cut-up cooked turkey
1 package (6 ounces) seasoned long
    grained and wild rice
1 can of our mushroom sauce (1 cup)
¼ cup chopped onion
½ teaspoon salt
2¼ cups boiling water

Heat oven to 350°. Mix all ingredients in ungreased 2-quart casserole. Cover tightly; bake about 50 minutes or until rice is tender. Uncover; bake 10 minutes longer.

We like Green and White Salad (page 55) with this easy oven casserole.

6 servings.

VARIATION

■ *Wild Rice and Chicken Casserole:* Substitute 2 cups cut-up cooked chicken for the turkey.

FRUITED TURKEY SALAD

1½ cups cut-up cooked turkey
1 can (8¼ ounces) green grapes, drained
1 can (5 ounces) water chestnuts,
    drained and chopped
1 can (11 ounces) mandarin orange
    segments, drained
½ cup mayonnaise or salad dressing
½ teaspoon salt
¼ teaspoon curry powder

Combine turkey, grapes, water chestnuts and orange segments. Mix remaining ingredients; toss with turkey mixture.

So pretty when served in a bowl lined with greens and garnished with toasted almonds.

3 or 4 servings.

Substitution

    For canned grapes: 1 cup fresh seedless green grapes.

VARIATION

■ *Fruited Chicken Salad:* Substitute 1½ cups cut-up cooked chicken for the turkey.

Fish and Seafood

BAKED FISH

2 pounds fish fillets or steaks
  Salt and pepper
2 tablespoons lemon juice
1 teaspoon grated onion
¼ cup butter or margarine, melted

Heat oven to 350°. If fillets are large, cut into serving pieces. Season with salt and pepper. Mix lemon juice, onion and butter; dip fish into butter mixture.

Arrange fish in greased baking pan, 9×9×2 inches. Pour remaining butter mixture on fish. Bake uncovered 25 to 30 minutes or until fish flakes easily with fork. Sprinkle with paprika if you like.

About 6 servings.

GOLDEN SOLE

1 package (16 ounces) frozen sole fillets
  Salt and pepper
1 tablespoon butter or margarine
1 can (19 ounces) asparagus spears, drained
1 can of our hollandaise sauce (1 cup)

Thaw fillets just until they can be separated. Heat oven to 475°. Arrange fish in ungreased baking dish, 11½×7½×1½ inches, leaving space in center of dish. Season fish with salt and pepper and dot with butter. Bake uncovered 15 minutes.

Remove from oven; arrange asparagus in center of dish. Pour hollandaise sauce on asparagus. Bake 5 minutes or until heated through. Like something a bit different? Sprinkle 1 cup French fried onion rings on fish and bake 2 minutes longer.

Serve with Country-style Waldorf Salad (page 58), a green vegetable and Dill Mashed Potatoes (page 69). Strawberry Cream (page 112) is the beverage-dessert.

3 or 4 servings.

HALIBUT WITH VEGETABLES

1½ to 2 pounds halibut fillets
1 teaspoon salt
¼ teaspoon pepper
¼ teaspoon paprika
2 carrots
3 stalks celery
6 green onions
1 teaspoon salt
¼ cup butter or margarine
1 tablespoon lemon juice

Heat oven to 350°. Arrange fish in ungreased baking pan, 13×9×2 inches. Season with 1 teaspoon salt, the pepper and paprika.

Cut carrots, celery and onions (with tops) into 1-inch lengths. Place in blender; add water to cover. Chop, watching carefully. Drain thoroughly. (Or carrots can be shredded and celery and onions finely chopped by hand.)

Spread vegetables on fish; season with 1 teaspoon salt. Dot with butter and sprinkle with lemon juice. Cover tightly; bake 30 minutes or until fish flakes easily with fork.

Herbed Zucchini (page 68) and Creamy Blackeye Peas (page 67) round out the main dish.

6 servings.

Note: This dish can be prepared ahead of time, refrigerated and baked later. Increase the baking time 15 minutes.

POACHED FISH

1 medium onion, sliced
3 slices lemon
3 sprigs parsley
1 bay leaf
1 teaspoon salt
2 peppercorns
1 pound fish fillets

Pour water (1½ inches) into large skillet; add onion, lemon slices, parsley, bay leaf, salt and peppercorns and heat to boiling.

Arrange fish in single layer in skillet. Cover tightly; simmer 4 to 6 minutes or until fish flakes easily.

2 or 3 servings.

BROILED FISH

2 pounds fish fillets or steaks,
  about 1 inch thick
1 teaspoon salt
⅛ teaspoon pepper
¼ cup butter or margarine, melted

Set oven control at broil and/or 550°. Grease broiler pan and place in oven to heat. If fillets are large, cut into serving pieces. Season with salt and pepper. If fish has not been skinned, arrange skin side up in broiler pan; brush with some of the butter.

Broil fish 2 to 3 inches from heat 5 to 8 minutes or until light brown. Brush with butter; turn carefully and brush again. Broil 5 to 8 minutes longer or until fish flakes easily with fork.

6 servings.

VARIATION

■ *Broiled Fish Italiano:* Omit salt, pepper and butter; brush fish with ¼ cup Italian salad dressing during broiling.

PARSLEYED FISH BROIL

1½ to 2 pounds fish fillets or steaks,
  ¾ to 1 inch thick
1 teaspoon salt
⅛ teaspoon pepper
½ cup butter or margarine, melted
¼ cup lemon juice
2 tablespoons snipped parsley

Set oven control at broil and/or 550°. Grease rack in broiler pan and place in oven to heat. Season fish with salt and pepper. Mix remaining ingredients; brush some of the butter mixture on fish.

Broil fish 2 to 3 inches from heat 3 to 5 minutes or until brown. Brush with butter mixture; turn carefully and brush again. Broil 3 to 5 minutes longer or until fish flakes easily with fork. Serve with remaining butter mixture.

Suggested go-withs: Sautéed Spinach (page 67), Perfection Salad (page 57) and Potatoes O'Brien (page 70).

6 servings.

CRISPY FISH STICKS

1 package (16 ounces) frozen fish sticks
¼ cup tomato French salad dressing
½ to ¾ teaspoon barbecue spice
1 tablespoon lemon juice
½ teaspoon prepared mustard

Arrange frozen fish sticks on ungreased baking sheet. Mix remaining ingredients; brush on fish. Bake or broil as directed on package.

Serve with Dilled Peas and Cauliflower (page 66) and an orange and grapefruit salad.

4 or 5 servings.

LIME-GLAZED FISH STICKS

1 package (8 ounces) frozen fish sticks
¼ cup lime marmalade, melted
2 tablespoons lime juice

Bake fish sticks as directed on package for oven method except—blend marmalade and juice; spoon onto fish sticks for the last 5 minutes of baking.

Peas and Almonds (page 66) are great with this quick fish fix-up.

3 servings.

VARIATION

■ *Orange-glazed Fish Sticks:* Substitute ¼ cup orange marmalade, melted, for the lime marmalade and 2 tablespoons lemon juice for the lime juice.

FISH STICKS
WITH MUSHROOMS AND PECANS

1 package (8 ounces) frozen fish sticks
1 can (4 ounces) mushrooms stems and
  pieces, drained
¼ cup chopped onion
¼ cup butter or margarine, melted
¼ cup chopped pecans

Arrange frozen fish sticks in jelly roll pan, 15½ × 10½ × 1 inch. Mix remaining ingredients and spoon onto fish sticks. Bake as directed on package.

Nice with our colorful Pineapple-Cheese Mold (page 58).

3 servings.

PANFRIED FISH

2 pounds fish fillets, steaks or
  pan-dressed fish
1 teaspoon salt
⅛ teaspoon pepper
1 egg
1 tablespoon water
1 cup Gold Medal Flour
  Shortening (part butter)

If fillets are large, cut into serving pieces. Season with salt and pepper. Beat egg and water slightly. Dip fish into egg, then coat with flour. Melt shortening (⅛ inch) in skillet; fry fish over medium heat, about 10 minutes.

4 to 6 servings.

Substitution

For flour: 1 cup Bisquick, cornmeal or grated Parmesan cheese.

VARIATION

■ *Fish Almondine:* Brown ¼ cup butter or margarine in small skillet; stir in ¼ cup toasted slivered blanched almonds, ¼ teaspoon salt and 2 teaspoons lemon juice. Just before serving, top fish with almond butter.

OVEN-FRIED FILLETS

2 pounds fish fillets or steaks
1 tablespoon salt
½ cup milk
1 cup dry bread crumbs
¼ cup butter or margarine, melted

Heat oven to 500°. If fillets are large, cut into serving pieces. Stir salt into milk. Dip fish into milk, then coat with bread crumbs. Arrange in well-greased baking pan, 13×9×2 inches.

Pour butter on fish. Place pan on rack slightly above middle of oven; bake uncovered 10 to 12 minutes or until fish flakes easily with fork.

6 servings.

HERBED SALMON STEAKS

Pictured on page 5.

3 packages (12 ounces each) frozen
  salmon steaks
¼ cup lemon juice
2 tablespoons butter or margarine, melted
2 teaspoons marjoram leaves
2 teaspoons onion salt
½ teaspoon seasoned pepper
  Paprika
  Lemon wedges
  Snipped parsley

Heat oven to 450°. Arrange frozen salmon steaks in greased baking pan, 13×9×2 inches. Mix lemon juice, butter, marjoram leaves, onion salt and seasoned pepper; brush on fish. Bake uncovered 35 minutes or until fish flakes easily with a fork. Sprinkle with paprika; garnish with lemon wedges and parsley.

Menu mates: Crunchy Creamy Spinach (page 67), sliced tomatoes and potato salad.

6 servings.

SCALLOP CASSEROLE

1 package (12 ounces) frozen scallops,
  thawed
¾ cup light cream (20%)
1 cup dry bread crumbs
½ cup butter or margarine, melted
2 teaspoons celery seed
1 teaspoon salt
¼ teaspoon pepper
  Paprika

Heat oven to 375°. If scallops are large, cut into 1½-inch pieces. Remove any shell particles and wash scallops. Arrange in greased baking dish, 11½×7½×1½ inches.

Pour about half the cream on scallops. Mix bread crumbs, butter and seasonings; sprinkle on scallops. Pour on remaining cream (liquid should come about ¾ of the way up on scallops). Sprinkle with paprika. Bake uncovered 25 to 30 minutes.

4 servings.

Substitution

For frozen scallops: ¾ pound fresh scallops.

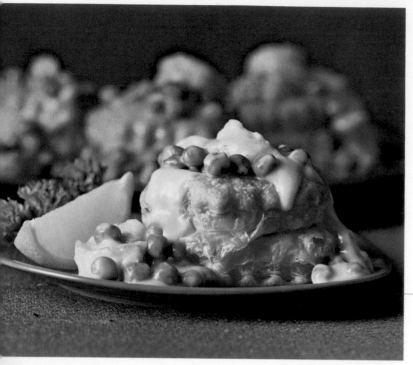

Creamy Shrimp and Peas

Skillet Paella

JIFFY LOBSTER NEWBURG

1 can (5½ ounces) lobster, drained
1 can of our Newburg sauce (1 cup)
2 or 3 slices toast

Break lobster meat into pieces. Heat Newburg sauce as directed on can. Stir in lobster; cook over low heat until heated through. Serve on hot toast.

Complete this classy canned dinner with asparagus, Orange and Onion Salad (page 58) and Chocolate-Cherry Parfait (page 85).

2 or 3 servings.

VARIATION

■ *Shrimp Newburg:* Substitute 1 can (4½ or 5 ounces) shrimp, rinsed and drained, for the lobster.

SKILLET PAELLA

1 package (12 ounces) frozen peeled shrimp
1 can (7 to 8 ounces) minced clams
1 can (5 ounces) boned chicken
1 can (16 ounces) tomatoes
1 package (10 ounces) frozen green peas, broken apart
2 cups uncooked instant rice
2 tablespoons instant minced onion
1 teaspoon paprika
1 teaspoon instant chicken bouillon
¼ teaspoon cayenne red pepper
⅛ teaspoon saffron

Rinse frozen shrimp under running cold water to remove ice crystals. Stir together all ingredients in large skillet. Heat to boiling, stirring occasionally. Reduce heat; simmer 5 minutes. Remove skillet from heat. Cover tightly; let stand about 10 minutes.

4 or 5 servings.

Substitutions

For frozen shrimp: 2 cans (4½ ounces each) jumbo shrimp, drained.

For canned chicken: ½ cup cubed cooked chicken.
For tomatoes: 1 can (16 ounces) stewed tomatoes.
For instant onion: ⅓ cup minced onion.
For instant bouillon: 1 chicken bouillon cube.

CREAMY SHRIMP AND PEAS

1 package (7 ounces) frozen peeled shrimp
1 can (10 ounces) frozen condensed
cream of shrimp soup, thawed
1 package (10 ounces) frozen green peas
2 tablespoons pasteurized process cheese
spread
2 tablespoons sherry
4 baked patty shells

Rinse frozen shrimp under running cold water to remove ice crystals. Heat shrimp, soup and peas to boiling. Boil and stir 5 minutes. Stir in cheese spread and sherry; cook, stirring until cheese is melted. Serve in patty shells.

Molded Waldorf Salad (page 57) adds color to the meal.

4 servings.

Substitutions

For sherry: 1 tablespoon plus 1 teaspoon sherry flavoring.
For patty shells: Toast points.

TUNA AND RICE MELANGE

1 small onion, thinly sliced
1 tablespoon salad oil
1 package (10 ounces) frozen
mixed vegetables
½ cup water
3 cups cooked rice (without salt)
2 cans (6½ ounces each) tuna, drained
1 cup thinly sliced celery
¼ cup soy sauce

In large skillet, cook and stir onion in oil until tender. Add frozen vegetables and water; heat to boiling. Reduce heat. Cover tightly; simmer 5 to 10 minutes or until vegetables are tender. Stir in remaining ingredients; heat through.

6 to 8 servings.

TUNA-NOODLE DINNER

1 package of our noodles almondine
1 can (6½ ounces) tuna, drained
1 package (10 ounces) frozen mixed
vegetables, broken apart

Heat oven to 350°. Prepare noodles almondine as directed on package for oven method except—use 2 cups boiling water; stir in tuna and vegetables. Bake uncovered about 25 minutes or until liquid is absorbed. Stir before serving; garnish with packet of almonds.

This complete meal-in-a-dish needs only the crunch of celery sticks.

4 servings.

Substitution

For frozen vegetables: 1 cup cooked mixed vegetables.

SALMON PUFF

2 cans (16 ounces each) salmon,
drained (reserve liquid)
About ¾ cup milk
2 eggs, slightly beaten
3 cups coarse cracker crumbs
¼ cup frozen chopped onion
1 teaspoon lemon pepper
¼ teaspoon salt

Heat oven to 350°. Flake salmon, removing bone and skin. Add enough milk to reserved salmon liquid to measure 1½ cups. Mix all ingredients. Pour into greased 2-quart casserole. Bake uncovered 45 minutes. Garnish with lemon twists or wedges.

We like this light, fluffy casserole with Best Tossed Salad (page 55) and Classic Bean Casserole (page 62)—baked in the same oven. Blender Orange-Raisin Cake (page 101) is the dessert choice.

6 to 8 servings.

Substitutions

For frozen onion: ¼ cup chopped onion.
For lemon pepper: 1 teaspoon lemon juice and ¼ teaspoon seasoned pepper.

Cheese-Spinach Soufflé

Jiffy Cheese Fondue

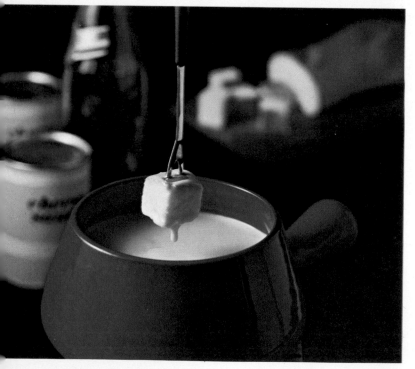

Cheese, Eggs and Beans

CHEESE-SPINACH SOUFFLÉ

1 package (12 ounces) frozen
    spinach soufflé, thawed
2 packages (12 ounces each) frozen
    cheese soufflé, thawed

Heat oven to 350°. Butter 8-cup soufflé dish or 2-quart casserole. (If using soufflé dish, make a 4-inch band of triple thickness aluminum foil 2 inches longer than circumference of dish; butter one side. Extend depth of dish by securing foil band, buttered side in, around outside top of dish.)

Pour spinach soufflé into soufflé dish. Top with cheese soufflés. Bake 1 hour or until knife inserted halfway between edge and center comes out clean. Serve immediately. Carefully remove foil band and divide soufflé into sections with 2 forks.

Let the soufflé star for company. Lead off with Guacamole Dip with Tacos (page 150), then serve the soufflé with Artichokes and Peas (page 61) and Sesame Rye Fingers (page 77). Offer Cookie Refrigerator Dessert (page 88) for dessert.

5 or 6 servings.

JIFFY CHEESE FONDUE

1 clove garlic
2 cans of our cheese sauce (2 cups)
⅓ cup dry white wine
    French bread

Rub cut clove of garlic around the inside of an earthenware fondue pot. Heat cheese sauce and wine. Pour into fondue pot and keep hot over low heat. Use long-handled forks to spear 1-inch cubes of French bread, then dip and swirl in fondue.

Bright Bean Salad (page 56) is an ideal side dish. Try other dippers for the fondue—cubes of cooked ham, cherry tomatoes, avocado chunks.

4 servings.

PIZZA RICE

12 slices bacon, diced
  Cooked instant rice (enough for
  4 servings)
1½ cups shredded Cheddar cheese
  (6 ounces)
¼ cup instant minced onion
2 tablespoons dried green pepper
1 can (10½ ounces) pizza sauce

Fry bacon until crisp; drain off fat. Stir in rice and cheese; sprinkle with onion and green pepper. Pour sauce on rice. Cover tightly, cook over low heat until cheese melts, about 10 minutes.

4 to 6 servings.

Substitutions

For instant rice: 2 cups cooked rice.
For instant onion: 1 large onion, chopped.
For dried green pepper: ⅓ cup chopped green pepper.

EGGS CONTINENTAL

¼ cup dry bread crumbs
1 tablespoon butter or margarine, melted
4 hard-cooked eggs, sliced
3 slices bacon, diced
1 cup dairy sour cream
1 tablespoon milk
1 tablespoon instant minced onion
½ teaspoon salt
¼ teaspoon paprika
⅛ teaspoon pepper
½ cup shredded Cheddar cheese

Heat oven to 350°. Toss bread crumbs in melted butter; divide among 4 buttered 10-ounce casseroles or baking dishes. Layer egg slices on crumbs.

Fry bacon until crisp; remove bacon and drain. Stir together bacon, sour cream, milk, onion and seasonings; spoon onto eggs. Top with cheese. Bake uncovered 10 to 15 minutes or until cheese is melted.

Buttered Brussels sprouts and rye toast make good go-withs.

4 servings.

Substitution

For instant onion: 3 tablespoons minced onion.

EGG FOO YONG

2 tablespoons salad oil
3 eggs
1 cup bean sprouts, drained
½ cup chopped cooked pork
2 tablespoons chopped onion
1 tablespoon soy sauce
  Sauce (below)

Heat oil in large skillet. Beat eggs until thick; stir in bean sprouts, pork, onion and soy sauce.

Pour ¼ cup mixture at a time into skillet; with broad spatula, push cooked egg up over meat to form a patty. When patties are set, turn to brown other side. Serve hot with Sauce.

5 servings.

SAUCE

1 teaspoon cornstarch
1 teaspoon sugar
1 teaspoon vinegar
2½ tablespoons soy sauce
½ cup water

Mix all ingredients in small saucepan. Cook, stirring constantly, until mixture thickens and boils. Boil and stir 1 minute.

CREAMED HAM AND EGGS

3 tablespoons butter or margarine
3 tablespoons flour
½ teaspoon dry mustard
¼ teaspoon salt
⅛ teaspoon pepper
2¼ cups milk
1 cup diced cooked ham
4 hard-cooked eggs, quartered
  Buttered toast

Melt butter in large saucepan over low heat. Blend in flour and seasonings. Cook over low heat, stirring until mixture is smooth and bubbly. Remove from heat. Stir in milk. Heat to boiling, stirring constantly. Boil and stir 1 minute. Gently stir in ham and eggs; heat through. Serve hot on toast.

6 servings.

Substitution

For toast: Toast cups, biscuits or hot fluffy rice.

CHEDDAR EGG BAKE

6 eggs, slightly beaten
1 cup shredded Cheddar cheese (4 ounces)
½ cup milk
2 tablespoons soft butter or margarine
1 teaspoon prepared mustard
½ teaspoon salt
¼ teaspoon pepper

Heat oven to 325°. Mix all ingredients. Pour into ungreased baking pan, 8×8×2 inches. Bake 25 to 30 minutes or until eggs are set.

6 servings.

COUNTRY CASSOULET

Pictured on page 5.

1 pound bulk pork sausage
1 cup sliced celery
½ cup chopped onion
½ cup chopped green pepper
⅛ teaspoon instant minced garlic
1 teaspoon salt
1 can (16 ounces) pork and beans
1 can (16 ounces) lima beans
1 can (6 ounces) tomato paste

Cook and stir sausage, celery, onion, green pepper, garlic and salt until meat is brown. Drain off fat. Stir in pork and beans (with sauce), lima beans (with liquid) and tomato paste. Simmer uncovered 10 minutes.

A tossed green salad—and lots of it—is all you need with this dinner in a dish.

5 or 6 servings.

LAZY MAN'S CHILI BEANS

4 slices bacon, diced
2 large onions, thinly sliced
2 cans (16 ounces each) kidney beans
1 can (15 ounces) chili without beans
¼ cup sugar
2 teaspoons salt
¼ teaspoon instant minced garlic

Fry bacon in large skillet until golden. Stir in onions; cook and stir until onion is tender. Stir in remaining ingredients. Simmer uncovered 25 to 30 minutes.

6 to 8 servings.

Substitution

For instant garlic: 2 cloves garlic, minced.

SPEEDY BAKED BEANS

2 cans (20 ounces each) baked beans
  (with pork)
¼ cup Bac*Os† chips
¼ cup chili sauce
1 tablespoon instant minced onion
1 teaspoon prepared mustard

Heat oven to 350°. Combine all ingredients in greased 1½-quart casserole. Bake uncovered 45 minutes or until bubbly.

6 servings.

†Reg. T.M. of General Mills, Inc.

Substitution

For instant onion: 3 tablespoons minced onion.

Pictured at right:

TOP
  Cheese Potato Casserole
  Snow Peas and Carrot Nuggets
  Saucy Spaghetti and Sprouts

CENTER
  Broccoli 'n Chips
  Best Tossed Salad
  Rice Medley

BOTTOM
  Twin Pan Rolls (Parmesan)
  Sweet and Sour Beets
  Molded Waldorf Salad

Serve-Withs
and Side Dishes

Salads

BOTTLED SALAD DRESSING FIX-UPS

Add the homemade touch to bottled dressing ease with any of the following combinations:

For vegetable salads:

¼ cup oil and vinegar salad dressing and ¼ teaspoon savory leaves, crushed

¼ cup oil and vinegar salad dressing and ¼ teaspoon oregano leaves, crushed

¼ cup oil and vinegar salad dressing and ¼ teaspoon thyme leaves, crushed

¼ cup oil and vinegar salad dressing and ¼ teaspoon chili powder

For cottage cheese salads:

¼ cup creamy French salad dressing and 1 tablespoon pickle sandwich spread

¼ cup creamy sour cream salad dressing and 1 teaspoon horseradish

¼ cup creamy blue cheese salad dressing and 1 tablespoon catsup or chili sauce

¼ cup creamy blue cheese salad dressing and ⅛ teaspoon curry powder (also good on fruit)

For fruit salads:

¼ cup creamy blue cheese salad dressing and 1 tablespoon apricot preserves

¼ cup creamy blue cheese salad dressing and 2 tablespoons creamy French salad dressing

¼ cup fruit salad dressing and ¼ teaspoon sesame seed

RUBY-RED FRUIT SALAD DRESSING

Beat ½ cup currant jelly and ¼ cup oil and vinegar salad dressing with rotary beater.

¾ cup.

Substitution

For currant jelly: ½ cup cranberry jelly.

VEGETABLE SALAD DRESSINGS

Catsup Mayonnaise: Blend ½ cup mayonnaise and ¼ cup catsup.

Chili Mayonnaise: Blend ½ cup mayonnaise, ¼ cup chili sauce, 1 drop Tabasco and dash chili powder.

Fluffy Mayonnaise: Blend ½ cup mayonnaise and ¼ cup frozen whipped topping (thawed).

¾ cup.

CREAMY LEMON DRESSING

⅓ cup frozen lemonade concentrate (thawed)

⅓ cup honey

⅓ cup dairy sour cream

1 teaspoon celery seed

Beat all ingredients with rotary beater. Perfect for fruit salads.

¾ cup.

Substitution

For dairy sour cream: ⅓ cup salad oil.

For Gorgeous Greens

A little TLC please. The beautiful greens deserve it. Buy them crisp and fresh, of course; store them, covered, in the refrigerator. And think twice about tossing away the outer leaves; that's where the vitamins are at their best.

Wash greens only as you need them. And do put aside that knife. Greens were meant to be torn, not cut—unless you're serving wedges, or want shredded leaves for slaw.

Avoid the head lettuce rut. Make friends with the whole family of leafy greens: romaine, endive, escarole, watercress. Use them together—the dark and the light, the crisp and the tender—and create your own splendid setting for vegetable sparkers and your favorite dressing.

But before you add these final fillips, make sure the greens are cold and dry. Then pour on the dressing at the very last moment—just enough to coat the leaves lightly—and toss. But ever so gently; that's all they need.

BEST TOSSED SALAD

Pictured on page 53.

1 small head lettuce
1 small bunch leaf lettuce
½ small bunch endive
½ bag (10-ounce size) spinach
¼ cup oil and vinegar salad dressing

Into large salad bowl or plastic bag, tear greens into bite-size pieces (12 cups). Toss with salad dressing until greens are well coated. If you like, toss in 1 cup herb-seasoned croutons.

6 to 8 servings.

GREEN AND WHITE SALAD

1 small head lettuce
½ small bunch endive
½ small cauliflower
1 jar (6 ounces) marinated artichoke hearts, drained (reserve marinade)
12 pitted ripe olives
2 tablespoons tarragon vinegar
1 teaspoon salt
1 teaspoon instant minced garlic

Into large salad bowl, tear greens into bite-size pieces (about 8 cups). Break cauliflower into flowerets, cut artichoke hearts in half and slice olives; add to greens.

Sprinkle with reserved artichoke marinade; toss until greens glisten. Sprinkle with vinegar, salt and garlic; toss until greens are well coated.

6 to 8 servings.

Substitutions

For endive: 4 cups bite-size pieces spinach (4 ounces).

For instant garlic: 1 clove garlic, minced.

TOSSED SALAD WITH CLASSIC DRESSING

1 medium head lettuce
1 medium cucumber, cut into thin slices
8 cherry tomatoes, cut into halves
1 tablespoon plus 1 teaspoon salad oil
½ teaspoon salt
  Dash garlic powder
  Dash pepper
2 teaspoons wine vinegar

Into salad bowl, tear lettuce into bite-size pieces. Add cucumber slices and tomato halves to salad bowl.

Sprinkle with oil; toss until lettuce glistens. Season with salt, garlic powder and pepper. Sprinkle with vinegar; toss until lettuce is well coated.

4 servings.

Note: For a pretty effect, run tines of fork down side of cucumber before slicing.

BLENDER COLESLAW

½ medium cabbage
1 small onion
⅔ cup dairy sour cream
¼ cup mayonnaise or salad dressing
½ teaspoon salt
½ teaspoon dry mustard
  Dash pepper

Cut cabbage into 2-inch pieces. Quarter onion. Place half the cabbage in blender; add water to cover. Chop, watching carefully. Drain thoroughly. Repeat with remaining cabbage and the onion. (Or vegetables can be shredded or finely chopped by hand.) Mix vegetables, sour cream, mayonnaise, salt, mustard and pepper. Chill.

6 to 8 servings.

VARIATIONS

■ *Dill Slaw:* Add ½ teaspoon dill weed.

■ *Herbed Slaw:* Omit mustard and pepper; add 1 teaspoon celery seed and ½ teaspoon chervil leaves.

■ *Pineapple-Marshmallow Slaw:* Omit onion; stir in 1 can (13½ ounces) pineapple tidbits, drained, 1 cup miniature marshmallows and 1 tablespoon lemon juice.

GREEN AND GOLD SALAD

1 package (10 ounces) frozen green peas
½ cup shredded natural Cheddar cheese
2 tablespoons chopped onion
2 tablespoons mayonnaise or salad dressing
1½ teaspoons prepared mustard
¼ teaspoon salt
  Crisp salad greens

Rinse peas with small amount of running cold water to separate and remove ice crystals; drain. Mix all ingredients except salad greens. Serve salad on greens.

4 or 5 servings.

Substitution

For frozen green peas: 1 can (8 ounces) green peas, drained.

MARINATED CUCUMBER SALAD

1 medium cucumber
1 small onion
½ cup vinegar
½ cup water
2 tablespoons sugar
¼ teaspoon salt
  Crisp salad greens

Run tines of fork lengthwise down side of unpared cucumber. Thinly slice cucumber and onion. Mix vinegar, water, sugar and salt; pour on cucumber and onion in glass bowl. Cover; refrigerate at least 2 hours. Drain and serve on salad greens.

4 to 6 servings.

BRUSSELS AND CARROTS SALAD

½ cup oil and vinegar salad dressing
1 package (10 ounces) frozen
  Brussels sprouts
1 can (16 ounces) sliced carrots, drained

In covered saucepan, heat salad dressing and Brussels sprouts to boiling. Reduce heat; cover and simmer 8 minutes. Add carrots; cook until Brussels sprouts are tender. Turn into serving dish. Cover; refrigerate at least 6 hours, stirring occasionally.

6 to 8 servings.

OKRA AND TOMATO SALAD

1 package (10 ounces) frozen whole okra
1 tomato, chopped
½ cup sliced celery
1 teaspoon cream-style horseradish
3 tablespoons oil and vinegar salad dressing
  Crisp salad greens

Cook okra as directed on package; drain and cut into ½-inch pieces. Mix all ingredients except salad greens. Cover; refrigerate at least 4 hours. Serve on salad greens.

4 or 5 servings.

BRIGHT BEAN SALAD

1 medium carrot
1 can (15½ ounces) French-style
  green beans, drained
2 tablespoons chopped onion
⅛ teaspoon salt
3 tablespoons oil and vinegar salad dressing

Cut carrot into 1-inch lengths; chop in blender, watching carefully. (Or carrot can be finely chopped by hand.) Mix all ingredients. Cover; refrigerate at least 4 hours.

4 servings.

Substitutions

For canned green beans: 1 package (9 ounces) frozen French-style green beans, cooked and drained.

For fresh onion: 1 tablespoon instant minced onion.

Yesterday's Vegetables—Today's Salads

You cooked too many peas yesterday? Great! You've got a headstart on a new salad: marinate them in oil and vinegar, with chopped green pepper, onion and celery for added flavor. Then garnish with pimiento to serve. Or if you have cooked cauliflowerets around, combine them with tomato wedges and cucumber slices. Let the flavors mingle in French dressing; serve in lettuce cups. And don't let leftover cooked potatoes throw you. Soak them in the liquid of marinated artichoke hearts—along with the hearts, of course—for a very fancy salad. The marinating time for each leftover vegetable, and its new-found friends, should be about 4 hours, in the refrigerator.

PERFECTION SALAD

1 cup boiling water
1 package (3 ounces) lemon-flavored
  gelatin
1 can (8½ ounces) crushed pineapple,
  drained (reserve syrup)
2 tablespoons lemon juice or vinegar
1 teaspoon salt
¼ medium cabbage
2 celery stalks
3 tablespoons chopped pimiento

Pour boiling water on gelatin in large bowl, stirring until gelatin is dissolved. Add enough water to reserved pineapple syrup to measure 1 cup; stir into gelatin with lemon juice and salt.

Cut cabbage into 2-inch pieces. Cut celery into 1½-inch lengths. Place half the cabbage in blender; add water to cover. Chop, watching carefully. Drain thoroughly. Repeat with remaining cabbage and the celery. (Or vegetables can be finely chopped by hand.)

Stir pineapple, vegetables and pimiento into gelatin. Pour into 4-cup mold or 10 to 12 individual molds. Chill until firm. If you like, garnish with curly endive and serve with mayonnaise or salad dressing.

6 to 8 servings.

To Keep That Perfect Shape

There's no mystique to unmolding a salad. Use the method that's easiest for you.

The warm water way: Dip mold in warm (not hot) water up to the depth of contents; loosen around edge with tip of knife. Place plate on mold and invert both. Jiggle the mold gently; lift off.

The hot towel treatment: Press hot, damp towel around mold and into any depressions. Shake mold gently; lift off. Repeat if necessary.

CUCUMBER RELISH MOLD

Pictured on page 59.

1 package (3 ounces) lime-flavored
  gelatin
1 medium cucumber
2 celery stalks
5 green onions
½ teaspoon salt

Prepare gelatin as directed on package except— decrease water to 1½ cups and chill until slightly thickened but not set.

Cut unpared cucumber lengthwise into quarters, then into 1½-inch lengths. Cut celery and onions into 1½-inch lengths. Place vegetables in blender; add water to cover. Chop, watching carefully. Drain thoroughly. (Or vegetables can be finely chopped by hand. Be sure to drain cucumber thoroughly.)

Stir vegetables and salt into gelatin. Pour into 4-cup mold or 6 individual molds. Chill until firm, at least 6 hours. For a festive touch, unmold on salad greens. A sour cream salad dressing offers an interesting contrast.

6 servings.

MOLDED WALDORF SALAD

Pictured on page 53.

1 cup boiling water
1 package (3 ounces) lemon-flavored
  gelatin
1 can (11 ounces) mandarin orange segments
1 can (8½ ounces) pineapple tidbits
1 medium apple, diced
1 medium banana, sliced
¼ cup nuts, coarsely chopped

Pour boiling water on gelatin in large bowl, stirring until gelatin is dissolved. Stir in orange segments (with syrup), pineapple tidbits (with syrup), apple, banana and nuts.

Pour into 5-cup mold or 8 to 10 individual molds. Chill until firm. Serve with your favorite fruit salad dressing.

6 to 8 servings.

PINEAPPLE-CHEESE MOLD

1 cup boiling water
1 package (3 ounces) lemon-flavored
  gelatin
1 can (8½ ounces) crushed pineapple,
  drained (reserve syrup)
2 tablespoons lemon juice or vinegar
1 cup shredded Cheddar cheese (4 ounces)
1 cup whipping cream, whipped

Pour boiling water on gelatin in large bowl, stirring until gelatin is dissolved. Add lemon juice and enough water to reserved pineapple syrup to measure 1 cup; stir into gelatin. Chill until slightly thickened but not set.

Stir in pineapple and cheese; fold in whipped cream. Pour into 4-cup mold or 8 individual molds. Chill until firm.

8 servings.

Substitution

For whipped cream: 1 envelope (about 2 ounces) dessert topping mix prepared as directed.

FROZEN COCKTAIL SALAD

2 cups dairy sour cream
¾ cup sugar
1 tablespoon plus 1 teaspoon lemon juice
1 can (30 ounces) fruit cocktail, drained
2 medium bananas, cut into ¼-inch slices
½ cup coarsely chopped walnuts
1 jar (10 ounces) maraschino cherries
  (¾ cup), halved

Mix sour cream, sugar and lemon juice. Stir in fruit cocktail, bananas, nuts and cherries. Pour into 2 refrigerator trays. Freeze 24 hours or until firm. (Upright or chest freezers will freeze salad in about 2 hours.)

About 15 minutes before serving, remove trays from freezer and place in refrigerator. Cut each salad into 8 pieces, 2×2¼ inches. Stemmed red cherries make a bright garnish.

16 servings.

Note: This salad can be kept covered in freezer 3 to 4 weeks.

CINNAMON-APPLESAUCE SALAD

¼ to ½ cup red cinnamon candies
½ cup water
1 package (3 ounces) lemon-flavored gelatin
1½ cups applesauce

Heat cinnamon candies and water, stirring frequently, until candies are melted. Pour on gelatin in bowl, stirring until gelatin is dissolved. Stir in applesauce.

Pour into 3- or 4-cup mold or into baking pan, 8×8×2 inches. Chill until firm. Try a garnish of cream cheese balls rolled in chopped nuts.

6 servings.

Note: For 12 servings, double amounts and pour into 6-cup mold or into baking pan, 13×9×2 inches.

ORANGE AND ONION SALAD

2 cans (11 ounces each) mandarin orange
  segments, drained
3 tablespoons finely chopped onion
  Crisp salad greens

Toss orange segments and onion. Serve on salad greens. Nice with Roquefort dressing.

4 servings.

COUNTRY-STYLE WALDORF SALAD

Pictured at right.

2 cups diced unpared apple
1 cup diced celery
1 can (8¼ ounces) seedless grapes, drained
⅓ cup coarsely chopped nuts
4 cups bite-size pieces lettuce
½ cup mayonnaise or salad dressing

Toss all ingredients. Garnish with slices of red apple for added color.

4 to 6 servings.

Substitution

For canned grapes: 1 cup fresh seedless green grapes.

Pictured at right:
Orange-Cauliflower Salad, Country-style
Waldorf Salad and Cucumber Relish Mold

ORANGE-CAULIFLOWER SALAD

Pictured on page 59.

2 cans (11 ounces each) mandarin orange
  segments, drained
2 cups uncooked cauliflowerets
¼ cup chopped green pepper
2 cups bite-size pieces spinach (about 2 ounces)
¼ cup French salad dressing
  Lettuce cups

Toss orange segments, cauliflowerets, green pepper, spinach and salad dressing. Serve in lettuce cups.

5 or 6 servings.

Substitution

For French salad dressing: Fruit salad dressing.

AMBROSIA SALAD

1 can (11 ounces) mandarin orange
  segments, drained
1 medium unpared apple, chopped
2 medium bananas, sliced
¼ cup chopped dates (sugar rolled)
2 tablespoons fruit salad dressing
  Lettuce cups
  Plain or toasted coconut

Toss orange segments, apple, bananas, dates and fruit salad dressing. Serve in lettuce cups. Sprinkle salads with coconut.

4 or 5 servings.

SEEDLESS GRAPE SALAD

1 can (8¼ ounces) seedless grapes, drained
1 cup diced celery
½ cup maraschino cherries, halved
¼ cup coarsely chopped nuts
2 tablespoons fruit salad dressing
  Lettuce cups

Toss grapes, celery, cherries, nuts and fruit salad dressing. Serve in lettuce cups.

2 or 3 servings.

Substitution

For canned grapes: 1 cup fresh seedless green grapes.

MACARONI FRUIT SALAD

1½ cups uncooked macaroni rings
1 tablespoon cornstarch
1 tablespoon sugar
1 can (30 ounces) fruit cocktail, drained
  (reserve ½ cup syrup)
2 tablespoons lemon juice
½ cup chilled whipping cream
1 tablespoon sugar
¼ cup maraschino cherries, halved

Cook macaroni rings as directed on package; drain. Blend cornstarch and 1 tablespoon sugar in saucepan. Gradually stir in reserved fruit cocktail syrup and the lemon juice. Cook over medium heat, stirring constantly, until mixture thickens and boils. Boil and stir 1 minute. Mix with hot macaroni rings. Cover; chill at least 4 hours.

Just before serving, beat cream and 1 tablespoon sugar in chilled bowl until stiff. Fold cream, fruit cocktail and cherries into macaroni rings.

4 to 6 servings.

Substitution

For whipping cream and 1 tablespoon sugar: 1 tablespoon sugar mixed into ½ cup dairy sour cream or unflavored yogurt, or ½ envelope (2-ounce size) dessert topping mix prepared as directed on package except—decrease milk to ¼ cup and mix in 1 tablespoon sugar.

PINEAPPLE-BANANA SALAD

2 small bananas
1 can (15¼ ounces) pineapple spears,
  drained
  Crisp salad greens
2 cups strawberries
⅓ cup mayonnaise or salad dressing
2 tablespoons chopped nuts

Cut bananas crosswise in half, then cut into lengthwise slices. On each salad plate, alternate banana slices and pineapple spears on greens. Divide strawberries among salads.

Top each salad with about 1 tablespoon mayonnaise; sprinkle with nuts.

5 or 6 servings.

Vegetables

BUTTERS FOR VEGETABLES

Almond Butter: Melt 1 tablespoon butter or margarine; stir in 2 or 3 drops almond extract.

Almondine Butter: Melt 1 tablespoon butter or margarine; add 1 tablespoon toasted slivered almonds.

Lemon Butter: Melt 1 tablespoon butter or margarine; stir in 1 teaspoon lemon juice.

Mustard-Dill Butter: Melt 1 tablespoon butter or margarine; add ⅛ teaspoon dry mustard and ¼ teaspoon dill weed.

Olive Butter: Melt 1 tablespoon butter or margarine; add 1 tablespoon sliced or chopped ripe olives.

Oriental Butter: Melt 1 tablespoon butter or margarine; stir in 1 teaspoon soy sauce.

Seasoned Butter: Melt 1 tablespoon butter or margarine; add ¼ teaspoon seasoned salt and dash pepper.

Enough for 1 package (9 or 10 ounces) frozen vegetables or 1 can (16 ounces) vegetables.

ARTICHOKES AND PEAS

1 package (10 ounces) frozen artichoke hearts
1 package (10 ounces) frozen green peas
¾ cup water
1 teaspoon salt
1 tablespoon butter or margarine, melted
1 tablespoon lemon juice

In covered saucepan, heat frozen vegetables, water and salt to boiling. Reduce heat and cook until peas and artichoke hearts are tender, 5 to 8 minutes; drain. Turn into serving dish; pour butter and lemon juice on vegetables.

4 or 5 servings.

ASPARAGUS WITH CHEESE SAUCE

1 package (10 ounces) frozen cut asparagus
½ can of our cheese sauce (½ cup)
½ cup canned French fried onion rings

Cook asparagus as directed on package; drain. Return to saucepan. Stir in cheese sauce; heat through. Turn into serving dish; top with onion rings.

4 servings.

Substitution

For French fried onion rings: ½ cup slivered almonds.

ASPARAGUS À LA POLONAISE

¼ cup seasoned croutons
1 tablespoon butter or margarine
2 cans (15 ounces each) cut asparagus
1 tablespoon butter or margarine, melted
1 hard-cooked egg, chopped

Cook and stir croutons in 1 tablespoon butter until brown. Heat asparagus; drain. Turn asparagus into serving dish; drizzle with melted butter and sprinkle with croutons and egg.

4 or 5 servings.

Substitution

For canned asparagus: 2 packages (9 ounces each) frozen cut asparagus, cooked as directed on package.

CHILLED ASPARAGUS

Cook 2 packages (10 ounces each) frozen asparagus spears as directed on package; drain. Season with ½ teaspoon seasoned salt and ⅛ teaspoon pepper. Cover; chill several hours. Serve as either the vegetable or the salad.

8 to 10 servings.

DELUXE BEAN CASSEROLE

2 packages (9 ounces each) frozen
   French-style green beans
1 can (15 ounces) bean sprouts, rinsed
   and drained
1 can (10½ ounces) condensed cream of
   mushroom soup
1 tablespoon soy sauce
1 teaspoon salt
1 cup canned French fried onion rings

Heat oven to 350°. Rinse beans with small amount of running cold water to separate and remove ice crystals; drain. Mix all ingredients except onion rings in ungreased 2-quart casserole. Bake uncovered 25 minutes. Top with onion rings; bake 5 minutes longer.

6 to 8 servings.

VARIATION

■ *Classic Bean Casserole:* Omit bean sprouts and soy sauce.

GREEN BEANS AND BACON

3 slices bacon
1 tablespoon chopped onion
⅛ teaspoon instant minced garlic
1 tablespoon soy sauce
1 can (16 ounces) French-style
   green beans, drained

Fry bacon until crisp; remove bacon and drain. Drain off all but 2 teaspoons fat. Cook and stir onion in fat until tender. Stir in remaining ingredients; heat through. Turn beans into serving dish; crumble bacon on beans.

4 servings.

Substitutions

For instant garlic: 1 clove garlic, minced.
For French-style green beans: 1 can (16 ounces) cut green beans, drained.

MUSHROOM ITALIAN GREEN BEANS

1 can (4 ounces) mushroom stems
   and pieces, drained (reserve liquid)
1 package (9 ounces) frozen Italian
   green beans
1 tablespoon butter or margarine
½ teaspoon salt

Add enough water to reserved mushroom liquid to measure ½ cup; pour into medium saucepan. Add beans, butter and salt; cook as directed on package or until beans are tender.

4 servings.

PERKY LIMA BEANS

1 package (10 ounces) frozen lima beans
2 tablespoons soft butter or margarine
1 teaspoon sugar
1 teaspoon dry mustard
1 teaspoon lemon juice
¼ teaspoon salt

Cook lima beans as directed on package; drain. Stir in remaining ingredients.

4 servings.

Substitution

For frozen lima beans: 1 can (15 ounces) lima beans, heated and drained.

HICKORY LIMAS

1 package (10 ounces) frozen lima beans
¼ cup pasteurized process cheese spread
   with hickory smoke flavor
2 tablespoons milk

Cook lima beans as directed on package; drain. Return to saucepan. Stir in cheese spread and milk; heat, stirring constantly, until cheese spread is melted and smooth.

4 servings.

Substitutions

For frozen lima beans: 1 can (15 ounces) lima beans, heated and drained.
For cheese spread: ¼ cup pasteurized process cheese spread with bacon or garlic.

SAVORY BEETS

1 can (16 ounces) whole or sliced beets
2 tablespoons butter or margarine
1 teaspoon salt
½ teaspoon savory
½ teaspoon basil

In covered saucepan, heat all ingredients to boiling. Reduce heat; simmer 10 minutes.

4 servings.

SWEET AND SOUR BEETS

Pictured on page 53.

1 jar (16 ounces) pickled beets, drained
  (reserve syrup)
1 tablespoon cornstarch
1 can (11 ounces) mandarin orange segments,
  drained

Blend reserved beet syrup and the cornstarch in medium saucepan. Cook, stirring constantly, until mixture thickens and boils. Boil and stir 1 minute. Stir in beets and orange segments; heat through.

4 servings.

Substitutions

For pickled beets and cornstarch: 1 jar (16 ounces) Harvard beets.

For mandarin orange segments: 1 can (8½ ounces) pineapple tidbits.

BROCCOLI ELEGANT

1 package (10 ounces) frozen broccoli
  spears
½ can of our cheese sauce (½ cup)
2 tablespoons sliced ripe olives

Cook broccoli as directed on package; drain. Return to saucepan. Stir in cheese sauce and olives; heat through.

4 servings.

Substitution

For cheese sauce: ½ can of our hollandaise sauce.

BROCCOLI 'N CHIPS

Pictured on page 53.

1 package (10 ounces) frozen chopped
  broccoli
¼ cup canned shoestring potatoes
2 teaspoons lemon juice

Cook broccoli as directed on package; drain. Turn into serving dish; top with shoestring potatoes and sprinkle with lemon juice.

4 servings.

SPROUTS SAUTÉ

1 package (10 ounces) frozen Brussels
  sprouts
½ cup water
1 teaspoon instant chicken bouillon
½ medium onion, sliced and separated
  into rings
2 tablespoons butter or margarine

In covered saucepan, heat Brussels sprouts, water and bouillon to boiling. Reduce heat; cook 5 minutes. Stir in onion and butter; cook uncovered until onion is tender, about 5 minutes.

3 servings.

Substitution

For instant bouillon: 1 chicken bouillon cube.

BOHEMIAN CABBAGE

1 medium cabbage (about 1½ pounds),
  shredded (about 5 cups)
¼ cup water
1 tablespoon instant minced onion
1 teaspoon salt
½ teaspoon caraway seed
¼ teaspoon pepper
½ cup dairy sour cream

Mix all ingredients except sour cream in skillet. Cover tightly; cook 5 minutes or until cabbage is crisp-tender. Stir in sour cream; heat through.

6 servings.

Substitution

For instant onion: 3 tablespoons minced onion.

Hot Vegetable Relishes

Cauliflower and Brussels Sprouts

HOT VEGETABLE RELISHES

1 can (16 ounces) whole carrots
2 stalks celery, cut into ¼-inch
diagonal slices (about 1 cup)
½ cup sweet pickle sticks
½ teaspoon salt

Mix carrots (with liquid), celery, pickle sticks and salt in saucepan; heat through.

4 servings.

Substitution

For sweet pickle sticks: ½ cup drained watermelon pickles.

CARROTS BOUILLON

1 can (16 ounces) carrot slices
2 teaspoons instant minced onion
1 teaspoon instant beef bouillon
1 bay leaf

In covered saucepan, heat carrot slices (with liquid), onion, bouillon and bay leaf to boiling. Reduce heat; simmer 5 minutes.

4 servings.

Substitutions

For instant onion: 2 tablespoons minced onion.
For instant bouillon: 1 beef bouillon cube.

CAULIFLOWER AND BRUSSELS SPROUTS

1 package (10 ounces) cauliflower
frozen in cheese sauce in cooking pouch
1 package (10 ounces) frozen Brussels sprouts
2 tablespoons crumble herb stuffing,
if desired

Cook each vegetable as directed on package. Drain Brussels sprouts and turn into serving dish. Pour cauliflower on sprouts; toss to mix. Sprinkle with stuffing.

5 or 6 servings.

Substitution

For Brussels sprouts: 1 package (10 ounces) frozen lima beans.

CREAMY CORN AND CUCUMBER

1 envelope (1½ ounces) white sauce mix
1 teaspoon instant chicken bouillon
1 medium cucumber
1 can (17 ounces) whole kernel corn, drained

Prepare white sauce as directed on package except—stir instant chicken bouillon into white sauce mix before adding milk.

Cut unpared cucumber lengthwise into quarters, then crosswise into 1-inch pieces. Stir cucumber and corn into white sauce; heat through.

5 servings.

CORN SESAME SAUTÉ

1 tablespoon butter or margarine
1 clove garlic, crushed
2 tablespoons sesame seed
½ teaspoon salt
¼ teaspoon basil leaves
⅛ teaspoon pepper
1 can (12 ounces) vacuum-pack whole
    kernel corn

In medium skillet, cook and stir all ingredients except corn over medium heat until sesame seed is toasted. Stir in corn; heat through.

4 servings.

OVEN-FRIED EGGPLANT

½ cup seasoned crumbs
1 teaspoon salt
1 small eggplant (about 1 pound), pared
1 egg, slightly beaten

Heat oven to 375°. Grease jelly roll pan, 15½× 10½×1 inch. Mix seasoned crumbs and salt. Cut eggplant into ½-inch slices. Dip slices into egg, then coat with crumbs. Arrange in pan. Bake uncovered 15 minutes; turn and bake 15 minutes longer.

4 servings.

Substitution

For seasoned crumbs: ½ cup dry bread crumbs and ¼ teaspoon pepper.

Creamy Corn and Cucumber

Oven-fried Eggplant

HOLLANDAISE ONIONS

Heat 2 cups frozen whole onions and ½ can of our hollandaise sauce (½ cup) over medium heat, stirring frequently, until tender, about 7 minutes.

4 servings.

CREAMED ONIONS AND BROCCOLI

1 package (10 ounces) frozen
   small onions in cream sauce
1 package (10 ounces) frozen broccoli spears
1 tablespoon creamy peanut butter

Cook each vegetable as directed on package except—stir peanut butter into onions until sauce is smooth. Drain broccoli and turn into serving dish; pour onions over broccoli.

4 or 5 servings.

VARIATION

■ *Nutmeg Creamed Onions and Broccoli:* Omit peanut butter and stir in ⅛ teaspoon nutmeg.

BROILED ONIONS AND POTATOES

Shape aluminum foil into a broiler pan, 10 × 7 × 1½ inches. Drain 1 can (16 ounces) whole onions and 1 can (16 ounces) whole potatoes. Place onions and potatoes in foil pan; dot with 1 or 2 tablespoons soft butter or margarine.

Set oven control at broil and/or 550°. Place pan on rack in broiler pan. Broil 3 inches from heat 4 minutes. Turn onions and potatoes; sprinkle with seasoned salt and paprika. Broil 3 minutes longer or until heated through.

4 servings.

PEAS WITH CELERY AND ONION

1 package (10 ounces) frozen green peas
1 stalk celery, sliced (about ½ cup)
1 small onion, thinly sliced

Cook peas, celery and onion as directed on package for peas; drain. If desired, toss vegetables with 1 tablespoon soft butter or margarine.

3 or 4 servings.

PEAS AND ALMONDS

¼ cup slivered almonds
1 tablespoon butter or margarine
1 package (10 ounces) frozen green peas,
   broken apart
½ teaspoon salt

Cook and stir almonds in butter until light brown, 2 to 3 minutes. Stir in peas and salt. Cook, stirring frequently, until peas are tender, 5 to 7 minutes.

3 servings.

DILLED PEAS AND CAULIFLOWER

1 package (8 ounces) frozen green peas
   with cream sauce
1 package (10 ounces) frozen cauliflower
⅔ cup water
1 tablespoon butter or margarine
½ teaspoon dill weed

In covered saucepan, heat all ingredients to boiling. Reduce heat; cook 5 to 8 minutes or until cauliflower is tender. Remove from heat; stir until sauce is smooth.

4 servings.

SNOW PEAS AND CARROT NUGGETS

Pictured on page 53.

1 package (7 ounces) frozen Chinese
   pea pods
1 package (10 ounces) carrot nuggets
   frozen in butter sauce in cooking pouch
2 teaspoons lemon juice

Cook each vegetable as directed on package. Drain pea pods and turn into serving dish. Pour carrots and lemon juice on pea pods; toss.

4 servings.

Substitution

For pea pods: 1 package (9 ounces) frozen Italian green beans.

CREAMY BLACKEYE PEAS

1 package (10 ounces) frozen
   blackeye peas
4 slices bacon, diced
1 can (10½ ounces) condensed
   cream of chicken soup
¼ teaspoon Worcestershire sauce
   Dash pepper

Cook peas and bacon as directed on package for peas; drain. Return to saucepan. Stir in remaining ingredients; heat through.

4 servings.

SPINACH AND BROCCOLI

1 package (10 ounces) frozen chopped
   spinach
1 package (10 ounces) frozen chopped
   broccoli
⅔ cup water
1 teaspoon salt
1 tablespoon butter or margarine, melted
1 tablespoon lemon juice

In covered saucepan, heat spinach, broccoli, water and salt to boiling, breaking vegetables apart with a fork. Reduce heat and cook 5 to 10 minutes or until vegetables are tender; drain. Turn into serving dish; toss with mixture of butter and lemon juice.

6 or 7 servings.

CRUNCHY CREAMY SPINACH

1 package (10 ounces) frozen chopped
   spinach
½ cup dairy sour cream
1 can (3½ ounces) French fried onion rings

Cook spinach as directed on package; drain. Stir in sour cream. Turn into serving dish; top with onion rings.

4 servings.

SAUTÉED SPINACH

2 slices bacon, diced
1 small onion, thinly sliced
1 package (10 ounces) frozen chopped
   spinach, broken apart
½ teaspoon salt
   Dash pepper

In medium skillet, cook and stir bacon and onion until bacon is crisp. Stir in spinach, salt and pepper. Cover tightly; cook until spinach is tender, 5 to 8 minutes.

4 servings.

HONEY-CHILI SQUASH

¼ cup honey
2 tablespoons butter or margarine
½ to 1 teaspon chili powder
½ teaspoon salt
1 can (15 ounces) squash
½ cup crumble herb stuffing

Heat oven to 350°. In small skillet, heat honey, butter, chili powder and salt just to boiling, stirring occasionally. Reserve 2 tablespoons of the honey mixture; pour remainder into ungreased 1-quart casserole.

Blend squash into honey mixture in casserole. Toss stuffing with reserved honey mixture; sprinkle on squash. Bake uncovered 25 minutes or until topping is brown.

4 or 5 servings.

Substitutions

For honey and butter: ⅓ cup honey butter.
For canned squash: 1 package (12 ounces) frozen squash, thawed.

VARIATIONS

■ *Crusty Pecan Squash Bake:* Omit chili powder and stir in ⅛ teaspoon nutmeg. Substitute ½ cup coarsely chopped pecans for the herb stuffing.

■ *Marshmallow Puff Squash Bake:* Blend all the honey mixture into squash. Omit herb stuffing and sprinkle ½ cup miniature marshmallows on squash. Bake 30 minutes or until marshmallows are puffed and golden brown.

NUTTY BAKED SQUASH

 2 acorn squash (1 pound each)
⅔ cup graham cracker crumbs
⅓ cup coarsely chopped pecans
⅓ cup soft butter or margarine
 3 tablespoons brown sugar
¼ teaspoon salt
¼ teaspoon nutmeg

Heat oven to 400°. Cut each squash in half; remove seeds and fibers. Stir together remaining ingredients. Spoon ¼ of the crumb mixture into each squash half.

Arrange squash halves in ungreased baking dish, 11½ × 7½ × 1½ inches. Pour water (¼ inch) into baking dish. Cover; bake 35 to 40 minutes or until squash is tender.

4 servings.

Substitution

For graham cracker crumbs: ⅔ cup soda cracker crumbs.

HERBED ZUCCHINI

Cut 2 pounds unpared zucchini into 1-inch slices. Heat 1 inch salted water (½ teaspoon salt to 1 cup water) to boiling. Add zucchini. Cover tightly; heat to boiling. Reduce heat and cook until tender, 5 minutes; drain. Sprinkle with oregano.

4 servings.

ITALIAN-STYLE ZUCCHINI

1½ pounds zucchini (about 6 small)
 1 tablespoon Italian salad dressing mix
¼ cup salad oil
  Grated Parmesan cheese

Cut unpared zucchini lengthwise into ½-inch slices. Place slices in skillet; sprinkle with salad dressing mix and pour oil on zucchini. Cover tightly; cook until zucchini is tender, 12 to 16 minutes. Turn into serving dish; sprinkle with Parmesan cheese.

4 or 5 servings.

TOMATO-CABBAGE SKILLET

1 teaspoon instant beef bouillon
1 can (16 ounces) tomato wedges in
  tomato juice, drained (reserve liquid)
1 small cabbage (about 1 pound), shredded
  (about 3 cups)

In medium skillet, heat bouillon and reserved tomato liquid until bouillon is dissolved. Stir in cabbage. Cover tightly; cook 3 minutes, stirring occasionally.

Stir in tomatoes. Cover; cook 3 to 5 minutes longer or until cabbage is crisp-tender and tomatoes are heated through.

4 servings.

Substitution

For instant bouillon: 1 beef bouillon cube.

BAKED STUFFED TOMATOES

 6 medium tomatoes (about 2 pounds)
⅔ cup crumble herb stuffing
¼ cup grated Parmesan cheese
  Parsley

Heat oven to 350°. Remove stem ends of tomatoes. Remove pulp, leaving ½-inch wall. Chop pulp; mix with stuffing and cheese.

Fill tomatoes with stuffing; arrange in ungreased baking dish, 8 × 8 × 2 inches. Bake 20 to 25 minutes or until tomatoes are heated through. Garnish with parsley.

6 servings.

BROILED TOMATOES

Wash 4 medium tomatoes (about 1½ pounds). Remove stem end from each; cut tomatoes crosswise in half.

Set oven control at broil and/or 550°. Dot each half with ½ teaspoon butter or margarine. Season with salt, pepper, basil leaves, oregano leaves or ground savory. Broil tomato halves cut side up 3 to 5 inches from heat 5 minutes or until tops are golden brown.

4 servings.

Potatoes

Starting with a mix...
MASHED POTATO STIR-INS

Prepare Potato Buds as directed on package for 4 servings. Just before serving, try one of the following additions:

- *Bacon:* Stir in 1 to 2 slices bacon, crisply fried and crumbled.
- *Blue Cheese:* Stir in 1 to 1½ tablespoons crumbled blue cheese.
- *Celery Seed:* Stir in ½ teaspoon celery seed.
- *Chives:* Stir in 1 tablespoon snipped chives.
- *Dill:* Stir in ¼ teaspoon dill weed.
- *Green Pepper:* Stir in 1 tablespoon chopped green pepper.
- *Mushroom:* Stir in 1 can (2 ounces) mushroom stems and pieces, drained.
- *Mustard:* Stir in 1½ teaspoons prepared mustard.
- *Olive:* Stir in 1½ tablespoons sliced pitted ripe olives or 1½ tablespoons sliced pimiento-stuffed olives.
- *Pimiento:* Stir in 1 tablespoon chopped drained pimiento.

CHEESE POTATOES

Prepare Potato Buds as directed on package for 8 servings except—omit butter; after stirring in Potato Buds, stir in 1 jar (5 ounces) pasteurized process sharp American cheese spread or flavored pasteurized Neufchâtel cheese spread (the latter is now available with a wide variety of added flavor sparkers; i.e., pineapple, pimiento, relish).

Note: To prepare in oven, turn potato mixture into 1½-quart casserole. Bake uncovered in 350° oven 15 to 20 minutes or until heated through.

CHEESE POTATO CASSEROLE

Pictured on page 53.

    Potato Buds (enough for 8 servings)
½ teaspoon garlic salt
1 tablespoon snipped parsley
1 cup shredded sharp Cheddar
    cheese (4 ounces)
1½ cups cornflakes, crushed
2 tablespoons soft butter
½ teaspoon dry mustard
½ teaspoon paprika
¼ teaspoon salt

Heat oven to 325°. Prepare Potato Buds as directed on package except—decrease salt to ½ teaspoon and add garlic salt. Stir in parsley and cheese. Turn into 1½-quart casserole. Stir remaining ingredients together; sprinkle on potatoes. Bake 20 minutes.

8 servings.

Starting with a mix...
AU GRATIN POTATO STIR-INS

Prepare 1 package of our au gratin potatoes as directed on package except—before baking, try one of the following additions:

- *Bacon:* Stir in 3 slices bacon, crisply fried and crumbled.
- *Blue Cheese:* Stir in 2 tablespoons crumbled blue cheese.
- *Dill:* Stir in ½ teaspoon dill weed.
- *Green Onion:* Stir in 2 tablespoons thinly sliced green onion.
- *Green Pepper:* Stir in ½ cup chopped green pepper.
- *Mushroom:* Stir in 1 can (3 ounces) sliced mushrooms, drained.
- *Mustard:* Stir in 1 tablespoon prepared mustard.
- *Olive:* Stir in ¼ cup sliced pitted ripe olives or ½ cup sliced pimiento-stuffed olives.
- *Pimiento:* Stir in 1 jar (2 ounces) sliced pimiento, drained.

Golden Potato Bake

Potatoes O'Brien

GOLDEN POTATO BAKE

½ cup cornflake crumbs
1 teaspoon salt
4 to 6 medium potatoes, pared
2 tablespoons butter or margarine, melted

Heat oven to 375°. Mix cornflake crumbs and salt. Brush potatoes with butter; coat with crumbs. Arrange in ungreased baking pan, 9×9×2 inches. Bake uncovered 1 to 1¼ hours or until potatoes are tender.

4 to 6 servings.

POTATOES O'BRIEN

⅓ cup chopped green pepper
2 tablespoons chopped pimiento
1 medium onion, chopped
¼ cup butter or margarine
1 package (16 ounces) frozen French fried potatoes, diced
1 teaspoon salt
⅛ teaspoon pepper

In large skillet, cook and stir green pepper, pimiento and onion in butter until onion is tender. Stir in potatoes, salt and pepper. Cook, stirring occasionally, until potatoes are brown and heated.

4 servings.

Substitution

For fresh green pepper: 2 tablespoons dried green pepper.

Starting with a mix...
SCALLOPED POTATO VARIATIONS

Prepare 1 package of our scalloped potatoes as directed on package except—try one of the following variations:

■ *Blue Cheese:* Stir in 2 tablespoons crumbled blue cheese with the butter.

■ *Mushrooms:* Stir in 1 can (3 ounces) sliced mushrooms, drained, or ½ cup sautéed sliced mushrooms.

■ *Sour Cream:* Substitute ⅔ cup dairy sour cream for the milk.

4 to 6 servings.

CREAMY SCALLOPED POTATOES

1 package of our scalloped potatoes
2 cups boiling water
1 can (10½ ounces) condensed cream of
   celery soup
2 tablespoons butter or margarine

Heat oven to 400°. Empty potato slices into ungreased 1½-quart casserole; sprinkle with sauce mix. Stir in water, soup and butter. Bake uncovered 35 to 40 minutes.

4 to 6 servings.

Substitution

For cream of celery soup: 1 can (10½ ounces) condensed cream of chicken soup or cream of mushroom soup.

SCALLOPED POTATO SALAD

1 package of our scalloped potatoes
3 cups water
2 tablespoons salad oil
⅔ cup water
2 tablespoons white wine tarragon
   vinegar
½ cup mayonnaise or salad dressing
¼ teaspoon prepared mustard
½ cup diced celery
½ cup finely chopped onion
4 hard-cooked eggs, chopped
2 tablespoons snipped parsley

Heat potato slices and 3 cups water to boiling. Reduce heat; simmer until tender, 15 to 20 minutes. Rinse with cold water; drain. Place in large bowl; cover and chill.

In saucepan, blend sauce mix and oil; stir in ⅔ cup water and the vinegar. Heat to boiling over medium heat, stirring constantly. Cover and chill.

Blend mayonnaise and mustard; mix with potatoes, celery, onion, eggs and parsley.

6 servings.

SWEET POTATO CASSEROLE

1 can (18 ounces) vacuum-pack
   sweet potatoes
1 can (8½ ounces) crushed pineapple
¼ cup chopped dates (sugar rolled)
1 tablespoon brown sugar
1 tablespoon butter or margarine
1 teaspoon salt
½ teaspoon nutmeg
1 cup miniature marshmallows

Heat oven to 350°. In ungreased 1½-quart casserole, mash sweet potatoes. Stir in remaining ingredients except ½ cup of the marshmallows; sprinkle with remaining marshmallows. Bake uncovered 30 minutes or until marshmallows are puffed and golden brown.

4 servings.

Substitution

For miniature marshmallows: 10 or 11 large marshmallows, cut up.

CARAMEL-GLAZED SWEET POTATOES

The skillet variation is pictured with the ham on page 5.

1 can (18 ounces) vacuum-pack
   sweet potatoes
½ teaspoon salt
⅓ cup caramel ice-cream topping

Heat oven to 350°. Arrange sweet potatoes in ungreased baking dish, 8×8×2 inches; season with salt. Spoon caramel topping on potatoes. Bake uncovered 25 to 30 minutes, basting occasionally with caramel topping in pan.

4 servings.

VARIATIONS

■ *Skillet-glazed Sweet Potatoes:* Arrange sweet potatoes in medium skillet; season with salt. Spoon ice-cream topping on potatoes. Heat just to boiling, stirring occasionally and carefully. (Don't cut or mash potatoes.) Reduce heat. Cook about 10 minutes longer, basting occasionally, until potatoes are heated through.

■ *Sweet Potatoes Orangé:* Substitute ⅓ cup orange marmalade for the caramel ice-cream topping.

Noodles and Spaghetti

NOODLE STIR-INS

Cook 8 ounces egg noodles as directed on package. Just before serving, try one of the following additions:

■ *Almonds:* Brown ¼ cup sliced almonds in 2 tablespoons melted butter; stir into noodles.

■ *Browned Crumbs:* Brown ½ cup fine bread crumbs in 2 tablespoons melted butter; stir into noodles.

■ *Herbs:* Stir ½ teaspoon each thyme leaves, basil leaves, snipped parsley and chopped chives or minced onion into 2 tablespoons melted butter; stir into noodles.

■ *Onion and Green Pepper:* Cook and stir ¼ cup chopped green pepper and 2 tablespoons chopped onion in 2 tablespoons melted butter until onion is tender; stir into noodles.

■ *Parmesan:* Stir in 2 tablespoons melted butter, then fold in ¼ cup grated Parmesan cheese.

■ *Poppy Seed:* Stir in 2 teaspoons poppy seed and 1 tablespoon soft butter.

BACON AND ONION NOODLES

3 teaspoons salt
5 ounces uncooked noodles (about 3 cups)
4 slices bacon
1 small onion, chopped

Heat 6 cups water and the salt to boiling. Add noodles; heat to boiling. Boil uncovered, stirring occasionally, 7 to 10 minutes or until tender; drain.

While noodles cook, fry bacon until crisp; remove bacon and drain. Drain off all but 2 tablespoons fat. Cook and stir onion in fat until tender. Toss hot noodles with onion and fat; crumble bacon on noodles.

4 to 6 servings.

TANGY NOODLES

3 teaspoons salt
5 ounces uncooked noodles (about 3 cups)
¼ cup Italian salad dressing

Heat 6 cups water and the salt to boiling. Add noodles; heat to boiling. Boil uncovered, stirring occasionally, 7 to 10 minutes or until tender; drain. Toss hot noodles with salad dressing.

4 to 6 servings.

Substitution

For Italian salad dressing: ¼ cup green goddess, creamy onion, blue cheese or oil and vinegar salad dressing.

CAULIFLOWER AND SPINACH NOODLES

1 small cauliflower (about 1 pound)
3 teaspoons salt
5 ounces uncooked spinach noodles
  (about 3 cups)
1 can of our hollandaise sauce (1 cup)
  Pimiento strips

Heat 1 inch salted water (½ teaspoon salt to 1 cup water) to boiling; add cauliflower. Cover tightly; heat to boiling. Reduce heat. Cook 15 to 20 minutes or until tender; drain.

While cauliflower cooks, heat 6 cups water and the 3 teaspoons salt to boiling. Add noodles; heat to boiling. Boil uncovered, stirring occasionally, 7 to 10 minutes or until tender; drain.

Heat hollandaise sauce as directed on can. Turn noodles onto platter; arrange cauliflower in center of noodles. Pour sauce on cauliflower and garnish with pimiento.

4 servings.

NOODLES ROMA

Prepare 1 package (5.5 ounces) of our noodles Romanoff as directed on package except—toss with ⅓ to ½ cup shredded Parmesan cheese before serving.

4 servings.

Starting with a mix...
NOODLES ROMANOFF STIR-INS

Prepare 1 package (5.5 ounces) of our noodles Romanoff as directed on package except—try one of the following additions:

■ *Cheese-Chive:* Stir in ½ cup cottage cheese and 1 tablespoon snipped chives.

■ *Chive or Green Onion:* Stir in 1 tablespoon snipped chives or chopped green onion.

■ *Mushroom:* Stir in 1 can (4 ounces) mushroom stems and pieces, chopped and drained, and 2 tablespoons toasted chopped almonds.

■ *Poppy Seed:* Stir in 1 teaspoon poppy seed.

SPINACH AND NOODLE COMBO

1 package (5.5 ounces) of our noodles
  Romanoff
1 package (10 ounces) frozen chopped
  spinach
⅓ cup milk
2 tablespoons soft butter or margarine

Cook noodles as directed on package; drain. Cook spinach as directed on package; drain. Toss spinach, noodles, milk, butter and sour cream-cheese sauce mix.

4 or 5 servings.

ITALIAN RICE AND SPAGHETTI

1 cup boiling water
1 cup tomato juice
½ envelope (2-ounce size) spaghetti sauce
  mix (about 2 tablespoons)
  About 2 ounces uncooked long spaghetti,
  broken into 3-inch lengths
⅓ cup uncooked converted rice
½ cup thinly sliced celery

Heat oven to 350°. Heat water, tomato juice and spaghetti sauce mix to boiling, stirring occasionally. Mix all ingredients in ungreased 1½-quart casserole.

Cover tightly; bake 35 to 40 minutes, stirring after 20 minutes of baking. Uncover; bake 5 minutes longer or until rice and spaghetti are tender.

5 servings.

SAUCY SPAGHETTI AND SPROUTS

Pictured on page 53.

1 package (10 ounces) frozen
  Brussels sprouts
1 can of our hollandaise sauce (1 cup)
3 teaspoons salt
  About 3½ ounces uncooked long spaghetti

Cook Brussels sprouts as directed on package except—decrease cooking time by 5 minutes; drain. Return to saucepan; stir in sauce. Cook over medium heat, stirring occasionally, 5 minutes or until sauce is heated through.

While Brussels sprouts cook, heat 6 cups water and the salt to boiling. Add spaghetti; heat to boiling. Boil uncovered, stirring occasionally, 7 to 10 minutes or until tender; drain. Turn spaghetti onto platter; top with Brussels sprouts and sauce.

4 or 5 servings.

Substitutions

For frozen Brussels sprouts and the hollandaise sauce: 1 package (10 ounces) frozen cauliflower with cheese sauce in cooking pouch.

For hollandaise sauce: 1 can of our cheese sauce.

TOMATOED MACARONI

1 can (16 ounces) tomatoes
2 tablespoons butter or margarine
1 teaspoon salt
¼ teaspoon oregano
3 teaspoons salt
2 cups uncooked elbow macaroni
  Grated Parmesan cheese

Heat tomatoes, butter, 1 teaspoon salt and the oregano to boiling. Reduce heat; simmer 10 to 12 minutes, stirring occasionally.

While tomato sauce cooks, heat 6 cups water and the 3 teaspoons salt to boiling. Add macaroni; heat to boiling. Boil uncovered, stirring occasionally, 7 to 10 minutes or until tender; drain. Turn macaroni into serving dish; pour sauce on macaroni and sprinkle with cheese.

6 servings.

Rice

OVEN STEAMED RICE

1 cup uncooked regular rice
2 cups boiling water
1 teaspoon salt

Heat oven to 350°. Mix all ingredients in ungreased 1- or 1½-quart casserole or in baking dish, 10×6×1½ or 11½×7½×1½ inches. Cover tightly; bake until liquid is absorbed and rice is tender, 25 to 30 minutes.

4 to 6 servings.

VARIATIONS

■ *Coconut Rice:* Decrease water to 1 cup and heat 1 cup milk and the water to boiling. Stir in ½ cup flaked coconut and 1 medium onion, thinly sliced.

■ *Mushroom-Herb Rice:* Increase salt to 1½ teaspoons; stir in 1 can (4 ounces) mushroom stems and pieces, drained, 1 tablespoon instant chicken bouillon, 1 medium onion, thinly sliced, 1 tablespoon butter or margarine and ½ to 1 teaspoon chervil or 1 teaspoon parsley flakes.

■ *Orange Rice:* Decrease water to 1⅓ cups and heat ⅔ cup orange juice and the water to boiling. Stir in ¼ teaspoon allspice.

FROZEN RICE IN COMBINATION

Cook 1 package (12 ounces) frozen rice risotto in cooking pouch and 1 package (12 ounces) frozen Spanish rice in cooking pouch as directed on package. Empty each pouch into serving bowl; toss rices to mix.

6 to 8 servings (4 cups).

Note: Try a mixture of cooked rice verdi and rice pilaf or make your own combinations of flavored frozen rice.

RICE MEDLEY

Pictured on page 53.

1 can (17 ounces) peas and tiny onions, drained (reserve liquid)
1½ cups uncooked instant rice
1 teaspoon butter or margarine
½ teaspoon salt
1 small carrot, shredded (about 3 tablespoons)

Add enough water to reserved liquid to measure 1½ cups; pour into 2-quart saucepan. Heat to boiling. Stir in peas, rice, butter, salt and shredded carrot; heat to boiling. Remove from heat. Cover tightly; let stand until liquid is absorbed and rice is tender, about 10 minutes.

4 to 6 servings.

SKILLET PILAF

3 tablespoons butter or margarine
Uncooked instant or converted rice (enough for 6 servings)
1 small onion, chopped
2 teaspoons instant beef bouillon
½ teaspoon salt
½ teaspoon ground cardamom
¼ teaspoon turmeric
¼ teaspoon allspice
⅛ teaspoon pepper

Melt butter in large skillet; cook and stir rice in butter until brown. Remove from heat. Stir in amount of water as directed on package for 6 servings and the remaining ingredients. Cook as directed on package or until liquid is absorbed and rice is tender.

6 servings.

Substitutions

For uncooked instant or converted rice: 1 package (about 7 ounces) beef-flavored rice; omit beef bouillon, salt and pepper.

For instant bouillon: 2 beef bouillon cubes.

VARIATION

■ *Mushroom Pilaf:* Stir in 1 can (4 ounces) mushroom stems and pieces, drained, with the water and seasonings.

CURRIED RICE

Uncooked instant or converted rice
(enough for 6 servings)
1 tablespoon instant minced onion
2 teaspoons instant chicken bouillon
1 teaspoon curry powder
¼ teaspoon pepper
⅛ teaspoon instant minced garlic

Cook rice as directed on package except—decrease
salt to ½ teaspoon and stir in remaining ingredients with the water. Cook until liquid is absorbed
and rice is tender.

6 servings.

Substitutions

For uncooked instant or converted rice: 1 package (7 ounces) chicken-flavored rice; omit onion,
chicken bouillon, pepper and garlic.

For instant onion: 3 tablespoons minced onion.

For instant bouillon: 2 chicken bouillon cubes.

For instant garlic: 1 clove garlic, minced.

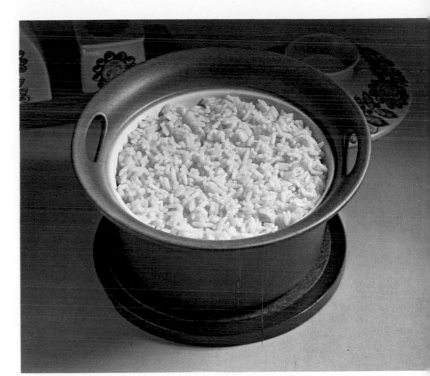

Curried Rice

Green Rice

GREEN RICE

¾ cup uncooked regular rice
1 package (10 ounces) frozen chopped
spinach, thawed and drained
1½ cups boiling water
1 tablespoon instant minced onion
1 tablespoon butter or margarine
1½ teaspoons salt

Heat oven to 350°. Mix all ingredients in ungreased
1- or 1½-quart casserole or in baking dish, 10 ×
6 × 1½ or 11½ × 7½ × 1½ inches. Cover tightly;
bake until liquid is absorbed and rice is tender, 25
to 30 minutes.

4 to 6 servings.

Note: This easy method requires the use of regular
rice for best results. Instant or converted rice
should not be substituted.

Substitutions

For frozen spinach: 1 package (10 ounces)
frozen chopped broccoli.

For instant onion: 3 tablespoons minced onion.

For boiling water: 1½ cups boiling chicken or
beef bouillon.

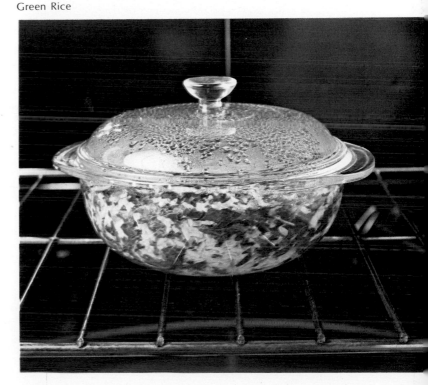

HOPPING JOHN

1 package (10 ounces) frozen
    blackeye peas
4 slices bacon, diced
2 cups water
1½ teaspoons salt
½ cup uncooked converted rice

In covered saucepan, heat all ingredients except rice to boiling. Reduce heat; cook 20 minutes. Stir in rice; cook 25 minutes longer or until liquid is absorbed and rice is tender.

4 or 5 servings.

CARIBBEAN RICE AND BEANS

Uncooked instant rice (enough for
    4 servings)
1 can (15½ ounces) kidney beans, drained
½ teaspoon salt
⅛ teaspoon pepper
⅛ teaspoon instant minced garlic
2 tablespoons salad oil
1 tablespoon snipped chives

Cook rice as directed on package. While rice cooks, cook and stir beans, salt, pepper and garlic in oil until beans are heated through. Stir chives into rice. Turn rice onto platter; top with beans.

4 servings.

Substitution

For instant garlic: 1 clove garlic, minced.

MEXI-BARLEY

¾ cup uncooked barley
1 can (16 ounces) tomatoes
1 cup boiling water
1 medium onion, thinly sliced
1 tablespoon sugar
1 teaspoon salt
½ teaspoon basil
⅛ teaspoon instant minced garlic
⅛ teaspoon cayenne red pepper

Heat oven to 400°. Mix all ingredients in ungreased 1½-quart casserole. Cover tightly; bake 1 to 1¼ hours or until liquid is absorbed and barley is tender.

4 to 6 servings.

BARLEY PILAF

2 tablespoons butter or margarine
1 cup barley
3 tablespoons instant chopped onion
2 teaspoons celery salt
1 can (8 ounces) mushroom stems
    and pieces, drained
⅛ teaspoon pepper
2 teaspoons instant chicken bouillon
2 cups water

Heat oven to 350°. Melt butter in small skillet; cook and stir barley in butter 1 minute (do not allow barley to become brown). Pour into ungreased 1½-quart casserole. Stir in remaining ingredients. Cover tightly; bake about 1 hour or until barley is tender.

4 to 6 servings.

Substitutions

For instant onion: ½ cup chopped onion.
For instant bouillon: 2 chicken bouillon cubes dissolved in the water.

BULGUR PILAF

2 tablespoons butter or margarine
1 cup bulgur wheat
1 teaspoon instant minced onion
2 teaspoons instant chicken bouillon
2 cups water
½ teaspoon salt
¼ teaspoon oregano
    Dash pepper

Melt butter in medium skillet; cook and stir bulgur wheat in butter until golden. Stir in remaining ingredients. Cover tightly; heat to boiling. Reduce heat; simmer 15 minutes.

4 or 5 servings.

Substitutions

For instant onion: 1 tablespoon minced onion.
For instant bouillon and water: 2 cups canned condensed chicken broth.

Dinner Breads

SESAME RYE FINGERS

Pictured on page 79.

Spread 4 to 6 slices of rye bread with soft butter or margarine and sprinkle with sesame seed. Cut each slice crosswise into 4 strips; arrange on ungreased baking sheet. Set oven control at broil and/or 550°. Broil 6 inches from heat 1½ to 2 minutes or until seeds are brown.

4 to 6 servings.

BUN STICKS

Heat oven to 425°. Cut split halves of 3 or 4 frankfurter buns into 1-inch strips. Spread both sides of each strip with soft butter or margarine; arrange on ungreased baking sheet. Bake 5 to 8 minutes or until light brown.

12 to 16 sticks.

GARLIC FRENCH BREAD STICKS

The Parmesan variation is pictured on page 79

¾ cup butter or margarine, melted
⅛ teaspoon instant minced garlic
1 loaf French bread, 19×3×2¼ inches

Heat oven to 425°. Mix butter and garlic. Cut bread into 5 pieces, each about 4 inches long; then cut each piece lengthwise into 6 sticks. Brush cut sides with garlic butter; arrange in ungreased jelly roll pan. Bake 8 minutes or until golden.

30 sticks.

VARIATIONS

■ *Dill French Sticks:* Omit garlic; sprinkle buttered sticks with 1 teaspoon dill weed.

■ *Parmesan French Sticks:* Omit garlic; sprinkle buttered sticks with ¼ cup Parmesan cheese.

ENGLISH MUFFIN DINNER ROUNDS

Parmesan Rounds are pictured on page 79.

½ cup soft butter or margarine
½ teaspoon garlic salt
6 English muffins, split
1 to 2 tablespoons sesame, poppy, celery or caraway seed

Mix butter and garlic salt; spread on cut surfaces of muffins. Sprinkle each with ¼ to ½ teaspoon sesame seed.

Set oven control at broil and/or 550°. Broil muffins 4 inches from heat 5 to 6 minutes or until golden brown.

12 rounds.

VARIATION

■ *Parmesan Rounds:* Substitute grated Parmesan cheese for the sesame seed.

HERB-TOPPED ROLLS

Heat oven to 400°. Brush tops of brown and serve rolls with melted butter or margarine. Sprinkle lightly with one of the following: parsley flakes or snipped chives, dill weed, onion salt or garlic salt or a mixture of 1 teaspoon each tarragon leaves, sweet basil leaves and thyme leaves and ½ teaspoon ground sage. Bake 10 to 12 minutes or until golden brown.

CHEESE PUFFS

Pictured on page 79.

1 package brown and serve rolls (about 10 medium)
2 cups shredded cheese (8 ounces)
2 tablespoons soft butter or margarine
½ teaspoon dry mustard
½ teaspoon salt
⅛ teaspoon pepper

Slice rolls lengthwise in half. Mix remaining ingredients. Place about 1 tablespoon cheese mixture on each half; arrange on baking sheet. Bake as directed on package.

20 puffs.

RICH DINNER BISCUITS

Heat oven to 450°. Mix 2 cups Bisquick and ⅔ cup light cream (20%) with fork until a soft dough forms. Gently smooth dough into a ball on floured cloth-covered board. Knead 5 times. Roll dough ½ inch thick. Cut with floured 2-inch cutter. Bake on ungreased baking sheet 8 to 10 minutes.

10 to 12 biscuits.

Substitution

For light cream: ½ cup milk and ¼ cup soft butter.

CHIVE DINNER MUFFINS

2 cups Bisquick
2 tablespoons shortening
1 egg
⅔ cup milk or water
¼ cup snipped chives

Heat oven to 400°. Grease 12 medium muffin cups (2¾ inches in diameter). Mix all ingredients with fork; beat vigorously ½ minute. Fill muffin cups ⅔ full. Bake 15 minutes.

12 muffins.

BISCUIT FAN-TANS

2 cups Bisquick
½ cup cold water
¼ cup butter or margarine, softened

Heat oven to 450°. Mix Bisquick and water with fork until a soft dough forms. Gently smooth dough into a ball on floured cloth-covered board. Knead 5 times. Roll dough ¼ inch thick.

Spread half the butter on half of dough; fold over. Spread remaining butter on half of dough; fold in half again. Roll dough ½ inch thick. Cut with floured 2-inch cutter. Place 2 biscuits on sides in each ungreased muffin cup. Bake about 10 minutes.

8 or 9 fan-tans.

VARIATION

■ *Bacon Fan-tans:* Stir ¼ cup crumbled crisply fried bacon into the dough.

TWIN PAN ROLLS

Pictured on page 53.

2 loaves frozen bread dough
½ teaspoon dill weed
½ teaspoon salt
2 tablespoons butter or margarine, melted
1 tablespoon parsley flakes
2 tablespoons butter or margarine, melted
  About ½ cup shredded Parmesan
  cheese

Let bread dough thaw and rise as directed on package except—grease 2 layer pans, 8 or 9 × 1½ inches. Shape each loaf into 18 equal balls. Arrange 18 balls in one pan.

Mix dill weed, salt and 2 tablespoons butter. Brush dill mixture on rolls in pan; sprinkle with parsley flakes. Dip remaining rolls into 2 tablespoons butter, then dip tops in cheese and arrange in other pan. Cover; let rise 20 minutes.

Heat oven to 375°. Bake 15 minutes or until golden.

3 dozen rolls.

ALMOND FLATBREAD

Pictured at right.

¾ cup toasted almonds
1 cup Gold Medal Flour*
1½ teaspoons sugar
½ teaspoon salt
¼ teaspoon soda
2 tablespoons butter or margarine, softened
¼ cup dairy sour cream
3 tablespoons milk

Heat oven to 400°. Grind nuts in blender, watching carefully. (Or nuts can be finely chopped by hand.) Mix all ingredients with fork. Pinch off 1-inch balls. Roll each ball into 4-inch circle on floured board. Bake on ungreased baking sheet 6 to 8 minutes or until golden brown.

About 2½ dozen rounds.

*Do not use Self-Rising Flour in this recipe.

Pictured at right:
From top to bottom—Sesame Rye Fingers, Parmesan Rounds, Almond Flatbread, Corn Sticks, Cheese Puffs, Parmesan French Sticks

PARMESAN SUPPER BREAD

1½ cups Bisquick
1 tablespoon sugar
1 tablespoon instant minced onion
1 egg
¼ cup milk
¼ cup white wine
½ teaspoon oregano
¼ cup grated Parmesan cheese

Heat oven to 400°. Grease layer pan, 8 × 1½ inches. Mix all ingredients except cheese with fork until a soft dough forms. Spread in pan; sprinkle with cheese. Bake 20 to 25 minutes. Cut into wedges.

6 to 8 servings.

Substitutions

For instant onion: 3 tablespoons finely chopped onion.

For wine: ¼ cup apple juice.

BREAD IN THE ROUND

4 cups Bisquick
1 envelope (1½ ounces) sour cream sauce mix
1¾ cups milk
2 eggs
   Poppy seed

Heat oven to 400°. Grease six 10-ounce custard cups. Mix all ingredients except poppy seed with fork until a soft dough forms; beat vigorously ½ minute. Spread in cups; sprinkle with poppy seed. Bake about 20 minutes.

6 rounds.

BISCUIT QUICK BREAD

Heat oven to 450°. Prepare Biscuit dough (enough for 10 to 12 biscuits) as directed on Bisquick package except—do not knead. Spread or roll dough on greased baking sheet into a rectangle, 10 × 8 inches. Spread dough with 1 tablespoon soft butter or margarine. Bake 10 minutes. Serve hot, broken into pieces or cut into squares.

6 servings.

VARIATION

■ *Caraway Quick Bread:* Stir 1 teaspoon caraway seed into dough. Sprinkle salt and paprika on buttered dough.

CORN BREAD

Corn Sticks are pictured on page 79.

2 eggs
1 cup Bisquick
1 cup white or yellow cornmeal
1½ cups buttermilk
2 tablespoons salad oil

Heat oven to 450°. Grease generously 12 medium muffin cups (2¾ inches in diameter), corn stick pans or baking pan, 9 × 9 × 2 inches. Heat in oven. Beat eggs with rotary beater until fluffy. Beat in remaining ingredients *just* until smooth. (Do not overbeat corn bread batter.)

Pour or spoon batter into hot pans until almost full. Bake muffins or corn sticks 15 to 20 minutes; corn bread 20 to 25 minutes. Serve piping hot.

12 servings.

Pictured at right:

TOP
   Chocolate Chip Bars/Sour Cream Brownies
   Fruit and Cheese Tray
   Apple Pandowdy

CENTER
   Broiled Fruit Kabobs
   Cotton Candy Angel Cake
   Cherry Cobbler

BOTTOM
   Rocky Road Pudding
   Orange Frost Soda
   Triple Fudge Cake

Desserts
and Confections

Fruit Desserts

FRUIT AND CHEESE TRAY

Pictured on page 81.

Arrange a variety of fresh fruit and cheese on a tray. Serve with dessert plates and small knives.

Select fresh fruits in season: apples, bananas, cherries, grapes, oranges, pears, pineapple, raspberries, strawberries, tangerines. Fill in with dates, figs, prunes and shell nuts.

As a guide to cheese selection, choose at least one soft, one semisoft and one firm-to-hard cheese, some mild and some sharp. Try one of the following combinations:

Gourmandise (soft; cherry brandy-flavored)
Port du Salut (semisoft; mild to robust)
Swiss (firm to hard; mild, nutty, sweet) or **Fontina** (firm to hard; mellow, scattered "eyes")

Liederkranz (soft; edible crust, pungent)
Bel Paese (semisoft; mild)
Cheddar (firm to hard; mild to very sharp) or **Gruyère** (firm to hard; nutty, sharper than Swiss)

Camembert (soft; edible crust, pungent) or **Brie** (soft; edible crust, pungent)
Roquefort (semisoft; sharp, salty)
Edam or Gouda (firm to hard; inedible casing, mild)

Or make substitutions or additions as desired from the following:

Club (soft; often flavored)
Cream (soft; very mild, chill slightly)
Blue (firm to hard; tangy, sharp)
Gorgonzola (firm to hard; piquant flavor, crumbly)
Kashkaval (firm to hard; salty)

FRUITED SHERBET

Sprinkle cubes of pineapple or other fresh fruit with confectioners' sugar; cover and refrigerate. Just before serving, scoop lime sherbet into individual serving dishes; surround with the fruit.

STRAWBERRIES TO DIP

Wash 1 pint fresh strawberries; do not hull. Chill. To serve, divide berries among individual serving dishes. Pass bowls of sour cream and brown sugar to be spooned onto dishes. Berries are first dipped into sour cream, then into sugar.

4 servings.

STRAWBERRIES ROMANOFF

1 quart strawberries, hulled
½ cup confectioners' sugar
1 cup chilled whipping cream
¼ cup Cointreau

Sprinkle strawberries with sugar; stir gently. Cover; refrigerate at least 2 hours.

Just before serving, beat cream in chilled bowl until stiff. Gradually stir in Cointreau. Fold in the strawberries.

6 servings.

Substitution

For Cointreau: ¼ cup orange juice.

MINTED GRAPEFRUIT

1 can (16 ounces) grapefruit sections
12 peppermint candy circles, crushed

Mix grapefruit (with syrup) and candy. Cover; refrigerate at least 1 hour.

4 servings.

Substitution

For canned grapefruit sections: 2 medium grapefruit, pared and sectioned (about 2 cups sections and juice).

PEARS AU CHOCOLAT

Chill can of pear halves. For each serving, put 2 well-drained pear halves together with 1 tablespoon of our chocolate ready-to-spread frosting in cavity. Stand pear upright in individual serving dish; chill.

Just before serving, melt 1 tablespoon chocolate frosting per serving (in custard cup placed in boiling water); pour on pears.

FRUIT IN SOUR CREAM

2 cups seedless green grapes
1 can (13½ ounces) pineapple tidbits,
   drained
¼ cup brown sugar (packed)
⅓ cup dairy sour cream

Mix grapes and pineapple. Reserving 1 tablespoon of the brown sugar, stir remaining sugar into sour cream. Toss with fruit; chill. Just before serving, sprinkle with reserved brown sugar.

4 servings.

Substitutions

For fresh grapes: 1 can (16 ounces) seedless grapes, drained.

For sour cream: ⅓ cup unflavored yogurt.

VARIATION

■ *Strawberries in Sour Cream:* Substitute 3 cups fresh strawberry halves (about 1 pint) for the grapes and pineapple.

PINEAPPLE ZIP

2 cans (about 8½ ounces each)
   pineapple tidbits
2 tablespoons maraschino cherry syrup
½ cup orange juice
¼ cup confectioners' sugar
⅛ teaspoon cinnamon

Mix pineapple tidbits (with syrup) and remaining ingredients. Cover; refrigerate at least 1 hour.

4 to 6 servings.

PINEAPPLE DATE DESSERT

Prepare 1 package of our date bar mix as directed on package except—decrease hot water to ¼ cup and stir 1 can (8½ ounces) crushed pineapple, drained, into date filling. Serve with sweetened whipped cream or frozen whipped topping (thawed).

9 servings.

RUBY-JEWELED PEARS

1 can (16 ounces) whole cranberry sauce
¼ cup sugar
2 tablespoons lemon juice
¼ teaspoon cinnamon
4 pears, pared and cored

Heat oven to 350°. Mix cranberry sauce, sugar, lemon juice and cinnamon in saucepan. Cook over low heat, stirring occasionally, until the sugar is dissolved.

Stand pears upright in ungreased baking pan, 8×8×2 inches; pour sauce on pears. Bake 30 minutes or until tender, basting occasionally.

4 servings.

HOT FRUIT COMPOTE

1 banana
   Corn syrup
1 jar (30 ounces) fruits for salad, drained
2 tablespoons brown sugar
1 tablespoon butter or margarine

Heat oven to to 350°. Slice banana; dip into corn syrup. Arrange all fruit in ungreased baking pan, 13×9×2 inches. Sprinkle with sugar; dot with butter. Bake 20 minutes. For an easy topping, mix 1 cup of our vanilla pudding and 2 tablespoons water.

4 to 6 servings.

Substitution

For fruits for salad: 2 cans (17 ounces each) fruits for salad.

BROILED FRUIT KABOBS

Pictured on page 81.

Set oven control at broil and/or 550°. Cut a variety of fresh or canned fruits into uniform pieces, about ¾-inch cubes. (Try pineapple, pitted cooked prunes, peaches, pears, maraschino cherries, bananas or apples.) Alternate fruits on long skewers; place on well-greased rack in broiler pan.

Blend ¼ cup honey and 1½ teaspoons lemon juice; brush on fruit. Broil kabobs about 5 inches from heat 1½ minutes or until light brown. Turn carefully; brush with honey mixture. Broil 1½ minutes longer or until heated through.

APPLE CRISP

Butter Crunch (below)
1 can (21 ounces) apple pie filling
1 teaspoon lemon juice
½ teaspoon cinnamon
1 or 2 drops aromatic bitters, if desired

Prepare Butter Crunch. Heat oven to 450°. Mix remaining ingredients. Place apple mixture in ungreased 9-inch pie pan or in baking dish, 8×8×2 inches. Sprinkle 1 cup of the Butter Crunch evenly on top. Bake 10 minutes or until golden brown and bubbly. Serve warm. Delicious topped with ice cream.

4 servings.

BUTTER CRUNCH

½ cup butter or margarine
¼ cup brown sugar (packed)
1 cup Gold Medal Flour*
½ cup chopped pecans, walnuts or coconut

Heat oven to 400°. Mix all ingredients with hands. Spread in ungreased baking pan, 13×9×2 inches. Bake 15 minutes. Stir with spoon; cool. (Store in covered container in refrigerator.)

°Do not use Self-Rising Flour in this recipe.

CARAMEL PEACH CRISPS

1 can (16 ounces) cling peach halves,
   drained
2 tablespoons brown sugar
⅔ cup Wheaties
¼ cup brown sugar (packed)
3 tablespoons butter or margarine, melted
2 tablespoons raisins
2 tablespoons broken pecans
   Vanilla ice cream

Set oven control at broil and/or 550°. Place peach halves cut side up in ungreased baking pan, 8×8×2 inches; sprinkle with 2 tablespoons brown sugar. Broil peaches 5 inches from heat 2 to 3 minutes or until light brown.

Mix remaining ingredients except ice cream; spoon onto peaches. Broil about 1 minute longer or until mixture is bubbly and brown. Serve with ice cream.

4 to 6 servings.

CHERRY COBBLER

Pictured on page 81.

1 can (21 ounces) cherry pie filling
½ teaspoon almond extract
1 cup Bisquick
1 tablespoon sugar
¼ cup milk
1 tablespoon soft butter
2 tablespoons toasted slivered
   blanched almonds

Heat oven to 400°. In 1½-quart casserole, mix pie filling and almond extract. Place in oven 15 minutes or until hot and bubbly.

Mix Bisquick, sugar, milk and butter with fork until a soft dough forms; beat vigorously 20 strokes. Stir in almonds. Drop 6 spoonfuls of dough onto hot cherry mixture. Bake 20 to 25 minutes or until topping is light brown. For a touch of tradition, serve with light cream.

6 servings.

VARIATIONS

■ *Blueberry Cobbler:* Omit cherry pie filling and almond extract; substitute 1 can (21 ounces) blueberry pie filling and ½ teaspoon grated orange peel.

■ *Peach Cobbler:* Omit cherry pie filling and almond extract; substitute 1 can (21 ounces) peach pie filling and ½ teaspoon cinnamon.

CHOCOLATE FONDUE

Heat 1 can of our chocolate ready-to-spread frosting over low heat, stirring frequently. Pour into fondue pot or chafing dish to keep warm. Offer pineapple chunks, banana slices, fresh strawberries and cubes of angel food cake to dip into the fondue.

VARIATIONS

■ *Almond Chocolate Fondue:* Stir ½ teaspoon vanilla and ¼ teaspoon almond extract into frosting.

■ *Mint Chocolate Fondue:* Stir ½ teaspoon mint extract into frosting.

Puddings

CHOCOLATE-CHERRY PARFAIT

For each serving, alternate layers of our canned chocolate pudding and cherry pie filling in parfait glass or individual serving dish. Garnish with whipped cream and a maraschino cherry.

ROCKY ROAD PUDDING

Pictured on page 81.

 1 can of our chocolate pudding (2 cups)
1½ cups miniature marshmallows
    Whipped cream

Mix pudding and marshmallows; pour into individual serving dishes. Garnish with whipped cream.

4 or 5 servings.

FRUIT DELIGHT

1 can (11 ounces) mandarin orange
    segments, well drained
1 can (13¼ ounces) pineapple tidbits,
    well drained
1 can of our vanilla pudding (2 cups)

Mix all ingredients. Spoon into individual serving dishes. Toasted coconut makes a nice garnish.

8 servings.

FRUIT 'N RICE DESSERT

1 can of our rice pudding (2 cups)
1 can (17 ounces) fruit cocktail, well drained
1 jar (12 ounces) apricot jam

Mix rice pudding and fruit cocktail; chill. Just before serving, heat apricot jam until melted, stirring occasionally. Spoon pudding into individual serving dishes and top with apricot sauce.

6 servings.

COCONUT PUDDING

Mix ½ cup flaked coconut and 1 can of our vanilla pudding (2 cups). Spoon into individual serving dishes. Garnish with sliced strawberries.

4 servings.

PUDDING-PIE DESSERT

For each serving, spoon ¼ cup apricot, blueberry, cherry, peach or strawberry pie filling into individual serving dish or glass. Top with ½ cup of our rice pudding. Garnish with a spoonful of pie filling.

4 servings.

RICH VANILLA PUDDING

1 cup dairy sour cream
1 can of our vanilla pudding (2 cups)
    Canned sliced peaches, drained

Fold sour cream into pudding; pour into individual serving dishes. Top with peaches.

5 or 6 servings.

LEMON PUDDING SHELLS

3 egg whites
¼ teaspoon cream of tartar
¾ cup sugar
1 can of our lemon pudding (2 cups),
    chilled
1 cup sweetened whipped cream
8 fresh strawberries

Heat oven to 275°. Cover baking sheet with heavy brown paper. In small mixer bowl, beat egg whites and cream of tartar until foamy. Beat in sugar, 1 tablespoon at a time; continue beating until stiff and glossy. Do not underbeat.

Drop meringue by ⅓ cupfuls onto brown paper. Shape mounds into circles with back of spoon, building up sides. Bake 1 hour. Turn off oven; leave meringues in oven with door closed 1½ hours. Remove from oven; finish cooling meringues away from draft.

Just before serving, fill each shell with ¼ cup pudding. Top with whipped cream and a strawberry.

8 servings.

Chilled and Frozen Desserts

RASPBERRY-RASPBERRY

Pictured at left.

1 cup boiling water
1 package (3 ounces) raspberry-flavored
  gelatin
4 to 6 ice cubes
1 carton (8 ounces) raspberry-flavored
  yogurt

Pour boiling water on gelatin in large bowl, stirring until gelatin is dissolved. Add ice cubes; stir until gelatin begins to thicken. Remove any remaining ice cubes.

Add yogurt; beat until smooth with rotary beater. Pour into individual serving dishes, glasses or molds. Chill until firm, about 45 minutes. Serve with a dollop of whipped topping.

5 or 6 servings.

Note: Try other gelatin and yogurt combinations.

STRAWBERRY ICE

1 package (3 ounces) strawberry-flavored
  gelatin
½ cup sugar
1½ cups boiling water
1 package (16 ounces) frozen sliced
  strawberries, partially thawed
¼ cup orange juice
¼ cup lemon juice

Blend gelatin and sugar; pour boiling water on gelatin mixture in large bowl, stirring until gelatin is dissolved. Stir in remaining ingredients.

Pour into 2 refrigerator trays; freeze until mushy, about 1 hour. Remove from trays; beat until smooth. Return to trays; freeze until firm, about 1 hour.

8 to 10 servings.

Pictured at left.
Individual Baked Alaska, Raspberry-Raspberry,
Creamy Lemon Sherbet—a trio of happy endings.

FRUIT DESSERT FREEZE

1 package of our creamy white
  frosting mix
2 cups whipping cream
1 large banana
1 can (8¾ ounces) crushed pineapple,
  drained
1 can (11 ounces) mandarin orange
  segments, drained
⅓ cup halved maraschino cherries, drained
⅓ cup cut-up dates
⅓ cup chopped pecans, if desired
2 tablespoons lemon juice

In small mixer bowl, chill frosting mix (dry) and whipping cream at least 1 hour. Beat until soft peaks form. Slice banana into frosting mixture; fold in remaining ingredients. Pour into 2 refrigerator trays or a baking pan, 9×9×2 inches. Freeze until firm. Cut into squares.

12 servings.

VARIATION

■ *Fruit Salad Freeze:* Fold ⅓ cup mayonnaise into beaten frosting mix and whipping cream.

CHERRIES SUPREME

½ cup butter or margarine, softened
¼ cup brown sugar (packed)
1 cup Gold Medal Flour*
½ cup chopped pecans
½ gallon vanilla ice cream, softened
1 can (21 ounces) cherry pie filling
2 tablespoons rum flavoring, if desired

Heat oven to 400°. Mix butter, brown sugar, flour and pecans with hands. Press mixture evenly in bottom of baking pan, 9×9×2 inches. Bake about 12 minutes or until light brown. Crumble with spoon; cool.

Reserving 1 cup of the crumbs, press remaining crumbs evenly in pan. Pack ice cream evenly on crumbs. Sprinkle reserved crumbs on top. Freeze until firm. Just before serving, heat pie filling and rum flavoring; spoon onto each serving.

9 servings.

*Do not use Self-Rising Flour in this recipe.

CREAMY LEMON SHERBET

Pictured on page 86.

1 can (13 ounces) evaporated milk, chilled
1 can (6 ounces) frozen lemonade
   concentrate, partially thawed
5 drops yellow food color

Beat chilled milk until stiff. Stir in lemonade concentrate and food color. Pour into 2 refrigerator trays; freeze until firm. If desired, serve with a sprinkling of chopped crystallized ginger.

6 to 8 servings.

COOKIE REFRIGERATOR DESSERT

   About twenty 2-inch vanilla wafers
1 envelope (about 2 ounces) dessert
   topping mix
½ cup flaked coconut, if desired
1 can of our vanilla pudding (2 cups)
¼ cup finely chopped nuts

Arrange vanilla wafers in bottom of ungreased baking pan, 9×9×2 inches. Prepare dessert topping as directed on package. Fold topping and coconut into pudding; spread on wafers. Sprinkle with nuts. Chill at least 1 hour or until firm.

9 servings.

Substitution

   For vanilla pudding: our chocolate pudding.

ICE-CREAM WAFFLES

1 package (5 ounces) frozen waffles
1 pint vanilla ice cream
1 pint strawberries, sliced and sweetened

Toast waffles as directed on package. Top each with scoop of ice cream. Spoon berries on ice cream.

6 servings.

Substitution

   For fresh strawberries: 1 package (16 ounces) frozen sliced strawberries, partially thawed.

VARIATION

■ *Sundae Waffles:* Omit strawberries. Pour warm chocolate sauce on ice cream; top with nuts.

PARTY PEACH MELBA

1 can (16 ounces) peach halves, drained
   Toasted almonds
1 package (10 ounces) frozen raspberries,
   partially thawed
1 pint vanilla ice cream

Place a peach half in each individual serving dish; sprinkle with almonds. Spoon raspberries on peach halves. Cover; refrigerate at least 1 hour. Just before serving, top each serving with a scoop of ice cream.

5 or 6 servings.

CHOCOLATE-MINT PARFAITS

¼ cup mint jelly
2 tablespoons water
½ cup chilled whipping cream
3 pints chocolate ice cream

Heat mint jelly and water until smooth, stirring constantly; cool. In chilled bowl, beat whipping cream until stiff; stir in jelly mixture. Alternate layers of ice cream and whipped cream mixture in parfait glasses or other individual serving dishes. Freeze until firm.

8 servings.

INDIVIDUAL BAKED ALASKAS

Pictured on page 86.

1 package sponge shortcakes (4)
1 pint ice cream
1 package of our fluffy white
   frosting mix

Cover baking sheet with aluminum foil. Arrange shortcakes on foil. Place scoop of ice cream in each shortcake; freeze at least 1 hour.°

Heat oven to 500°. Prepare frosting as directed on package. Completely cover shortcake and ice cream with frosting, sealing it to foil on baking sheet. Bake on lowest rack in oven 3 to 5 minutes or until frosting is light brown. Serve immediately.

4 servings.

°*Shortcakes can be frozen up to 24 hours at this point.*

Cookies

Starting with a mix...
BROWNIE VARIATIONS

Prepare 1 package (15.5 ounces) of our fudge brownie mix as directed on package except—try one of the following variations:

■ *Almond:* Stir in ½ teaspoon almond extract.

■ *Cherry:* Stir in ¼ cup drained chopped maraschino cherries (about 16).

■ *Coconut:* Omit nuts; stir in 1 cup flaked coconut.

■ *Date:* Omit nuts; stir in 1 cup chopped dates. Coat baked squares with confectioners' sugar.

■ *Fruit:* Stir in ⅓ cup chopped candied fruit.

■ *Mint:* Immediately after removing brownies from oven, place 16 chocolate-covered mint patties (about 1½ inches in diameter) on top. Allow mints to soften; spread evenly.

■ *Mocha:* Add 1½ tablespoons powdered instant coffee.

■ *Peanut:* Stir in ½ cup chopped peanuts. Frost with a peanut butter icing.

■ *Peanut Butter:* Omit nuts; add 3 tablespoons chunky peanut butter.

■ *Peppermint:* Add ¼ teaspoon peppermint extract.

SOUR CREAM BROWNIES

Pictured on page 81.

**1 package (22.5 ounces) of our
  fudge brownie mix
2 eggs
¾ cup dairy sour cream**

Heat oven to 350°. Grease baking pan, 13×9×2 inches. Mix brownie mix (dry), eggs and sour cream. Spread in pan. Bake 23 to 27 minutes. Cool; cut into 1½-inch squares.

4 dozen cookies.

GINGERBREAD DROPS

Heat oven to 375°. Blend 1 package of our gingerbread mix (dry) and ½ cup water. Drop by teaspoonfuls about 2 inches apart onto lightly greased baking sheet. Bake 10 to 12 minutes.

About 3 dozen cookies.

VARIATIONS

■ *Chocolate Chip Ginger Drops:* Stir in 1 package (6 ounces) semisweet chocolate pieces and ½ cup chopped nuts.

■ *Coconut Ginger Drops:* Stir in 1 cup shredded coconut.

■ *Date-Nut Ginger Drops:* Stir in ½ cup cut-up dates and ½ cup chopped nuts.

■ *Fruit Ginger Drops:* Stir in 1 cup cut-up candied fruit and ½ cup sugared chopped nuts.

■ *Jeweled Ginger Drops:* Stir in ⅔ cup cut-up gumdrops and ½ cup chopped nuts.

■ *Mincemeat Ginger Drops:* Stir in 1 cup prepared mincemeat and ½ cup chopped nuts.

■ *Orange-Coconut Ginger Drops:* Omit water; stir in 1 cup shredded coconut, 1 tablespoon grated orange peel and the juice from 1 orange plus enough water to measure ½ cup.

■ *Peanut Butter Ginger Drops:* Add ½ cup peanut butter.

■ *Peanut Ginger Drops:* Stir in 1 cup chopped peanuts.

■ *Raisin-Nut Ginger Drops:* Stir in 1 cup raisins and ½ cup chopped nuts.

The Case for Keeping Cookies

Soft cookies: Store in any container with a tight-fitting cover. To keep them soft, tuck in a fresh slice of bread or apple every couple of days.

Crisp cookies: Store in any container, but cover loosely. If they soften, recrisp by placing them in a 300° oven for 3 to 5 minutes. Crunch!

Freezing? Arrange baked cookies in a foil- or plastic wrap-lined box, separating the layers with foil or wrap. Or, store small batches in freezer bags, plastic wrap or foil. They'll keep for 9 to 12 months!

Starting with a mix...
DATE BAR VARIATIONS

Prepare 1 package of our date bar mix as directed on package except—try one of the following easy variations:

- *Almond:* Stir ¾ teaspoon almond extract into date filling.

- *Apple:* Stir ½ cup finely chopped pared tart apples into date filling.

- *Apricot:* Stir ½ cup finely cut dried apricots into date filling.

- *Cherry:* Stir ¼ cup drained chopped maraschino cherries (about 16) into date filling.

- *Coffee:* Stir 1 tablespoon powdered instant coffee into date filling.

- *Raisin:* Stir ½ cup raisins into date filling.

- *Spice:* Stir 1 teaspoon cinnamon, ¼ teaspoon cloves or ½ teaspoon nutmeg into date filling.

- *Walnut:* Stir ½ cup chopped walnuts into date filling.

FUDGE CRINKLES

 2 eggs
 ⅔ cup shortening
 1 package of our devils food cake mix
 1 package of our chocolate fudge
   frosting mix

Heat oven to 375°. Beat eggs, shortening and half the cake mix (dry) until light and fluffy. Stir in remaining cake mix.

Shape into 1-inch balls. Place about 2 inches apart on ungreased baking sheet. Bake 10 to 12 minutes. Cool slightly before removing from baking sheet.

Prepare frosting as directed on package; frost cooled cookies. You can decorate with raisins, red cinnamon candies, colored nonpareils or candy corn. Or, put cookies together in pairs with frosting.

4 dozen cookies (2 dozen cookie sandwiches).

REFRIGERATOR COOKIES

 1 package of our creamy white
   frosting mix
 2 cups Gold Medal Flour*
 1 cup butter or margarine, softened
 ½ cup chopped pecans
 1½ tablespoons butter or margarine,
   softened
 2 tablespoons hot water

Measure 1½ cups of the frosting mix (dry) into large bowl. With hands, mix in flour, 1 cup butter and the pecans. Divide dough in half; shape each half into roll, about 1½ inches in diameter and about 7½ inches long. Wrap; chill at least 4 hours.

Heat oven to 400°. Cut rolls into ⅛-inch slices. Place 1 inch apart on ungreased baking sheet. Bake 4 to 6 minutes. Cool slightly before removing from baking sheet.

Mix remaining frosting mix, 1½ tablespoons soft butter and the water until smooth. (Add 1 to 2 teaspoons water if necessary.) Frost cookies. (Enough frosting for about 4 dozen cookies.)

About 8 dozen cookies.

°Do not use Self-Rising Flour in this recipe.

VARIATION

- *Chocolate Refrigerator Cookies:* Substitute our chocolate fudge frosting mix for the creamy white frosting mix.

PEANUT BUTTER COOKIES

 1 cup crunchy peanut butter
 ⅓ cup water
 2 eggs
 1 package of our yellow cake mix

Heat oven to 375°. Beat peanut butter, water, eggs and half the cake mix (dry) until smooth. Stir in remaining cake mix.

Drop dough by teaspoonfuls 3 inches apart onto ungreased baking sheet. Press floured thumb deeply into center of each mound. Bake 8 to 10 minutes or until golden brown. Cool slightly before removing from baking sheet.

4 dozen cookies.

GOLDEN GOOD BARS

   2 cups Bisquick
2⅓ cups brown sugar (packed)
   4 eggs
   1 teaspoon vanilla
   1 cup chopped nuts
   ½ cup flaked coconut

Heat oven to 350°. Grease and flour baking pan, 13×9×2 inches. Mix Bisquick, brown sugar, eggs and vanilla. Stir in chopped nuts and flaked coconut. Pour into pan. Bake 25 to 30 minutes. Cool; cut into bars, 2×1 inch.

4½ dozen cookies.

BUTTER PECAN COOKIES

   1 package of our butter pecan muffin mix
   ⅓ cup salad oil
   1 egg
   2 tablespoons milk

Heat oven to 375°. Mix muffin mix (dry), oil, egg and milk. Drop by teaspoonfuls 2 inches apart onto ungreased baking sheet. Flatten slightly with bottom of glass that has been greased and dipped in sugar. Bake 8 to 10 minutes or until light brown on edges. Immediately remove from baking sheet.

About 3 dozen cookies.

ALMOND SHORTBREADS

   1 packet of our free-flowing pie crust mix
   1 cup confectioners' sugar
   ½ cup chopped blanched almonds
   1 teaspoon almond extract

Heat oven to 350°. Prepare pastry for Two-crust Pie as directed on package except—before adding water to pie crust mix, mix in sugar, nuts and almond extract.

Roll dough ½ inch thick on lightly floured board. Cut into 1¼-inch diamonds. Place ½ inch apart on ungreased baking sheet. Bake about 15 minutes or until set. Immediately remove from baking sheet.

About 3 dozen cookies.

Substitution

   For free-flowing pie crust mix: 2 sticks of our pie crust mix.

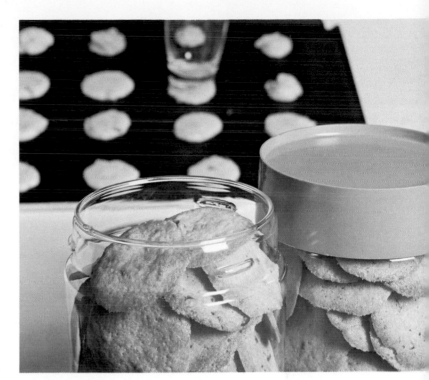

Butter Pecan Cookies

Almond Shortbreads

CHOCOLATE CHIP BARS

Pictured on page 81.

⅓ cup shortening
⅓ cup butter or margarine, softened
½ cup granulated sugar
½ cup brown sugar (packed)
1 egg
1 teaspoon vanilla
1½ cups Gold Medal Flour*
½ teaspoon soda
½ teaspoon salt
½ cup chopped pecans
1 package (6 ounces) semisweet chocolate pieces

Heat oven to 375°. Mix shortening, butter, sugars, egg and vanilla. Stir in remaining ingredients.

Spread in ungreased baking pan, 13×9×2 inches. Bake 20 to 25 minutes or until light brown. Cool; cut into bars, about 3×1 inch.

About 3 dozen cookies.

*If using Self-Rising Flour, omit soda and salt.

APPLESAUCE BARS

1 cup Gold Medal Flour*
⅔ cup brown sugar (packed)
1 teaspoon soda
1 teaspoon pumpkin pie spice
½ teaspoon salt
¼ cup shortening
1 cup applesauce
1 egg
½ cup raisins
    Browned Butter Icing (below)

Heat oven to 350°. Grease baking pan, 13×9×2 inches. Mix all ingredients except icing. Spread in pan. Bake about 25 minutes. Cool; frost with icing. Cut into bars, about 3×1 inch.

32 cookies.

*If using Self-Rising Flour, decrease soda to ½ teaspoon and omit salt.

BROWNED BUTTER ICING

Heat 3 tablespoons butter over medium heat until golden. Remove from heat; blend in 1½ cups confectioners' sugar, 1 teaspoon vanilla and about 1 tablespoon milk. Beat until smooth.

COCONUT-TOFFEE BARS

¼ cup butter or margarine, softened
¼ cup shortening
½ cup brown sugar (packed)
1 cup Gold Medal Flour*
    Almond-Coconut Topping (below)

Heat oven to 350°. Cream butter, shortening and sugar. Blend in flour. Press evenly in bottom of ungreased baking pan, 13×9×2 inches. Bake 10 minutes.

Spread Almond-Coconut Topping on baked layer. Bake 25 minutes longer or until topping is golden brown. Cool cookies slightly; cut into bars, about 3×1 inch.

32 cookies.

*If using Self-Rising Flour, omit baking powder and salt from Almond-Coconut Topping.

ALMOND-COCONUT TOPPING

2 eggs
1 cup brown sugar (packed)
1 teaspoon vanilla
2 tablespoons flour
1 teaspoon baking powder
½ teaspoon salt
1 cup shredded coconut
1 cup chopped almonds

Beat eggs in large mixing bowl; stir in remaining ingredients.

PEANUT BREAK

1 cup butter or margarine, melted
1½ cups brown sugar (packed)
2 cups Gold Medal Flour*
¼ cup dark corn syrup
1 egg
2 cups salted peanuts

Heat oven to 375°. Line jelly roll pan, 15½×10½×1 inch, with waxed paper. Cream butter and sugar. Mix in flour, syrup and egg. Stir in peanuts.

Spread in pan. Bake about 25 minutes or until light brown. Loosen layer from sides of pan; invert onto wire rack. Carefully remove paper. Cool; break into pieces.

*Self-Rising Flour can be used in this recipe.

POLYNESIAN COOKIES

    1 cup shortening
 1½ cups sugar
    1 egg
    1 can (8½ ounces) crushed pineapple
 3½ cups Gold Medal Flour*
    1 teaspoon soda
   ½ teaspoon salt
   ¼ teaspoon nutmeg
   ½ cup chopped macadamia nuts

Heat oven to 400°. Mix shortening, sugar and egg. Stir in pineapple (with syrup) and remaining ingredients.

Drop dough by teaspoonfuls about 2 inches apart onto ungreased baking sheet. Bake 8 to 10 minutes or until golden brown and no imprint remains when touched lightly with finger.

About 5 dozen cookies.

If using Self-Rising Flour, omit soda and salt.

Substitution

For macadamia nuts: ½ cup chopped walnuts or pecans.

VARIATIONS

■ *Pineapple Coconut Cookies:* Omit nutmeg; stir in 1 cup flaked coconut.

■ *Pineapple Raisin Cookies:* Stir in 1 cup raisins.

Take Care with Your Cookie-baking

☐ Make sure your baking sheets are in good condition—nice and smooth. They should be at least 2 inches narrower and shorter than your oven.
☐ Don't grease unless the recipe tells you so.
☐ Always place cookie dough on a cool sheet.
☐ It's best to bake cookies one sheet at a time, in the center of the oven.
☐ With drop cookies, you can take a trial run: bake a test cookie. If it spreads more than you like, add 1 or 2 tablespoons flour to the dough. If it's too dry or crumbly, add 1 or 2 tablespoons cream or milk.
☐ Don't overbake. Check cookies at the end of the minimum baking time. One minute can make a big difference.
☐ When cookies are done, remove from the baking sheet immediately—unless the recipe directs otherwise. Cool on a wire rack.

CHOCOLATE CHIP COOKIES

   ⅔ cup shortening
   ⅔ cup butter or margarine, softened
    1 cup granulated sugar
    1 cup brown sugar (packed)
    2 eggs
    2 teaspoons vanilla
    3 cups Gold Medal Flour*
    1 teaspoon soda
    1 teaspoon salt
    1 cup chopped nuts
    2 packages (6 ounces each) semisweet
      chocolate pieces

Heat oven to 375°. Mix shortening, butter, sugars, eggs and vanilla. Stir in remaining ingredients. (For a softer, rounder cookie, add ½ cup flour.)

Drop dough by rounded teaspoonfuls 2 inches apart onto ungreased baking sheet. Bake 8 to 10 minutes or until light brown. Cool slightly before removing from baking sheet.

About 7 dozen cookies.

If using Self-Rising Flour, omit soda and salt.

VARIATION

■ *Salted Peanut Cookies:* Substitute 2 cups salted peanuts for the chopped nuts and chocolate pieces. Before baking, flatten each cookie with bottom of glass that has been greased and dipped in sugar.

BROWN SUGAR PECAN ROUNDS

   ½ cup butter or margarine, softened
 1¼ cups brown sugar (packed)
    1 egg
 1¼ cups Gold Medal Flour*
   ¼ teaspoon soda
   ⅛ teaspoon salt
   ½ cup coarsely chopped pecans

Heat oven to 350°. Mix butter, brown sugar and egg. Stir in remaining ingredients.

Drop dough by teaspoonfuls about 2 inches apart onto ungreased baking sheet. (Dough will flatten and spread.) Bake 12 to 15 minutes or until set.

About 3 dozen cookies.

If using Self-Rising Flour, omit soda and salt.

Candies

CHOCOLATE FUDGE

2 tablespoons butter or margarine
3 tablespoons water
1 package of our chocolate fudge
   frosting mix

Butter loaf pan, 9×5×3 inches. In medium saucepan, melt butter in water. Blend in frosting mix (dry). Heat over low heat, stirring constantly, about 5 minutes or until smooth and glossy. Spread mixture evenly in buttered pan. Cool until firm. Cut into 1-inch squares.

32 candies.

VARIATION

■ *Chocolate-Nut Fudge:* Stir in ½ cup chopped nuts.

OPERA FUDGE

3 tablespoons butter or margarine
3 tablespoons milk
1 package of our creamy white
   frosting mix
½ cup chopped nuts

Butter loaf pan, 9×5×3 inches. In medium saucepan, melt butter in milk. Blend in frosting mix (dry). Heat over low heat, stirring constantly, about 5 minutes or until smooth and glossy. Remove from heat; stir in nuts.

Spread mixture evenly in buttered pan. Cool until firm. Cut into 1-inch squares.

32 candies.

VARIATION

■ *Cherry Opera Fudge:* Stir in ½ cup candied cherry halves with the nuts.

FUDGE CLUSTERS

2 tablespoons butter or margarine
3 tablespoons water
1 package of our chocolate fudge
   frosting mix
1 cup pecans or salted peanuts

In medium saucepan, melt butter in water. Blend in frosting mix (dry). Heat over low heat, stirring constantly, about 5 minutes or until smooth and glossy. Remove from heat; stir in nuts.

Drop by teaspoonfuls onto waxed paper. (Keep mixture warm, stirring occasionally, while making candies.) Cool until firm.

3 to 4 dozen candies.

CRUNCHY MOCHA DROPS

3 tablespoons butter or margarine
3 tablespoons milk
1 package of our creamy white
   frosting mix
1 to 2 tablespoons powdered
   instant coffee
1½ cups toasted flaked coconut

In medium saucepan, melt butter in milk. Blend in frosting mix (dry) and instant coffee. Heat over low heat, stirring constantly, about 5 minutes or until smooth and glossy. Remove from heat; stir in coconut.

Drop by teaspoonfuls onto waxed paper. (Keep mixture warm, stirring occasionally, while making candies.) Cool until firm.

4 to 5 dozen candies.

MARGUERITES

1 package of our fluffy white
   frosting mix
1 cup chopped nuts
   About 4 dozen soda crackers

Heat oven to 350°. Prepare frosting as directed on package. Fold in nuts. Drop by tablespoonfuls onto soda crackers. Bake 4 to 6 minutes or until light brown.

About 4 dozen confections.

PEANUT BUTTER FUDGE BALLS

1 package of our chocolate fudge
  frosting mix
½ cup creamy peanut butter
¼ cup butter or margarine, softened
2 tablespoons hot water
½ teaspoon vanilla
2 cups Cheerios

In large bowl, mix frosting mix (dry), peanut butter, butter, water and vanilla until blended. Mix in Cheerios. Shape into 1-inch balls.

About 4 dozen candies.

CHOCOLATE BONBONS

1 package of our chocolate fudge
  frosting mix
½ cup butter or margarine, softened
1 teaspoon vanilla

Mix frosting mix (dry), butter and vanilla with fork. Work into a ball with hands. Knead 20 to 30 times on board lightly dusted with confectioners' sugar. Wrap fondant around candied fruit such as cherries, ginger, pineapple or walnut halves.

Garnish candies with finely chopped coconut pressed on top or roll in finely chopped nuts, chocolate shot and the like. Store in tightly covered container in cool place.

4 to 5 dozen candies.

VARIATION

■ *Vanilla Bonbons:* Substitute 1 package of our creamy white frosting mix for the chocolate fudge frosting mix. Tint fondant with food color if desired.

ALMOND DROPS

1 can of our vanilla ready-to-spread
  frosting
¾ teaspoon almond extract
½ teaspoon vanilla
½ cup slivered almonds, toasted

Mix all ingredients. Drop by level teaspoonfuls onto waxed paper-covered baking sheet. Chill until set, about 4 hours. Store in refrigerator.

7 dozen candies.

CREAMY VANILLA FONDANT

Mix 1 package of our creamy white frosting mix (dry), ½ cup butter or margarine, softened, and 1 teaspoon vanilla with fork. Work into a ball with hands. Knead 20 to 30 times on board lightly dusted with confectioners' sugar. (Fondant can be divided and tinted with various food colors; knead again to distribute color evenly in each portion.)

Shape mixture into 1-inch balls. Press tops into, or roll completely in, finely crushed peppermint-stick candy, chopped nuts, multicolored candies or flaked coconut.

About 4 dozen candies.

VARIATIONS

■ *Peppermint Creams:* Substitute ½ teaspoon peppermint extract for the vanilla.

■ *Toasted Almond Bonbons:* Omit vanilla and stir in ½ cup finely chopped toasted almonds. Roll balls in finely chopped toasted almonds if desired.

CHOCOLATE NUT CREAMS

1 package of our chocolate fudge
  frosting mix
½ cup butter or margarine, softened
1 teaspoon vanilla
½ cup finely chopped nuts

Mix frosting mix (dry), butter and vanilla with fork. Stir in nuts. Work into a ball with hands. Knead 20 to 30 times on board lightly dusted with confectioners' sugar.

Shape mixture into 1-inch balls. (If desired, roll in mixture of 1 teaspoon cinnamon and 1 tablespoon granulated sugar.) Store in tightly covered container in cool place.

About 5 dozen candies.

VARIATION

■ *Vanilla Nut Creams:* Substitute 1 package of our creamy white frosting mix for the chocolate fudge frosting mix.

Toasted Coconut Yellow Cake with Chocolate Frosting

Lemon Butter Crunch Cake

Cakes

Starting with a mix...
YELLOW CAKE VARIATIONS

Prepare 1 package of our yellow cake mix as directed on package except—try one of the following variations:

■ *Banana:* Use ¼ cup less water and add 1 cup mashed banana (2 to 3 medium) and ⅛ teaspoon soda. Stir in ½ cup finely chopped nuts.

■ *Maple-Nut:* Add 2 teaspoons maple flavoring and stir in ⅓ cup finely chopped nuts.

■ *Nutmeg-Mace:* Add ½ teaspoon each nutmeg and mace.

■ *Orange:* Add 2 tablespoons grated orange peel.

■ *Toasted Coconut:* Stir in 1 to 1½ cups toasted flaked coconut.

LEMON BUTTER CRUNCH CAKE

1 package of our yellow cake mix
½ can of our lemon pudding (1 cup)
1 cup crushed peanut brittle

Bake cake in baking pan, 13×9×2 inches, as directed on package. Cool; spread lemon pudding on cake. Sprinkle with peanut brittle.

PEANUT BUTTER CAKE

Prepare 1 package of our yellow cake mix as directed on package except—before blending, add 1 cup peanut butter. Cool.

Prepare 1 package of our creamy white frosting mix as directed on package except—substitute peanut butter for the butter. If frosting is too thick, add a few drops of hot water. Frost cake.

Note: Irregular surface and crack on top of layers is characteristic of this cake.

Starting with a mix...

WHITE CAKE VARIATIONS

Prepare 1 package of our white cake mix as directed on package except—try one of the following variations:

■ *Cherry:* Stir in ½ cup drained finely chopped maraschino cherries.

■ *Cherry-Nut:* Stir in ½ cup finely chopped nuts and ½ cup drained finely chopped maraschino cherries.

■ *Coconut:* Stir in 1 to 1½ cups flaked coconut.

■ *Mint:* Add ¼ teaspoon peppermint extract and stir in red or green food color.

■ *Orange:* Add 2 tablespoons grated orange peel.

STRAWBERRY CHANTILLY TORTE

1 package of our white cake mix
1 package of our creamy white frosting mix
1 package (8 ounces) cream cheese, softened
1 tablespoon milk
1 teaspoon almond extract
1 pint strawberries

Bake cake in 2 layer pans, 8 or 9×1½ inches, as directed on package. Cool; split to make 4 layers.

In small mixer bowl, beat frosting mix (dry), cream cheese, milk and almond extract until smooth. Slice strawberries lengthwise, reserving ½ cup of the outer slices for top layer.

Stack layers, spreading each with about ½ cup frosting and about ½ cup strawberries. Place reserved strawberry slices cut side down on top layer. Chill at least 1 hour before serving. Because of the cream cheese, refrigerate leftover cake.

BUSY DAY CUPCAKES

Bake cupcakes in paper baking cups as directed on 1 package of our white, yellow or devils food cake mix. Place chocolate-covered thin mint candy on each cupcake.

Set oven control at broil and/or 550°. Broil cupcakes 3 inches from heat 1 to 2 minutes or until candy is soft. Spread candy to frost cupcakes.

Cherry-Nut White Cake with pink-tinted Creamy White Frosting

Strawberry Chantilly Torte

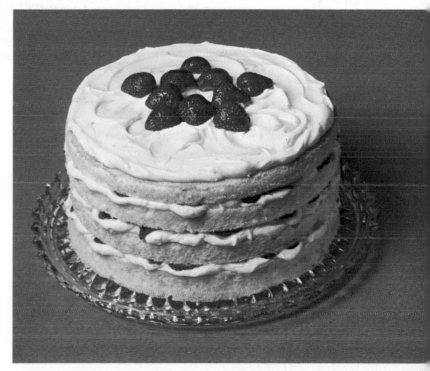

Starting with a mix...
DEVILS FOOD CAKE VARIATIONS

Prepare 1 package of our devils food cake mix as directed on package except—try one of the following variations:

■ *Banana:* Use ¼ cup less water and add ¾ cup mashed banana (1½ to 2 medium) and ⅛ teaspoon soda. Stir in ½ cup chopped nuts.

■ *Cherry Chocolate:* Stir in ½ cup well-drained chopped maraschino cherries.

■ *Fudge Nut:* Stir in ½ cup chopped nuts.

■ *Mocha:* Use 1 cup cold strong coffee for part of the water and add 3 tablespoons instant coffee.

■ *Peppermint:* Stir in ¼ teaspoon peppermint extract.

TRIPLE FUDGE CAKE

Pictured on page 81.

1 package of our devils food cake mix
1 can of our chocolate fudge pudding
   (2 cups)
1 egg
½ cup semisweet chocolate pieces
½ cup coarsely chopped nuts

Heat oven to 350°. Grease and flour baking pan, 13×9×2 inches. Beat cake mix (dry), pudding and egg 1 to 2 minutes.

Pour into pan. Sprinkle batter with chocolate pieces and nuts. Bake 35 to 40 minutes. If you like, serve with whipped cream.

PARTY DEVILS FOOD CAKE

1 package of our devils food cake mix
1 package of our fluffy white frosting mix
8 maraschino cherries, chopped
1 can (4 ounces) shredded coconut
½ teaspoon almond extract

Bake cake in 2 layer pans, 8 or 9×1½ inches, as directed on package. Cool.

Prepare frosting as directed on package except—fold in almond extract; frost cake. Mix cherries and coconut until coconut is a delicate pink. Sprinkle on frosted cake.

BROWNIE FUDGE CAKE

1 package (15.5 ounces) of our
   fudge brownie mix
2 eggs
½ cup water
½ cup finely chopped nuts
   Creamy Cocoa Frosting (below)

Heat oven to 350°. Grease baking pan, 9×9×2 inches. In small mixer bowl, blend brownie mix (dry), eggs and ¼ cup of the water on low speed, scraping bowl constantly. Beat 1 minute medium speed, scraping bowl occasionally. Add remaining ¼ cup water; beat 1 minute longer. Stir in nuts.

Pour into pan. Bake about 30 minutes or until top springs back when touched lightly with finger. Cool and frost.

CREAMY COCOA FROSTING

1 cup confectioners' sugar
2 tablespoons cocoa
1 tablespoon soft butter or margarine
1½ tablespoons milk

Beat all ingredients until smooth.

COUNTRY LOAF CAKE

Heat oven to 350° (325° for glass pans). Grease and flour 2 loaf pans, 9×5×3 inches. Prepare 1 package of our layer cake mix (chocolate, yellow or white) as directed on package except—use 2 tablespoons less water.

Pour into pans. Bake 30 to 35 minutes or until wooden pick inserted in center comes out clean. Cool. If desired, dust cake with confectioners' sugar or frost with your favorite frosting and trim with candied fruits or chopped nuts.

VARIATION

■ *Cake Sandwiches:* Cut loaf cake into ½-inch slices; put slices together in pairs with favorite pudding, marshmallow crème or slice of ice cream.

Starting with a mix...
POUND CAKE VARIATIONS

Prepare 1 package of our golden pound cake mix as directed on package except—try one of the following variations:

- *Chocolate-Nut:* Stir in 2 squares (1 ounce each) unsweetened chocolate, grated, and ½ cup nuts.

- *Fruit-Nut:* Stir in ½ cup finely chopped mixed candied fruit and ½ cup finely chopped nuts.

- *Lemon:* Stir in 1 tablespoon grated lemon peel.

- *Pecan:* Stir in 1 cup finely chopped pecans.

- *Raisin-Nut:* Stir in ½ cup finely chopped raisins and ½ cup chopped nuts.

FUDGY PECAN PUDDING CAKE

  1 package of our butter pecan muffin mix
  ½ cup milk
  1 cup brown sugar (packed)
  ¼ cup cocoa
  1¼ cups hot water

Heat oven to 350°. Grease baking pan, 9×9×2 inches. Stir together muffin mix (dry) and milk just until mix is moistened. Spread in pan.

Mix sugar and cocoa; sprinkle evenly on batter. Pour hot water carefully on batter. (Do not stir.) Bake 35 minutes. Cool slightly; cut into squares. Invert onto dessert plates and top with sauce.

9 servings.

QUICK DATE CAKE

  1 package of our date bar mix
  ½ cup hot water
  2 eggs
  1 teaspoon baking powder
  ½ cup chopped walnuts

Heat oven to 375°. Grease baking pan, 8×8×2 inches. Mix date filling and hot water. Stir in crumbly mix, eggs, baking powder and nuts.

Spread in pan. Bake about 30 minutes or until top springs back when touched lightly with finger. Cool.

Note: Recipe can be doubled and baked in greased baking pan, 13×9×2 inches.

HAWAIIAN CREAM PIE

  1 package of our pineapple upside-down
     cake mix
  ½ can of our vanilla pudding (1 cup)
     Brown Sugar Glaze (below)

Heat oven to 350°. Drain pineapple from 1 package of our pineapple upside-down cake mix; fold into 1 cup of our vanilla pudding. Chill.

Generously grease and flour layer pan, 8×1½ inches. Prepare cake as directed on package. Pour into pan. Bake 35 to 40 minutes or until wooden pick inserted in center comes out clean. Cool slightly; remove from pan. Cool thoroughly. Split layer; fill with pudding mixture and refrigerate.

Just before serving, spread with hot Brown Sugar Glaze. (If glaze hardens, stir over low heat.) Because of the pudding, refrigerate leftover pie.

BROWN SUGAR GLAZE

Mix Topping Mix, 2 tablespoons butter and 1 tablespoon light cream in small saucepan. Heat to boiling, stirring constantly.

TRIPLE LEMON CAKE

Bake 1 package of our lemon chiffon cake mix as directed on package. Cool; split to make 3 layers. Stack layers, filling each with ½ can of our lemon pudding (1 cup).

Prepare 1 package of our lemon fluff frosting mix as directed on package. Frost side and top of cake. Because of the pudding, refrigerate leftover cake.

The Cake Pan Counts—a Lot

Obvious but important, use the right size pan. Shiny metal ones give you tender, light brown crusts. (With heat-resistant glass pans, just lower the oven temperature 25°.) Non-stick finishes are great, too. Simply do as the manufacturer says.

For layer or loaf cakes (mix or scratch), grease pans generously with shortening—not butter, margarine or oil. Dust with abandon, shaking out the excess flour. Place pans on the middle rack of the oven and don't let them touch—the sides or each other.

ROOT BEER ANGEL CAKE

The Cotton Candy variation is pictured on page 83.

Prepare 1 package of our angel food cake mix as directed on package except—substitute root beer-flavored carbonated beverage for the water. Cool. Pour or spoon small amount of Root Beer Glaze (below) at a time on cake and spread, allowing some to drizzle unevenly down side.

ROOT BEER GLAZE

Melt ⅓ cup butter or margarine in saucepan. Remove from heat. Blend in 2 cups confectioners' sugar and ¼ cup finely crushed root beer-flavored hard candies. Stir in 2 to 4 tablespoons root beer-flavored carbonated beverage, 1 tablespoon at a time, until glaze is of proper consistency.

VARIATION

■ *Cotton Candy Angel Cake:* Substitute strawberry-flavored soda for the root beer-flavored carbonated beverage. In the glaze, omit crushed hard candies and use water or strawberry-flavored soda.

MOCK PISTACHIO CAKE

½ cup diced almonds
4 or 5 drops green food color
1 package of our angel food cake mix
  Glaze (below)

Heat oven to 375°. In plastic bag or tightly covered jar, shake almonds and food color until almonds are evenly colored. Spread in ungreased baking pan. Bake 8 to 10 minutes. Cool.

Prepare cake as directed on package except—fold almonds into batter. Cool.

Pour or spoon small amount of Glaze at a time on top of cake and spread, allowing some to drizzle unevenly down side. (Glaze will set within ½ hour.)

GLAZE

Mix 1½ cups confectioners' sugar and 1 to 2 tablespoons water until smooth.

VARIATION

■ *Chocolate Chip Angel Cake:* Omit almonds and green food color. Fold in ½ cup chocolate shot.

GRAHAM CRACKER TORTE

⅔ cup walnuts
1¼ cups graham cracker crumbs
1 tablespoon plus 1 teaspoon flour
1½ teaspoons baking powder
2 eggs
⅓ cup butter or margarine, softened
⅔ cup sugar
½ cup milk
1 can of our chocolate pudding
  (2 cups)
  Dessert topping or whipped cream
  Chopped crystallized ginger

Heat oven to 350°. Grease and flour layer pan, 9 × 1½ inches. Chop nuts 10 seconds in blender. Mix nuts, crumbs, flour and baking powder in bowl.

In blender, whip eggs, butter and sugar ½ minute while adding milk. Whip 1 minute longer, adding crumb mixture and stopping blender occasionally to scrape sides and guide mixture toward blades.

Pour batter into pan. Bake 40 minutes. Cool 10 minutes in pan; remove and cool. Split to make 2 layers. Fill layers and frost top with pudding. Garnish with dessert topping and ginger. Because of the pudding, refrigerate leftover torte.

8 to 10 servings.

Substitution

For chocolate pudding: 1 can of our vanilla or butterscotch pudding or 2 cups sweetened whipped cream.

Note: To make graham cracker crumbs in blender, use 18 to 20 graham crackers. Break 5 or 6 crackers at a time into blender; grind 10 seconds and empty into measuring cup. Repeat until crumbs measure 1¼ cups.

BLENDER ORANGE-RAISIN CAKE

    1 orange
    1 egg
    ⅓ cup shortening
    ¾ cup milk
    1 teaspoon vanilla
    1¼ cups Gold Medal Flour*
    1 cup sugar
    1½ teaspoons baking powder
    ½ teaspoon salt
    ½ cup walnuts
    ½ cup raisins
      Creamy Orange Frosting (below)

Heat oven to 350°. Grease and flour baking pan, 9×9×2 or 8×8×2 inches. With vegetable parer, remove thin outer layer of peel from orange. (Set orange aside and use for juice in frosting.) Place peel in blender; chop on low speed and set chopped peel aside.

In order listed, measure egg, shortening, milk, vanilla, flour, sugar, baking powder, salt, walnuts and raisins into blender; add 1 tablespoon of the chopped peel (reserve ½ teaspoon chopped peel for frosting). Mix ½ minute on high speed, stopping blender occasionally to scrape sides with rubber spatula. (Batter may be slightly lumpy.)

Pour batter into pan. Bake 9-inch square about 35 minutes, 8-inch square about 40 minutes or until wooden pick inserted in center comes out clean. Cool; frost with Creamy Orange Frosting.

*If using Self-Rising Flour, omit baking powder and salt.

Note: To prepare cake with electric mixer, measure all ingredients except orange and frosting into large mixer bowl, using 1 teaspoon grated orange peel, ½ cup chopped walnuts and ½ cup chopped raisins. Blend ½ minute on low speed, scraping bowl constantly. Beat 3 minutes high speed, scraping bowl occasionally.

CREAMY ORANGE FROSTING

    ⅓ cup butter or margarine, softened
    1½ teaspoons vanilla
    2 tablespoons orange juice
    ½ teaspoon reserved chopped orange peel
    2 cups confectioners' sugar

Mix all ingredients until smooth.

SPICE CAKE

    1¼ cups Gold Medal Flour*
    1 cup sugar
    1½ teaspoons baking powder
    1 teaspoon cinnamon
    ½ teaspoon salt
    ½ teaspoon nutmeg
    ¼ teaspoon cloves
    ¾ cup milk
    ⅓ cup shortening
    1 egg
      Browned Butter Icing (below)

Heat oven to 350°. Grease and flour baking pan, 8×8×2 or 9×9×2 inches. Measure all ingredients except Browned Butter Icing into large mixer bowl. Blend ½ minute on low speed, scraping bowl constantly. Beat 3 minutes high speed, scraping bowl occasionally.

Pour into pan. Bake 35 to 40 minutes or until wooden pick inserted in center comes out clean. Cool; frost with Browned Butter Icing.

*If using Self-Rising Flour, omit baking powder and salt.

BROWNED BUTTER ICING

    3 tablespoons butter or margarine
    1½ cups confectioners' sugar
    1 teaspoon vanilla
      About 1 tablespoon milk

Heat butter in saucepan over medium heat until a delicate brown. Blend in sugar. Stir in vanilla and milk; beat until frosting is smooth and of spreading consistency.

Substitution

    For Gold Medal Flour: 1½ cups Softasilk Cake Flour.

Hideaways for Frosted Cakes

With a creamy-type frosting: Keep under a cake safe or an inverted large bowl. Or cover *loosely* with foil, plastic wrap or waxed paper.

With a fluffy-type frosting: Eat right away! If you must store, or have some left over, use a cake safe. But keep a knife under the edge to let a bit of air in.

With a whipped cream-type frosting: Store in the refrigerator no need to cover. Do the same for any cake with a cream filling or topping.

Starting with a mix...
CHOCOLATE FROSTING VARIATIONS

Prepare 1 package of our chocolate fudge frosting mix as directed on package except—try one of the following variations:

- *Mocha:* Add 1 tablespoon powdered instant coffee.
- *Peppermint:* Sprinkle top of frosted cake with ½ cup crushed peppermint candy.
- *Peppermint Fudge:* Stir in ¼ to ½ teaspoon peppermint extract.
- *Rocky Road:* Stir in ½ cup miniature marshmallows and ½ cup chopped nuts.

Starting with a mix...
CREAMY WHITE FROSTING VARIATIONS

Prepare 1 package of our creamy white frosting mix as directed on package except—try one of the following variations:

- *Browned Butter:* Lightly brown butter over low heat.
- *Chocolate:* Add ½ cup cocoa.
- *Cocoa Mocha:* Substitute strong coffee for the water and add ½ cup cocoa.
- *Lemon, Orange or Lime:* Substitute lemon, orange or lime juice for the water.
- *Peppermint:* Add ½ teaspoon peppermint extract and 3 to 4 drops food color.
- *Raisin-Nut:* Stir in ½ cup cut-up raisins and ½ cup finely chopped nuts.
- *Raspberry or Strawberry:* Substitute crushed fresh or thawed frozen raspberries or strawberries for the water.

Pictured at left:
Chocolate Cake with Chocolate Chip Fluffy White Frosting—a double dose of chocolate.

Starting with a mix...
FLUFFY WHITE FROSTING VARIATIONS

Prepare 1 package of our fluffy white frosting mix as directed on package except—try one of the following variations:

- *Almond:* Fold in ½ teaspoon almond extract.
- *Cherry-Nut:* Fold in ⅓ cup drained chopped maraschino cherries and ½ cup chopped nuts.
- *Chocolate Chip:* Fold in ½ cup semisweet chocolate pieces.
- *Cinnamon:* Add 1 teaspoon cinnamon.
- *Clove:* Add ¼ teaspoon cloves.
- *Lemon:* Fold in ½ teaspoon lemon extract.
- *Maple-Nut:* Fold in ½ teaspoon maple flavoring and ½ cup chopped pecans.
- *Mocha:* Add 2 teaspoons powdered instant coffee.
- *Nutmeg:* Add ½ teaspoon nutmeg.
- *Orange-Coconut:* Fold in 1 tablespoon grated orange peel and ½ cup finely cut-up coconut.
- *Orange-Raisin:* Fold in ½ cup chopped nuts, 1½ cups raisins and 2 tablespoons coarsely grated orange peel.
- *Peppermint:* Fold in ¼ teaspoon peppermint extract. Red or green food color can be added.
- *Spice:* Add ½ teaspoon cinnamon, ¼ teaspoon nutmeg and ¼ teaspoon cloves.

Frosting a Layer Cake?

Is the cake nice and cool? Okay, begin. Lift one layer in your hand. With your free hand, brush the sides and edges gently to remove excess crumbs. Do the same with the other layer.

Place one layer upside down on the cake plate. Use about ½ cup frosting to fill—but don't spread to the edge; leave about ¼ inch free of filling. Then place the second layer right side up on the filling.

Now to the business of frosting. Do the sides first. Start with a thin coat to seal in the crumbs, then once again lavishly. Bring the frosting up high on the side, forming a ridge above the top. Spread the remaining frosting on top, meeting the ridge. It's picture pretty this way—agree?

VANILLA BUTTER FROSTING

⅓ cup soft butter or margarine
3 cups confectioners' sugar
1½ teaspoons vanilla
   About 2 tablespoons milk

Blend butter and sugar. Stir in vanilla and milk; beat until frosting is smooth and of spreading consistency.

Fills and frosts two 8- or 9-inch layers or frosts a 13 × 9-inch cake.

VARIATIONS

■ *Browned Butter Frosting:* Heat butter in saucepan over medium heat until a delicate brown.

■ *Cherry Butter Frosting:* Stir in 2 tablespoons drained chopped maraschino cherries and 2 drops red food color.

■ *Orange Butter Frosting:* Omit vanilla and substitute orange juice for the milk; stir in 2 teaspoons grated orange peel.

■ *Peanut Butter Frosting:* Substitute peanut butter for the butter; increase milk to ¼ to ⅓ cup.

CHOCOLATE BUTTER FROSTING

⅓ cup soft butter or margarine
2 ounces melted unsweetened chocolate
   (cool)
2 cups confectioners' sugar
1½ teaspoons vanilla
   About 2 tablespoons milk

Mix thoroughly butter and cooled chocolate. Blend in sugar. Stir in vanilla and milk; beat until frosting is smooth and of spreading consistency.

Fills and frosts two 8- or 9-inch layers or frosts a 13 × 9-inch cake.

VARIATIONS

■ *Chocolate-Nut Butter Frosting:* Stir in ¼ cup finely chopped nuts.

■ *Cocoa Butter Frosting:* Substitute ⅓ cup cocoa for the chocolate.

■ *Mocha Butter Frosting:* Blend in 1½ teaspoons powdered instant coffee with the sugar.

CHOCOLATE GLAZE

In small bowl, blend ¼ cup of our chocolate ready-to-spread frosting and 2 teaspoons hot water. If necessary, add a few drops of water until of desired consistency.

Glazes an 8- or 9-inch layer cake.

BUTTERSCOTCH BROILED TOPPING

¼ cup soft butter or margarine
⅔ cup brown sugar (packed)
1 cup finely chopped nuts
2 tablespoons milk

Mix thoroughly butter, brown sugar and nuts. Stir in milk. Spread mixture evenly on warm 13 × 9-inch cake.

Set oven control at broil and/or 550°. Place cake 5 inches from heat; broil about 3 minutes or until topping bubbles and browns slightly. (Watch carefully—mixture burns easily.)

Frosts a 13 × 9-inch cake.

VARIATIONS

■ *Coconut Broiled Topping:* Decrease nuts to ½ cup; add 1 cup flaked coconut with the nuts and increase milk to 3 tablespoons.

■ *Crunchy Broiled Topping:* Decrease nuts to ½ cup; add ½ cup Wheaties with the nuts and increase milk to 3 tablespoons.

BROWN SUGAR MERINGUE

2 egg whites (¼ cup)
1 cup brown sugar (packed)
1 tablespoon lemon juice
½ cup finely chopped nuts

Just before cake is removed from oven, beat egg whites until foamy. Gradually beat sugar and lemon juice into egg whites, beating until stiff. Carefully spread on hot 13 × 9-inch cake. Sprinkle with nuts. Bake in 400° oven 8 to 10 minutes or until brown.

Frosts a 13 × 9-inch cake.

Pies

APPLE-CHEESE PIE

Pastry for 9-inch Two-crust Pie (page 110)
1 cup shredded Cheddar cheese (4 ounces)
2 cans (21 ounces each) apple pie filling

Heat oven to 425°. Prepare pastry except—add cheese before mixing. Fill pastry-lined pie pan with apple pie filling.

Cover with top crust which has slits cut in it; seal and flute. Cover edge with 2- to 3-inch strip of aluminum foil to prevent excessive browning; remove foil for the last 15 minutes of baking. Bake 35 to 40 minutes.

Starting with a frozen pie...
APPLE PIE FIX-UPS

Bake 8-inch frozen ready-to-bake apple pie as directed on package except—try one of the following variations:

■ *Cheesey Apple Pie:* Five minutes before end of baking time, spread ½ cup pasteurized process cheese spread on pie.

■ *Raspberry-glazed Apple Pie:* Five minutes before end of baking time, spread 2 tablespoons raspberry jam on pie.

■ *Vanilla Apple Pie:* After baking, pour 2 teaspoons vanilla into slits in crust. Best served warm.

■ *Orange-glazed Apple Pie:* Mix ½ cups confectioners' sugar, 2 teaspoons grated orange peel and 1 tablespoon orange juice. Spoon on warm baked pie; garnish with orange slices.

APPLE PANDOWDY

Pictured on page 81.

Pastry for 8- or 9-inch Two-crust Pie (page 110)
1 can (20 ounces) apple slices, drained
½ cup brown sugar (packed)
3 tablespoons butter or margarine, melted
6 tablespoons maple-flavored syrup

Heat oven to 425°. Prepare pastry. Mix apple slices and brown sugar. Fill pastry-lined pie pan with apple mixture; top with butter and 3 tablespoons of the syrup.

Cover with top crust which has slits cut in it; seal and flute. Bake 15 minutes. Remove from oven; make crisscross cuts about 1 inch apart through top crust and apples. Pour remaining syrup on crust.

Cover edge with 2- to 3-inch strip of aluminum foil to prevent excessive browning. Bake 25 minutes. Serve warm and, if you like, with maple-flavored syrup.

VARIATION

■ *Molasses Pandowdy:* Substitute 3 tablespoons corn syrup for first 3 tablespoons maple-flavored syrup and 3 tablespoons molasses for the second.

RASPBERRY PIE

Pastry for 9-inch Two-crust Pie (page 110)
¼ cup sugar
3 tablespoons flour
3 packages (10 ounces each) frozen raspberries, thawed and drained (reserve ½ cup syrup)
2 tablespoons butter or margarine

Heat oven to 425°. Prepare pastry. Combine sugar and flour; mix with raspberries and reserved syrup. Pour into pastry-lined pie pan; dot with butter.

Cover with top crust which has slits cut in it; seal and flute. Cover edge with 2- to 3-inch strip of aluminum foil to prevent excessive browning; remove foil for the last 15 minutes of baking. Bake 35 to 40 minutes.

BERRY BASKET PIE

9-inch Cookie Pat Crust (page 110)
4 cups fresh strawberries (about 2 pints)
1 envelope (about 2 ounces) dessert topping mix
1 can of our lemon pudding (2 cups)

Bake crust; cool. Reserve about 8 strawberries for garnish. Arrange remaining whole berries in baked crust. Prepare dessert topping as directed on package. Fold topping into pudding; pour on berries in crust. Chill at least 4 hours. Garnish with reserved berries. For easier cutting, let stand at room temperature 10 minutes before serving.

Substitution

For Cookie Pat Crust: Vanilla Wafer Cookie Crumb Crust (page 110).

PERFECT PINEAPPLE PIE

Pastry for 9-inch Two-crust Pie (page 110)
3 eggs
⅓ cup butter or margarine, melted
2 tablespoons lemon juice
½ cup water
1 cup sugar
¼ cup Gold Medal Flour*
¼ teaspoon salt
1 can (20½ ounces) crushed pineapple, drained

Heat oven to 400°. Prepare pastry. In small mixer bowl, beat eggs until blended. Add butter, lemon juice and water; blend on low speed. Add sugar, flour and salt; beat until smooth. Stir in pineapple. Fill pastry-lined pie pan with pineapple mixture.

Cut second half of pastry into ten ½-inch strips. Arrange 5 pastry strips 1 inch apart across filling. Weave first cross-strip through center. Add another cross-strip, first folding back every other strip going the other way. Continue weaving until lattice is complete.

Fold lower crust over ends of pastry strips, building up edge; seal and flute. Cover edge with 2- to 3-inch strip of aluminum foil to prevent excessive browning; remove foil for the last 15 minutes of baking. Bake 35 to 40 minutes.

If using Self-Rising Flour, omit salt.

Starting with a frozen pie...
CHERRY PIE FIX-UPS

Bake 8-inch frozen ready-to-bake cherry pie as directed on package except—try one of the following variations:

■ *Candy-topped Cherry Pie:* Five minutes before end of baking time, sprinkle 1 bar (1⅛ ounces) chocolate toffee candy, chopped, on pie. After baking, pour 1 tablespoon crème de cacao or chocolate syrup into slits in crust.

■ *Lemon-glazed Cherry Pie:* Ten minutes before end of baking time, spread pie with Lemon Glaze: Mix ½ cup confectioners' sugar, 1 teaspoon grated lemon peel and 1 tablespoon lemon juice until smooth. (Be sure to drizzle some of the glaze into slits in crust.)

ORANGE-CHERRY PIE

Pastry for 8-inch Two-crust Pie (page 110)
1 tablespoon finely shredded orange peel
1 can (21 ounces) cherry pie filling
½ cup confectioners' sugar
1 teaspoon shredded orange peel
1 tablespoon orange juice

Heat oven to 425°. Prepare pastry except—add 1 tablespoon orange peel. Mix remaining ingredients. Fill pastry-lined pie pan with cherry mixture.

Cut second half of pastry into eight ½-inch strips. Arrange 4 pastry strips 1 inch apart across filling. Weave first cross-strip, folding back every other strip going the other way. Continue weaving cross-strips in this manner until lattice is complete.

Fold lower crust over ends of pastry strips, building up edge; seal and flute. Cover edge with 2- to 3-inch strip of aluminum foil to prevent excessive browning; remove foil for the last 15 minutes of baking. Bake 35 to 40 minutes.

Pictured at right:
Orange-Cherry Pie

PECAN PIE

3 eggs
⅔ cup sugar
½ teaspoon salt
⅓ cup butter or margarine, melted
1 cup light or dark corn syrup
1 cup pecan halves or broken pieces
9-inch frozen ready-to-bake pie crust shell

Heat oven to 375°. Beat eggs, sugar, salt, butter and syrup with rotary beater. Stir in nuts. Pour into frozen pie crust shell. Bake 40 to 50 minutes or until filling is set.

Substitution

For ready-to-bake pie crust shell: Pastry for 9-inch One-crust Pie (page 110).

Starting with a frozen pie...
PUMPKIN PIE FIX-UPS

Bake 8-inch frozen ready-to-bake pumpkin pie as directed on package. Then try one of the following variations:

■ *Maple Pumpkin Pie:* Cool pie about 30 minutes. Drizzle 2 tablespoons maple-flavored syrup on warm pie; sprinkle with 2 tablespoons chopped pecans. Serve warm.

■ *Pumpkin Pie with Rum Whipped Topping:* Cool pie about 1 hour. Mix ½ carton (8-ounce size) whipped cream cheese, 2 tablespoons confectioners' sugar and 1 tablespoon rum or ½ teaspoon rum flavoring; spread topping on warm pie. Serve immediately.

Starting with a frozen pie...
MINCEMEAT PIE FIX-UPS

Bake 8-inch frozen ready-to-bake mincemeat pie as directed on package. Then try one of the following variations:

■ *Mincemeat Pie with Hard Sauce:* Cool pie about 1 hour. In small mixer bowl, beat ¼ cup soft butter at high speed until very creamy and light in color, about 5 minutes. Gradually beat in ½ cup confectioners' sugar; stir in 1 teaspoon rum or ½ teaspoon rum flavoring. Just before serving, spread on warm pie.

■ *Pudding-topped Mincemeat Pie:* Cool pie about 1 hour. Mix ½ cup of our vanilla pudding and 3 or 4 drops almond extract; just before serving, spread on warm pie.

Pastry a Problem?

It needn't be—if you follow directions carefully and add these tips to your repertoire:

Rolling out: Keep the pastry circle round by pushing in gently around the edge with slightly cupped hands.

Patching up: Moisten the edge or tear; press the pastry patch into place. Who can tell?

Transferring: Fold the pastry round in quarters, then place in the pie pan with the point at center; unfold. It's an easy job this way.

LEMON MERINGUE PIE

8-inch frozen ready-to-bake pie crust shell
1 can of our lemon pudding (2 cups)
⅓ cup water
2 tablespoons cornstarch
Meringue (below)

Bake pie crust shell as directed on package. Stir pudding, water and cornstarch in saucepan. Cook over high heat, stirring constantly, until mixture thickens and boils. Boil and stir 1 minute. Immediately pour into pie shell.

Heap Meringue onto hot pie filling; spread over filling, carefully sealing Meringue to edge of crust to prevent shrinking or weeping. Set oven control at broil and/or 550°. Broil 3 to 5 inches from heat until light brown.

MERINGUE

In small mixer bowl, beat ⅔ cup of our fluffy white frosting mix (dry) and ¼ cup boiling water on highest speed until stiff peaks form, 3 to 5 minutes.

Substitution

For ready-to-bake pie crust shell: 8-inch Baked Pie Shell (page 110).

BANANA CREAM PIE

9-inch Cookie Pat Crust (page 110)
1 banana, sliced
1 cup miniature marshmallows
1 can of our vanilla pudding (2 cups)

Bake crust; cool. Fold banana slices and marshmallows into pudding; pour into baked crust. Chill at least 4 hours. For easier cutting, let stand at room temperature 10 minutes before serving.

Substitution

For Cookie Pat Crust: 9-inch Graham Cracker Crust (page 110).

STRAWBERRY CREAM PIE

9-inch Graham Cracker Crust (page 110)
1 package (10 ounces) frozen strawberries
1 package (3 ounces) strawberry-flavored gelatin
1 pint vanilla ice cream

Bake crust; cool. Heat strawberries to boiling, breaking apart with fork. Stir in gelatin until dissolved. Mix in ice cream until melted. Chill until thickened but not set.

Pour into baked crust. Chill until firm, about 2 hours. If desired, serve with frozen dessert topping (thawed) or sweetened whipped cream.

Substitution

For Graham Cracker Crust: 9-inch purchased graham cracker crust, baked.

RICH CHOCOLATE PIE

9-inch Cookie Pat Crust (page 110)
½ cup dairy sour cream
1 can of our chocolate or chocolate fudge pudding (2 cups)
Sweetened whipped cream
Chocolate curls

Bake crust; cool. Fold sour cream into 1 cup of the pudding; pour into baked crust. Spread remaining pudding on top. Chill at least 8 hours.

Garnish with whipped cream and chocolate curls. For easier cutting, let stand at room temperature 10 minutes before serving.

GRASSHOPPER PIE

Chocolate Wafer Cookie Crumb Crust (page 110)
3 cups miniature marshmallows
½ cup milk
1½ cups chilled whipping cream
¼ cup crème de menthe
3 tablespoons white crème de cacao
Few drops green food color

Bake crust; cool. Melt marshmallows in milk over low heat, stirring constantly. Chill until thickened.

In chilled bowl, beat cream until stiff. Stir marshmallow mixture to blend; stir in liqueurs and fold into cream. Fold in food color. Pour into baked crust. If desired, sprinkle grated semisweet chocolate on top. Chill at least 4 hours.

Substitution

For miniature marshmallows: 32 large marshmallows, cut up.

Getting the Edge on Pastry

You don't have to be a pro to put a fancy fluting on your pie. All you need is a fork, a spoon or your fingers. Here's how:

Fork Edge: Press tines all around edge—press firmly.

Spoon Scallop: Leaving a ½-inch overhang at rim, cut scallops with tip of inverted teaspoon.

Pinch Edge: With one index finger inside upright pastry fold and other index finger and thumb outside, pinch into V-shape.

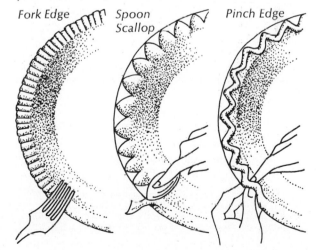

Fork Edge   Spoon Scallop   Pinch Edge

ELECTRIC MIXER PASTRY

8- OR 9-INCH ONE-CRUST PIE
1 cup Gold Medal Flour*
½ teaspoon salt
⅓ cup plus 1 tablespoon shortening
2 to 3 tablespoons cold water

8- OR 9-INCH TWO-CRUST PIE
2 cups Gold Medal Flour*
1 teaspoon salt
⅔ cup plus 2 tablespoons shortening
4 to 5 tablespoons cold water

Measure flour, salt and shortening into large mixer bowl; blend 1 minute on low speed, scraping bowl constantly. Add water; mix until all flour is moistened and dough begins to gather into beaters, about 10 seconds. (If using Wondra Flour, dough will begin to gather into beater in about 1 minute.) Scrape bowl constantly.

Press dough firmly into a ball. Shape into flattened round on lightly floured cloth-covered board. (For Two-crust Pie, divide dough in half and shape into 2 flattened rounds.) With floured stockinet-covered rolling pin, roll dough 2 inches larger than inverted pie pan.

Fold pastry into quarters; unfold and ease into pan.

For One-crust Pie: Trim overhanging edge of pastry 1 inch from rim of pan. Fold and roll pastry under, even with pan; flute. Fill and bake as directed in recipe.

For Baked Pie Shell: Prick bottom and side thoroughly with fork. Bake in 475° oven 8 to 10 minutes.

For Two-crust Pie: Pour desired filling into pastry-lined pie pan. Trim overhanging edge of pastry ½ inch from rim of pan. Roll second round of dough. Fold into quarters; cut slits so steam can escape. Place over filling and unfold. Trim overhanging edge of pastry 1 inch from rim of pan. Fold and roll top edge under lower edge, pressing pastry on rim of pan to seal; flute. Bake as directed in recipe.

If using Self-Rising Flour, omit salt. Pie crusts made with Self-Rising Flour differ in flavor and texture from those made with plain flour.

GRAHAM CRACKER CRUST

1½ cups graham cracker crumbs
   (about 20 crackers)
 3 tablespoons sugar
 ⅓ cup butter or margarine, melted

Heat oven to 350°. Mix crumbs, sugar and butter. (If desired, reserve 2 to 3 tablespoons crumb mixture for a garnish.) Press mixture firmly and evenly against bottom and side of 9-inch pie pan. Bake 10 minutes. Cool.

COOKIE CRUMB CRUST

1½ cups cookie crumbs (vanilla or
   chocolate wafers or gingersnaps)
 2 tablespoons sugar
 ¼ cup butter or margarine, melted

Heat oven to 350°. Mix crumbs, sugar and butter. (If desired, reserve 2 to 3 tablespoons crumb mixture for a garnish.) Press mixture firmly and evenly against bottom and side of 9-inch pie pan. Bake 10 minutes. Cool.

COOKIE PAT CRUST

1 cup Gold Medal Flour*
½ cup butter or margarine, softened
¼ cup finely chopped pecans
¼ cup confectioners' sugar

Heat oven to 400°. With hands, mix all ingredients to form a soft dough. Press firmly and evenly against bottom and side of 9-inch pie pan. (Do not press on rim.) Bake 12 to 15 minutes or until light brown. Cool.

Self-Rising Flour can be used in this recipe. If using Wondra, add 1 tablespoon milk.

Pastry from a Package

Skip the preliminaries. Get right down to the pastry rolling with a never-fail pie crust mix—either our pie crust sticks or our free-flowing mix. And since a mix puts you a jump ahead, think about this: do two shells at one time—one for today's pie and one to freeze, baked or unbaked.

Beverages

DEMITASSE

Prepare coffee, using ¼ cup ground coffee for each ¾ cup water. Serve with a twist of lemon peel. Sugar may be used but cream is usually shunned.

2 servings (about ⅓ cup each).

INSTANT DEMITASSE

Measure ½ cup instant coffee into heatproof container. Stir in 1 quart boiling water. Cover; let stand 5 minutes.

12 servings (about ⅓ cup each).

MOCHA DESSERT COFFEE

For each serving, place 1 to 2 tablespoons of our chocolate ready-to-spread frosting in cup. Fill with hot coffee; stir until blended. If desired, garnish with whipped topping.

RED-HOT CINNAMON COFFEE

For each serving, place 1 tablespoon red cinnamon candies in mug. Fill with hot coffee; stir. Serve with a cinnamon stick.

CAFÉ MEXICAN

⅛ teaspoon cinnamon
⅛ teaspoon nutmeg
1 cup frozen whipped topping (thawed)
2 cups hot strong coffee

Fold spices into whipped topping. Serve coffee in demitasse cups and top with the spiced whipped topping.

6 servings (about ⅓ cup each).

CALIFORNIA COFFEE

For each serving, pour 1 ounce (2 tablespoons) brandy into mug. Fill ⅔ full with hot strong coffee. Top with a small scoop of chocolate ice cream.

IRISH COFFEE

1 cup chilled whipping cream
¼ cup confectioners' sugar
1 teaspoon vanilla
¾ cup ground coffee
3 cups water
4 ounces (½ cup) Irish whiskey or brandy
4 to 8 teaspoons granulated sugar

In chilled bowl, beat cream, confectioners' sugar and vanilla until stiff; refrigerate.

Prepare coffee, using the ¾ cup ground coffee and 3 cups water.

Heat 4 mugs by rinsing with boiling water; drain. Mix 1 ounce (2 tablespoons) whiskey and 1 to 2 teaspoons granulated sugar in each mug; add hot coffee. Top with the whipped cream.

4 servings (¾ cup each).

COFFEE À LA MODE

For each serving, fill mugs about ¾ full with steaming hot strong coffee. Top with a small scoop of vanilla or coffee ice cream. Serve at once.

SPICED TEA

4 cups boiling water
4 teaspoons loose tea
6 whole cloves, broken into pieces
½ teaspoon dried orange peel
⅛ teaspoon cinnamon

Pour boiling water over tea, cloves, orange peel and cinnamon in heatproof container. Cover tightly; let steep 3 to 5 minutes. Stir and strain.

6 servings (⅔ cup each).

ICE-CREAM SODA

For each serving, place 2 to 3 tablespoons any flavor syrup (or ice-cream topping) or ¼ cup crushed fruit with 1 teaspoon sugar in tall glass. Fill ½ full with chilled sparkling water. Top with a scoop of ice cream; stir vigorously. Fill with sparkling water.

FRUIT FIZZ

For each serving, place ¼ cup chilled pineapple juice and 1 scoop vanilla ice cream in tall glass. Fill with chilled sparkling water; stir lightly.

Substitution

For pineapple juice: ¼ cup grape, cherry or raspberry juice or cranberry cocktail.

STRAWBERRY CREAM

For each serving, blend ½ pint vanilla ice cream (1 cup) and ½ cup chilled strawberry soda in blender or with rotary beater.

ORANGE FREEZE

For each serving, place 2 tablespoons frozen orange juice concentrate (thawed) and 1 scoop vanilla ice cream in tall glass. Fill with chilled ginger ale; stir lightly. Serve with a halved orange slice.

ORANGE FROST SODA

Pictured on page 81.

1 quart orange sherbet
2 bottles (14 ounces each)
   carbonated orange beverage, chilled

Place 2 scoops orange sherbet in each of 5 tall glasses. Fill with orange beverage.

5 servings.

CRANBERRY FROST

For each serving, place 1 scoop lime sherbet in tall glass. Fill with chilled cranberry cocktail.

Substitution

For lime sherbet: Lemon or orange sherbet.

CREAMY PEACH CUP

1 package (12 ounces) frozen
   sliced peaches
¼ cup of our canned vanilla pudding
¾ cup milk
¼ teaspoon almond extract

Thaw peaches just until they can be removed from package; cut into chunks. Pour into blender; blend until thoroughly chopped. Add remaining ingredients; mix until smooth. Serve immediately in chilled cups or individual serving dishes.

3 or 4 servings.

Pictured at right:

TOP
   Mulled Apricot Nectar
   Oven French Toast
   Breakfast Bars

CENTER
   Home-style Scrambled Eggs
   Rolled Egg/Canadian-style Bacon/Jam Crumpet
   Marmalade Pinwheels

BOTTOM
   Honey Bee Ambrosia
   Soup 'n Cereal
   Baked Breakfast Burgers

Breakfasts and Brunches

Hot soup for breakfast? A strawberry sundae on your cereal? How about fish sticks on a bun? Why not! There are no hard and fast rules about breakfast—except that you have a nutritious one, every day.

Try Some Surprises

Face it, the merrier the menu, the more likely your family is to sit down and eat it. Milk shakes, for instance, are deliciously nutritious. Likewise peanut butter sandwiches. And if you're a finicky eater, age 4, that's really good news. Bring on Breakfast Burgers (page 122) to snag a reluctant teenager. You speak his language; he gets his morning protein. And if Dad has a passion for apple pie, go ahead—slip him a piece, à la mode, before he gets out the door. Counting calories? Think about open-face grilled cheese sandwiches with a bunch of grapes alongside, or cottage cheese with orange slices.

Or be conventional, almost. Don't just serve a glass of fruit juice—stage it as a breakfast cocktail, on the rocks. Dress up the cereal bowl, too, with fruit or a scoop of ice cream. How about some eggstravaganzas: a fancy Rolled Egg (page 121); or Shirred Eggs (page 119), baked and brought to the table in individual ramekins. When you can spare an extra 15 minutes, add a new twist to your breakfast repertoire with Chicken Livers with Mushrooms (page 122) or Jam Grill (page 125). Above all, don't be a slave to custom. You have nothing to lose but breakfast boredom.

Make It a Big Deal Meal

Nutritionally speaking, breakfast should provide $1/4$ to $1/3$ of your daily food requirements. So, no matter what you decide to serve your family, make sure it's something wholesome and nutritious. And be careful not to confuse eating lots with eating well. (To brush up on nutritional needs, see page 152.)

Plan ahead. Each member of your family deserves a well-balanced meal to start off his day. After all, what with late nights at the office and those can't-be-missed football practices, chances are that breakfast is one of the few meals that a family's sure to eat at home. And it's one of the easiest for you to prepare. So go ahead—seize the opportunity to wake up those sleepy morning appetites. How you do it and the foods you choose are up to you and the willingness of your family to try something new.

Buy Extra Time in the A.M.

It happens in the most organized household— you grab a few extra winks and the breakfast scene falls apart at the seams. So stay a jump ahead. Set the table the night before; have cereals out, fruits chilled. Rely on convenience foods. Think about pre-preparation: mix up the batter for Potato Pancakes (page 128) or put together a Dried Fruit Compote (page 116) or bake muffins on the weekend, tuck them in the freezer and reheat them during the week. And if the family simply must eat on the run, plan ahead for Breakfast Bars (page 117). Or, at that eat-and-run moment, pour out a breakfast in a glass. You'll find a different one for every day of the week on page 131.

Morning Time...Party Time?

Turn a late-morning breakfast into two meals in one—otherwise known as brunch. Stick strictly to traditional breakfast menus, ending with coffee cake or doughnuts for dessert; or try something continental like Quiche Lorraine (page 121). It's elegant, but simple to do. Serve with a salad; finish with fruit. Think about it. It's one of the easiest ways to entertain.

Now who says breakfast is a bore? Not you. You believe in giving that early-morning meal lots of encouragement. And it shows on those happy faces going out your door.

Breakfast Fruits

HONEY BEE AMBROSIA

Pictured on page 113.

4 medium oranges, chilled
1 medium banana
½ cup orange juice
¼ cup honey
2 tablespoons lemon juice
¼ cup flaked coconut

Pare oranges and cut into thin slices. Peel banana and cut into slices. Mix fruits carefully. Blend orange juice, honey and lemon juice; pour on fruit. Sprinkle with coconut.

4 to 6 servings.

FRUIT WITH YOGURT

1 can (30 ounces) fruit cocktail, drained
½ cup unflavored yogurt
2 tablespoons honey
2 teaspoons lemon juice
 Dash aromatic bitters, if desired

Spoon fruit into individual serving dishes. Blend yogurt, honey, lemon juice and bitters; pour over fruit. Nice served with Almond Flatbread (page 78).

4 or 5 servings.

Substitutions

For fruit cocktail: 1 can (30 ounces) apricot halves or peach halves or about 4 cups cut-up fresh fruit.
For yogurt: ½ cup dairy sour cream.

PAPAYA

Cut 2 large ripe papayas in half lengthwise; remove seeds. Pare and cut into slices. Serve with lime wedges.

4 servings.

FROZEN FRUIT SLICES

Remove wrapping from 1 package (16 ounces) frozen melon balls. Cut frozen fruit into ⅜- to ½-inch slices with serrated knife. Place slices on salad plates with curly endive or sprigs of water cress or parsley.

4 or 5 servings.

Substitution

For melon balls: 1 package (10 ounces) frozen peach slices, 1 package (10 ounces) frozen strawberry halves or 1 can (13½ ounces) frozen pineapple chunks.

STRAWBERRY-RHUBARB COMPOTE

½ cup water
1 package (16 ounces) frozen rhubarb
2 tablespoons sugar
2 cups fresh strawberries
⅛ teaspoon ginger

Heat water to boiling; stir in rhubarb and sugar. Reduce heat; simmer 5 minutes, breaking fruit apart with fork. Remove from heat; stir in strawberries and ginger. Serve warm or cold.

Remember this fruit refresher as a first course for dinner, too.

6 servings.

MELON AND PROSCIUTTO

Cut a ripe cantaloupe, casaba, honeydew or Spanish melon (about 3 pounds) in half; scoop out seeds and fibers. Cut each half into 6 lengthwise wedges. Remove rind. Cut crosswise slits 1½ inches apart in each melon wedge.

Cut ¼ pound sliced prosciutto (Italian ham) into 1-inch strips. Place several strips of ham on each wedge; push ham into slits.

12 servings.

VARIATION

■ *Bite-size Melon and Prosciutto:* Cut pared melon into bite-size pieces. Wrap each piece in strips of prosciutto; secure with picks.

DRIED FRUIT COMPOTE

1 package (10 ounces) mixed dried fruit
    One 3-inch stick cinnamon
¼ cup brown sugar (packed)
3 slices lemon
2 cups water
1 can (21 ounces) cherry pie filling

Mix dried fruit, cinnamon stick, sugar, lemon slices and water in saucepan. Heat to boiling, stirring occasionally. Reduce heat; simmer uncovered 30 minutes. Stir in cherry pie filling. Serve warm or cold. This fruit combo also makes a particularly nice accompaniment for ham or roast beef.

4 to 6 servings.

VARIATION

■ *Currant-Raspberry Compote:* Omit cherry pie filling. Drain cooked fruit, reserving liquid. Measure reserved liquid and, if necessary, add enough water to measure 2½ cups. Prepare 1 package (4¾ ounces) currant-raspberry-flavored dessert mix as directed on package for fruit sauce except—substitute the reserved 2½ cups liquid for the water.

CINNAMON FRUITS

Drain 1 can (16 ounces) peaches or pears, reserving ½ cup syrup. In small saucepan, heat reserved syrup and ¼ cup red cinnamon candies to boiling; boil 1 minute. Remove from heat. Cover tightly; let stand 10 minutes or until candies are dissolved. Stir in fruit. Serve warm or chilled.

4 servings.

HOT BREAKFAST FRUITS

¼ cup butter or margarine
¼ cup brown sugar (packed)
1 tablespoon lemon juice
1 can (30 ounces) fruits for salad, drained

Melt butter in medium skillet over low heat; blend in sugar and lemon juice. Cook until smooth and bubbly. Stir in fruit; heat through.

Nice to serve on oatmeal or farina. Good for dessert, too—on rice pudding, custard or ice cream.

4 or 5 servings.

CRUNCHY BROILED GRAPEFRUIT

2 grapefruit, halved
1 cup Wheaties, crushed
⅓ cup brown sugar (packed)
¼ cup butter or margarine, melted

Remove seeds from grapefruit halves. Cut around edges and sections to loosen; remove centers. Mix Wheaties, sugar and butter; spread on grapefruit.

Set oven control at broil and/or 550°. Broil grapefruit 5 inches from heat 3 to 4 minutes or until golden brown.

4 servings.

BROILED HONEY GRAPEFRUIT

2 grapefruit, halved
¼ cup honey
10 drops aromatic bitters

Remove seeds from grapefruit halves. Cut around edges and sections to loosen; remove centers. Mix honey and bitters; spoon about 1 tablespoon honey mixture on each grapefruit half.

Set oven control at broil and/or 550°. Broil grapefruit 5 inches from heat about 5 minutes.

4 servings.

MARSHMALLOW APRICOTS

Heat oven to 400°. Divide 1 can (17 ounces) apricot halves among 4 or 5 individual ovenproof dishes (about 3 apricot halves and 1 tablespoon syrup per dish). Top each with 6 to 8 miniature marshmallows. Bake 5 minutes or until puffed.

4 or 5 servings.

BAKED BANANAS

Heat oven to 375°. For each serving, peel a large firm banana and cut lengthwise in half. Place halves cut side down in buttered baking dish. Brush with lemon juice. Sprinkle each half with ½ teaspoon grated lemon peel and ½ tablespoon brown sugar. Drizzle each banana with ½ tablespoon butter, melted. Bake 20 minutes. Serve warm. Top with ice cream, for dessert or breakfast.

Cereals

MOCK APPLE DUMPLINGS

2 cups Wheaties, crushed
2 tablespoons sugar
⅛ teaspoon salt
⅛ teaspoon nutmeg
⅛ teaspoon cinnamon
3 cups applesauce
  Milk

Mix Wheaties, sugar, salt, nutmeg and cinnamon. Spoon applesauce into individual serving dishes. Sprinkle Wheaties mixture on applesauce. Serve with milk.

4 servings.

SOUP 'N CEREAL

Pictured on page 113.

½ soup can milk
½ soup can water
1 can (10¾ ounces) condensed tomato soup
¼ teaspoon salt
  Favorite unsweetened dry cereal

In saucepan, gradually stir milk and water into soup and salt. Heat through over low heat, stirring frequently. Serve on cereal immediately.

3 servings.

FRUITED HOT CEREAL

Prepare cereal as directed on package except—when heating water to boiling, add one of the following for each serving:

  2 tablespoons raisins

  4 to 5 dried apricot halves, cut up

  4 to 5 prunes, cut up

  3 to 4 dates, cut up

PEANUT MALLOW CHEWS

⅓ cup butter or margarine
3 cups miniature marshmallows
½ cup peanut butter
5 cups Trix

In large saucepan, melt butter and marshmallows over low heat, stirring constantly. Stir in peanut butter until melted. Remove from heat; fold in cereal, stirring until evenly coated.

With buttered hands, pat evenly into buttered baking pan, 9×9×2 inches. Cool; cut into bars, about 3×2 inches.

12 bars.

Substitutions

  For miniature marshmallows: 32 large marshmallows, cut up.
  For Trix: 5 cups Cheerios, Kix or Sugar Jets.

BREAKFAST BARS

Pictured on page 113.

½ cup butter or margarine
3 cups miniature marshmallows
½ cup peanut butter
½ cup nonfat dry milk
¼ cup orange-flavored instant
  breakfast drink
1 cup raisins
4 cups Cheerios

In large saucepan, melt butter and marshmallows over low heat, stirring constantly. Stir in peanut butter until melted. Mix in milk and breakfast drink.

Remove from heat; fold in raisins and Cheerios, stirring until evenly coated. With buttered hands, pat evenly into buttered baking pan, 9×9×2 inches. Cool; cut into bars, about 3×1 inch.

Two bars and a glass of skimmed milk make a nutritious breakfast-on-the-run, furnishing ¼ of the Minimum Daily Requirements.

24 bars (12 servings).

Substitution

  For miniature marshmallows: 32 large marshmallows, cut up.

Hot Cereal Stir-ins

Cereal Sweeteners

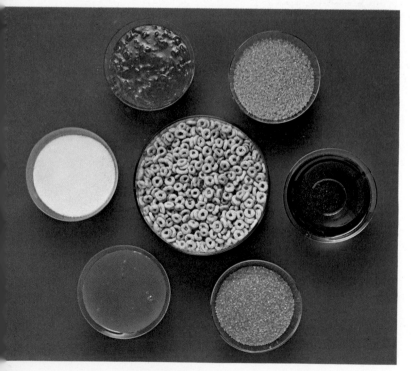

HOT CEREAL STIR-INS

Prepare your favorite hot cereal as directed on package except—for each serving, stir in one of the following:

> 1 teaspoon fruit-flavored gelatin (swirled in)
>
> ¼ cup miniature marshmallows
>
> 1 to 2 tablespoons maple syrup, light molasses or honey
>
> 1 tablespoon instant cocoa mix
>
> 1 to 2 tablespoons jam, jelly or marmalade
>
> 2 tablespoons brown sugar
>
> 2 tablespoons applesauce and 1 tablespoon brown sugar
>
> 2 tablespoons mandarin orange segments and 1 tablespoon brown sugar

CEREAL TOPPINGS

Try one of these flavored milks on your favorite unsweetened cereal. To ¾ cup milk in blender, add one of the following:

> ½ banana, cut up
>
> 2 teaspoons sugar and 1 teaspoon powdered instant coffee
>
> ½ teaspoon sugar-sweetened soft drink mix
>
> 1 or 2 canned peach halves
>
> 1 tablespoon peanut butter and 1 teaspoon sugar

CEREAL SWEETENERS

Substitute one of the following for sugar on your favorite unsweetened cereal:

> Mixture of 2 teaspoons sugar and 1 teaspoon cinnamon
>
> Brown sugar
>
> Maple syrup
>
> Ice-cream sundae topping
>
> Instant cocoa mix
>
> Fruit-flavored gelatin
>
> Jam or jelly
>
> Colored sugars

Eggs

SOFT-COOKED EGGS

Place eggs in saucepan; add enough cold water to come at least 1 inch above eggs. Heat rapidly to boiling. Remove from heat. Cover tightly; let stand 1 to 3 minutes, depending on desired doneness.

Immediately cool eggs in cold water several seconds to prevent further cooking. Cut eggs in half; scoop from shell.

HARD-COOKED EGGS

Place eggs in saucepan; add enough cold water to come at least 1 inch above eggs. Heat rapidly to boiling. Remove from heat. Cover tightly; let stand 25 minutes.

Immediately cool eggs in cold water to prevent further cooking. Tap egg to crackle shell. Roll between hands to loosen shell, then peel. Hold egg under running cold water to help ease off shell.

FRIED EGGS

In heavy skillet, heat butter or bacon fat (⅛ inch deep) until just hot enough to sizzle a drop of water. Break each egg into a measuring cup or saucer; carefully slip eggs one at a time into skillet. Immediately reduce heat to low.

Cook slowly, spooning butter on eggs until whites are set and a film forms over yolks (sunny-side up). Or when whites are set, turn eggs over gently and cook until desired doneness.

VARIATION

■ *Poached-fried Eggs:* Heat just enough butter or bacon fat to grease skillet. Cook eggs over low heat until edges turn white. Add ½ teaspoon water for 1 egg, decreasing the proportion slightly for each additional egg. Cover tightly.

POACHED EGGS

In saucepan or skillet, heat water, bouillon or milk (1½ to 2 inches) to boiling; reduce to simmer. Break each egg into a measuring cup or saucer; carefully slip eggs one at a time into water. (Eggs shouldn't touch each other while cooking.)

Cook 3 to 5 minutes or until desired doneness. Lift eggs from water with slotted spatula. Season with salt and pepper.

Note: To poach eggs in an egg poacher, pour water into poacher to just below bottom of egg cups; heat water to boiling. Butter metal egg cups; break eggs into cups. Set egg cups in frame over boiling water. Cover tightly; steam 3 to 5 minutes or until desired doneness.

BAKED (SHIRRED) EGGS

Heat oven to 325°. For each serving, break an egg carefully into buttered 5- or 6-ounce baking dish. Season with salt and pepper. If desired, top each egg with 1 tablespoon milk or light cream, dot with soft butter or sprinkle with 1 tablespoon shredded Cheddar cheese.

Bake eggs uncovered 15 to 18 minutes, depending on desired doneness and depth of baking dish. Whites should be set, but yolks soft. Serve in baking dish.

EGGS ON CORNED BEEF HASH

1 can (15 ounces) corned beef hash
6 eggs
  Salt and pepper
⅓ cup shredded Cheddar cheese

Heat oven to 350°. In each of six 5- or 6-ounce baking dishes, press about ¼ cup hash against bottom and side. Break an egg on hash in each dish. Season with salt and pepper. Sprinkle each with about 1 tablespoon cheese. Bake uncovered 20 to 25 minutes, depending on desired doneness.

6 servings.

GOLDEN EGGS ON TOAST

1 can of our cheese sauce (1 cup)
½ cup milk
6 hard-cooked eggs, sliced
6 slices toast
⅓ cup Bac*Os chips

Heat cheese sauce and milk, stirring occasionally. Gently stir in egg slices; heat through. Spoon on toast; sprinkle with Bac°Os chips. For extra color and flavor, garnish with snipped chives.

4 to 6 servings.

SCRAMBLED EGGS

For each serving, break 2 eggs into bowl; add 2 tablespoons milk or cream, ¼ teaspoon salt and dash pepper. Mix with fork, stirring thoroughly for a uniform color, or mixing just slightly if streaks of white and yellow are preferred.

Heat ½ tablespoon butter or margarine in skillet over medium heat until just hot enough to sizzle a drop of water. Pour egg mixture into skillet.

As mixture begins to set at bottom and side, gently lift cooked portions with spatula so that thin, uncooked portion can flow to bottom. Avoid constant stirring. Cook until eggs are thickened throughout but still moist, about 3 to 5 minutes.

VARIATIONS

■ *Creamy Scrambled Eggs:* Cook egg mixture in top of double boiler over simmering, not boiling, water. Stir occasionally until thick and creamy.

■ *Flavored Scrambled Eggs:* For each serving, stir one of the following into egg mixture in bowl:

   2 tablespoons shredded Cheddar,
   Monterey (Jack) or Swiss cheese

   2 tablespoons chopped mushrooms

   2 tablespoons snipped chives

   2 tablespoons snipped parsley

   2 tablespoons crisply fried and
   crumbled bacon*

   2 tablespoons finely shredded dried beef*

   2 tablespoons chopped cooked ham*

°*Omit salt in egg mixture.*

POTATO SCRAMBLE

6 slices bacon, diced
2 cups diced cooked potatoes
1 medium onion, diced
1 teaspoon salt
¼ teaspoon pepper
4 eggs, beaten

Fry bacon until crisp; drain off all but 3 tablespoons fat. Cook and stir potatoes, onion, salt and pepper in fat until light brown. Pour eggs into skillet. Cook uncovered until eggs are thickened.

4 servings.

Substitution

For cooked potatoes: 1 package (9 ounces) frozen French fried potatoes, diced.

HOME-STYLE SCRAMBLED EGGS

Pictured on page 113.

4 eggs
1 tablespoon instant minced onion
¾ teaspoon salt
3 tablespoons water
¼ cup butter or margarine
1 cup diced tomatoes
1 cup diced cooked potatoes
1 cup diced zucchini

Beat eggs, onion, salt and water. Melt butter in large skillet over medium heat; cook and stir vegetables in butter 2 minutes. Pour on egg mixture.

As mixture begins to set at bottom and side, gently lift cooked portions with spatula so that thin, uncooked portion can flow to bottom. Avoid constant stirring. Cook until eggs are thickened throughout but still moist, 3 to 5 minutes.

3 servings.

Substitutions

For instant onion: 3 tablespoons minced onion.
For zucchini: ½ cup chopped green pepper.

VARIATION

■ *Eggs Mexicali:* Decrease salt to ½ teaspoon. Omit instant onion and vegetables; stir ⅔ cup crushed corn chips into butter. Serve with hot green chili relish.

ROLLED EGG

Pictured on page 113.

For each Rolled Egg, beat 1 egg and ⅛ teaspoon salt until foamy. Melt 2 teaspoons butter, margarine or bacon fat in hot 10-inch skillet; rotate pan to coat bottom with butter.

Pour egg into skillet; slowly rotate pan to spread mixture into thin circle. Cook over medium heat about 2 minutes. Loosen edge; roll up, using small spatula and fork.

When preparing more than one, keep Rolled Eggs warm on ungreased baking sheet in 275° oven. Nice served with our cheese or mushroom sauce.

VARIATION

■ *Cheese Egg Roll:* Before rolling circle, sprinkle with 1 tablespoon Parmesan cheese.

QUICHE LORRAINE

12 slices bacon (about ½ pound),
   crisply fried and crumbled
 1 cup shredded natural Swiss cheese
   (4 ounces)
⅓ cup minced onion
   9-inch frozen ready-to-bake pie crust shell
 4 eggs
 2 cups whipping cream or light cream (20%)
¾ teaspoon salt
¼ teaspoon sugar
⅛ teaspoon cayenne red pepper

Heat oven to 425°. Sprinkle bacon, cheese and onion in frozen pie crust shell. Beat eggs slightly; beat in remaining ingredients. Pour cream mixture into pie shell. Bake 15 minutes.

Reduce oven temperature to 300° and bake 30 minutes longer or until knife inserted 1 inch from edge comes out clean. Let stand 10 minutes before cutting. Serve in wedges.

6 main-dish servings (8 appetizer servings).

Substitution

For ready-to-bake pie crust shell: Pastry for 9-inch One-crust Pie (page 110).

HAM AND CHEESE OVEN OMELET

8 eggs
1 cup milk
½ teaspoon seasoned salt
1 package (3 ounces) thin-sliced ham
1 cup shredded Cheddar cheese (4 ounces)
1 tablespoon instant minced onion

Heat oven to 325°. Beat eggs, milk and seasoned salt. Tear ham in small pieces into egg mixture. Stir in cheese and onion.

Pour into greased baking dish, 11½ × 7½ × 1½ or 8 × 8 × 2 inches. Bake uncovered 40 to 45 minutes or until omelet is set and top is golden brown.

4 to 6 servings.

Note: Remember this for a late-evening supper. Prepare mixture ahead of time and refrigerate until needed.

Substitutions

For ham: 1 package (3 ounces) thin-sliced corned beef or dried beef.

For Cheddar cheese: 1 cup shredded mozzarella, Swiss or other cheese.

For instant onion: 3 tablespoon minced onion.

PUFFY CHEESE BAKE

 4 slices bread, buttered
 2 eggs
 1 cup light cream (20%)
 2 tablespoons butter or margarine, melted
 ½ teaspoon salt
 ½ teaspoon dry mustard
 ¼ teaspoon paprika
   Dash cayenne red pepper
1½ cups shredded process
   American cheese (6 ounces)

Heat oven to 350°. Butter baking dish, 8 × 8 × 2 inches. Cut each slice of bread diagonally into 4 triangles. Line bottom and sides of baking dish with bread triangles. (For a crown effect, place 8 triangles upright against sides of dish. Arrange remaining triangles on bottom of dish.)

Beat eggs slightly; add remaining ingredients and mix well. Pour mixture into baking dish. Bake uncovered 30 to 40 minutes.

4 servings.

Breakfast Meats

FINNAN HADDIE

1 package (16 ounces) frozen finnan
  haddie, thawed
¼ cup butter or margarine

Cut fish into serving pieces. Melt butter in skillet. Add fish; reduce heat. Cover tightly; simmer 30 minutes or until fish flakes easily with a fork. To serve, spoon butter over fish.

Traditionally served on buttered toast—but why not try an English muffin and cinnamon apple rings.

4 servings.

Substitution

For finnan haddie: 1 package (16 ounces) frozen wall-eye pike, Northern pike or pollack. Rinse under cold water to remove wrapping. Let fish stand 5 minutes, then saw into serving pieces. Brush with 2 tablespoons liquid smoke; add to butter in skillet. Cover tightly; simmer 30 minutes.

MEAT 'N POTATO ROLL-UPS

  Potato Buds (enough for 4 servings)
 1 tablespoon finely chopped green pepper
¼ teaspoon instant chopped onion
½ teaspoon prepared mustard
 8 slices large bologna

Heat oven to 350°. Prepare Potato Buds as directed on package. Stir in green pepper, onion and mustard.

Place about ¼ cup potato mixture on each bologna slice; roll up and secure with wooden pick. Place on ungreased baking sheet. Bake 10 to 15 minutes or until heated through.

An unusual lunch, brunch or hearty breakfast served with Frozen Fruit Slices (page 115).

4 servings.

CHICKEN LIVERS WITH MUSHROOMS

¼ cup butter or margarine
½ pound chicken livers, halved
¼ pound fresh mushrooms, sliced
¼ teaspoon salt
2 teaspoons Worcestershire sauce

Melt butter in large skillet; brown livers. Push livers to one side. Add mushrooms; cook and stir until mushrooms are light brown. Mix livers and mushrooms.

Sprinkle with salt and Worcestershire sauce. Reduce heat. Cover tightly; simmer 5 minutes or until liver is done.

Serve with an omelet or scrambled eggs for a special brunch.

2 or 3 servings.

Substitution

For fresh mushrooms: 1 can (4 ounces) mushroom stems and pieces, drained.

BREAKFAST BURGERS

The baked variation is pictured on page 113.

1 pound ground beef
¼ cup applesauce
1 teaspoon salt
1 teaspoon Worcestershire sauce
½ teaspoon allspice

Mix all ingredients. Shape mixture by tablespoonfuls into 2-inch patties. Cook in skillet over medium-high heat, about 2 to 3 minutes on each side.

6 to 8 servings.

VARIATION

■ *Baked Breakfast Burgers:* Shape mixture into 5 patties, about 3 inches in diameter and ½ inch thick. Bake in 350° oven 20 minutes. Serve on a bun or toasted French bread.

Pictured at right:
Chicken Livers with Mushrooms

FISH STICK BREAKFAST

1 package (16 ounces) frozen fish sticks
1 can (8½ ounces) sliced pineapple, drained
2 tablespoons cranberry-orange relish
4 English muffins, split and toasted

Arrange fish sticks and pineapple slices on lightly buttered baking sheet. Fill each pineapple slice with a rounded teaspoonful of cranberry-orange relish.

Set oven control at broil and/or 550°. Broil fish sticks and pineapple slices 5 inches from heat about 5 minutes or until fish sticks are golden. Serve with English muffins. And don't forget to serve this treat for lunch or dinner sometime.

4 servings.

BACON

To Panfry: Place bacon slices in cold skillet. Cook over low heat 8 to 10 minutes, turning to brown evenly.

To Bake: Place separated slices of bacon on rack in broiler pan. Bake in 400° oven 10 minutes or until brown. Do not turn.

To Broil: Place separated slices of bacon on rack in broiler pan. Set oven control at broil and/or 550°. Broil bacon 3 inches from heat until brown, about 2 minutes. Turn slices; broil 1 minute longer.

CANADIAN-STYLE BACON

To Panfry: Place ⅛-inch slices of Canadian-style bacon in cold skillet. Cook over low heat 8 to 10 minutes, turning to brown evenly.

To Bake: If necessary, remove casing from 2-pound piece of Canadian-style bacon. Place bacon fat side up on rack in open shallow baking pan. Insert meat thermometer so tip is in center of bacon. Bake uncovered in 325° oven 1 to 1¼ hours or until thermometer registers 160°.

To Broil: Place ¼-inch slices Canadian-style bacon on rack in broiler pan. Set oven control at broil and/or 550°. Broil bacon 2 to 3 inches from heat until brown, about 3 minutes. Turn slices; broil 3 minutes longer.

SAUSAGE (Uncooked Smoked or Fresh)

To Panfry: Place sausage links or patties in cold skillet. Add 2 to 4 tablespoons water. Cover tightly; cook slowly 5 to 8 minutes, depending on size or thickness of sausages. Uncover; cook until well done, turning to brown evenly.

To Bake: Arrange sausages in single layer in un-ungreased shallow baking pan. Bake uncovered in 400° oven 20 to 30 minutes or until well done, turning sausages to brown evenly. Drain off fat as it accumulates.

YORKSHIRE SAUSAGE

1 cup Gold Medal Flour*
½ teaspoon salt
1 cup milk
2 eggs
1 package (10 ounces) brown and serve smoked sausages (10)

Heat oven to 425°. Butter baking pan, 9×9×2 inches. Mix flour, salt, milk and eggs with rotary beater just until smooth. (Do not overbeat.) Pour into pan. .

Arrange sausages on batter. Bake 25 minutes or until puffed and brown. Delicious with warm applesauce. For a complete breakfast add a glass of orange juice and a glass of milk.

4 or 5 servings.

*Do not use Self-Rising Flour in this recipe.

Substitution

For salt: ½ teaspoon favorite seasoned salt.

Merry Up the Menu—Maybe Then They'll Eat

Soup for breakfast? Why not! It's filling...and fast. Try any of the soups on page 134, or even those in our lunch chapter. And how about breakfast sandwiches? Plain old peanut butter goes over big with You Know Who, and Breakfast Burgers (page 122) are sure to draw the teenagers to the scene. And Denvers (page 140). They ought to give you a full table. Another day, surprise them with Baked Meatballs (page 16) or Oven-fried Fillets (page 47). Morning monotony? Not for your family!

Breakfast Breads

FLAVORED OVEN TOAST

Heat oven to 400°. Cut unsliced loaf of bread into desired number of 1-inch slices. Spread both sides of slices with butter. Arrange on ungreased baking sheet. Bake 10 to 12 minutes or until golden brown. Sprinkle with one of the following:

Chocolate-flavored malted milk (dry)

Instant cocoa

Orange-flavored instant breakfast drink (dry)

Fruit-flavored gelatin

Substitution

For 1-inch slices bread: Commercially sliced bread; bake 3 or 4 minutes, then turn and bake 4 or 5 minutes or until golden brown.

BREAKFAST HOT SWEETS

Heat oven to 400°. Cut unsliced nut bread into desired number of ½-inch slices. Spread with soft butter or margarine. Arrange buttered side up on ungreased baking sheet. Bake 6 to 8 minutes or until light brown.

JAM CRUMPETS

Pictured on page 113 with the Rolled Egg.

6 English muffins, split
¼ cup soft butter or margarine
¼ cup jam or preserves
¼ cup brown sugar (packed)
¼ cup flaked coconut or sliced almonds

Heat oven to 450°. Spread cut surface of each muffin half with 1 teaspoon each butter and jam. Sprinkle with brown sugar and coconut. Bake on ungreased baking sheet 5 minutes or until bubbly and brown.

12 crumpets.

JAM GRILL

For each serving, spread 1 slice bread with 2 tablespoons strawberry or raspberry jam; top with second slice bread. Spread outside of sandwich with about 1 tablespoon soft butter or margarine. Cook on both sides in skillet or on grill. Sprinkle with confectioners' sugar.

PEANUTTY POP-UPS

Heat oven to 350°. For each serving, spread peanut butter on flat side of your favorite toaster pop-up; top with second pop-up, flat side down. Arrange on ungreased baking sheet. Bake about 10 minutes or until heated through.

Note: Remember pop-ups for a quick dessert, too. Toast in oven. Top each with ice cream and ice-cream topping.

VARIATION

■ *Cheese Pop-ups:* Substitute pasteurized process cheese spread for the peanut butter.

MARMALADE PINWHEELS

Pictured on page 113.

2 cups Bisquick
½ cup cold water
½ cup orange marmalade
1 tablespoon butter or margarine, melted
1 tablespoon sugar

Heat oven to 425°. Grease 9-inch pie pan or 10 medium muffin cups. Stir Bisquick and water with fork until a soft dough forms. Gently smooth dough into a ball on floured cloth-covered board. Knead 5 times. Roll dough into rectangle, 12×9 inches. Spread with marmalade; roll up, beginning at wide side. Pinch edge of dough into roll to seal well.

Cut roll into 10 slices. Place cut side up with sides touching in pan. Brush with butter; sprinkle with sugar. Bake about 15 minutes or until golden brown.

10 pinwheels.

CARROT-ORANGE MUFFINS

1 package of our orange muffin mix
1 cup shredded carrot
½ cup raisins
¼ teaspoon cinnamon
¼ teaspoon nutmeg
¼ teaspoon allspice

Prepare muffin mix as directed on package except —stir in carrot, raisins and spices. Bake about 20 minutes.

About 15 muffins.

STREUSEL COFFEE CAKE

Heat oven to 400°. Grease baking pan, 9×9×2 inches. Prepare any flavor of our muffin mixes except corn as directed on package. Spread in pan. Sprinkle with Streusel Topping (below). Bake 20 to 25 minutes or until wooden pick inserted in center comes out clean. Serve warm.

9 servings.

STREUSEL TOPPING

Mix ½ cup brown sugar (packed), ⅓ cup Gold Medal Flour, ¼ cup firm butter and ½ teaspoon cinnamon until crumbly.

PEANUT BUTTER AND JELLY COFFEE CAKE

2 cups Bisquick
2 tablespoons sugar
¼ cup creamy peanut butter
⅔ cup milk
1 egg
½ cup favorite jam or jelly

Heat oven to 400°. Grease layer pan, 9×1½ inches. Mix Bisquick and sugar; cut in peanut butter. Mix in milk and egg; beat vigorously ½ minute.

Spread in pan; spread with jam. Bake 20 to 25 minutes or until light brown.

9 servings.

Substitution

For jam or jelly: ½ cup orange marmalade.

ORANGE ROLLS

1 loaf (1 pound) frozen bread dough
  Salad oil
3 tablespoons soft butter or margarine
1 tablespoon grated orange peel
2 tablespoons orange juice
1½ cups confectioners' sugar

Brush frozen loaf with oil. Place on lightly greased baking sheet; cover and thaw up to 12 hours in refrigerator or about 3 hours at room temperature.

Beat butter, orange peel, juice and confectioners' sugar until creamy and smooth. On lightly floured board, roll dough into rectangle, 15×8 inches. Spread with half the orange mixture; roll up, beginning at wide side. Pinch edge of dough into roll to seal well. Stretch to make even.

Cut roll into 15 slices. Place slightly apart in greased baking pan, 13×9×2 inches, or in greased muffin cups. Let rise until double, about 1 hour.

Heat oven to 350°. Bake 35 to 40 minutes or until golden brown. While warm, remove from pan and frost with remaining orange filling.

15 rolls.

VARIATIONS

■ *Caramel Rolls:* Before rolling dough, melt ¼ cup butter or margarine; stir in ½ cup brown sugar (packed), 2 tablespoons corn syrup and ½ cup pecan halves and spread over bottom of baking pan. Omit orange peel, juice and confectioners' sugar. Spread rectangle with 3 tablespoons butter; sprinkle with mixture of ¼ cup granulated sugar and 2 teaspoons cinnamon. After baking, immediately turn pan upside down on large tray. Let pan remain on a minute so caramel drizzles over rolls.

■ *Cinnamon Rolls:* Omit orange peel, orange juice and confectioners' sugar. Spread rectangle with 3 tablespoons butter and sprinkle with mixture of ¼ cup sugar, 2 teaspoons cinnamon and ½ cup chopped nuts. While rolls are warm, frost with mixture of 1½ cups confectioners' sugar and 1 tablespoon milk.

ORANGE PECAN BREAD

Heat oven to 350°. Grease and flour 2 loaf pans, 9×5×3 inches. Prepare 1 package of our orange cake mix as directed on package except—use 2 tablespoons less water and add ½ cup chopped pecans. Pour into pans. Bake 35 to 40 minutes or until wooden pick inserted in center comes out clean. Cool thoroughly before slicing. Nice served with hard sauce.

BLUEBERRY-ORANGE BREAD

2 eggs
1 cup milk
1 package of our orange muffin mix
1 package of our blueberry muffin mix

Heat oven to 350°. Grease loaf pan, 9×5×3 inches. Blend eggs and milk; add muffin mixes (dry). Stir with fork. (Batter will be slightly lumpy.) Pour into pan. Bake 50 to 60 minutes or until wooden pick inserted in center comes out clean. Cool thoroughly before slicing.

HAM WAFFLES

2 cups Bisquick
2 tablespoons shortening, melted, or salad oil
1⅓ cups milk
1 egg
1 package (3 ounces) smoked pressed ham

Heat waffle iron. Beat Bisquick, shortening, milk and egg with rotary beater until smooth. Stir in ham. Pour batter from cup or pitcher onto center of hot waffle iron. Bake about 5 minutes or until steaming stops. Lift waffle carefully with fork.

Three 9-inch waffles.

Note: To freeze waffles, bake, cool and wrap individually in foil. To reheat, unwrap and arrange on baking sheet. Bake in 400° oven 8 to 10 minutes or until hot.

VARIATION

■ *Orange-Nut Waffles:* Omit ham. Substitute orange juice for the milk and stir ¾ cup finely chopped nuts into batter.

Orange Rolls

Ham Waffles

Starting with a mix...
PANCAKE VARIATIONS

Prepare Pancakes as directed on Bisquick package except—try one of the following variations:

■ *Cheese:* Fold in ½ to 1½ cups shredded sharp cheese.

■ *Corn:* Fold in 1 cup drained whole kernel corn and ½ teaspoon paprika.

■ *Ham:* Fold in 1 to 1½ cups ground or chopped cooked ham.

OVEN FRENCH TOAST

Pictured on page 113.

4 slices white bread, 1 inch thick
3 eggs, slightly beaten
¾ cup milk
1 tablespoon sugar
¼ teaspoon salt

Heat oven to 500°. Arrange bread in ungreased baking dish, 13½×9×2 inches. Beat eggs, milk, sugar and salt. Pour egg mixture on bread; turn each slice to coat well.

With pancake turner, arrange bread on greased baking sheet. Bake about 8 minutes. Turn and bake about 8 minutes longer or until golden brown. Serve with warm cranberry sauce.

4 servings.

Note: The toast can also be cooked in buttered skillet or on a griddle.

Substitution

For 1-inch slices bread: 4 to 6 ½-inch slices white bread or 8 1¼-inch slices French bread; cover baking dish and refrigerate at least 8 hours.

VARIATION

■ *Waffled French Toast:* Heat waffle iron. Use 1-inch or ½-inch slices white bread; arrange on hot ungreased waffle iron and bake 3 to 5 minutes or until golden brown.

Note: To freeze Waffled French Toast, bake, cool and wrap individually in foil. To reheat, unwrap and arrange on baking sheet. Heat in 400° oven 8 to 10 minutes.

CONTINENTAL BRUNCH TOAST

½ loaf (1-pound size) French bread
3 eggs
⅓ cup sugar
½ teaspoon cinnamon
  Dash salt
1½ cups milk
2 tablespoons raisins
2 tablespoons brown sugar

Butter baking pan, 9×9×2 inches. Into pan, tear bread into 1- to 1½-inch pieces, each with a little crust (about 8 cups). Beat eggs, sugar, cinnamon and salt; stir in milk and raisins. Pour egg mixture on bread pieces; sprinkle with brown sugar. Cover; refrigerate at least 8 hours for best results. (Can be baked immediately if you like.)

Heat oven to 325°. Bake uncovered 1 hour or until crust is golden brown. Serve warm.

6 or 7 servings.

Note: For 8 to 10 servings, double amounts of all ingredients except French bread; bake 1 hour in buttered baking pan, 13×9×2 inches.

POTATO PANCAKES

1¾ cups boiling water
1 package of our hash browns with onions
¼ cup salad oil
2 eggs
2 tablespoons flour
1 teaspoon salt

Pour boiling water over potatoes; set aside about 30 minutes, tossing occasionally, until liquid is absorbed. (At this point, potatoes can be covered and refrigerated up to 12 hours.)

Pour oil over potatoes; toss. Beat eggs, flour and salt; pour over potatoes and mix. For each pancake, spread ¼ cup batter into 4-inch round on medium-hot griddle. Cook 3 to 4 minutes; turn and cook 3 to 4 minutes longer or until golden brown.

12 pancakes.

VARIATION

■ *Corned Beef-Potato Pancakes:* Flake 1 can (12 ounces) corned beef; mix into batter.

Breakfast Beverages

BREAKFAST PUNCH

1 cup orange juice, chilled
½ cup lemon juice, chilled
2 cups apple cider, chilled
¼ cup sugar

Stir juices and sugar until sugar is dissolved. Pour over ice cubes. Garnish with mint leaves.

4 or 5 servings.

MULLED APRICOT NECTAR

Pictured on page 113.

1 can (46 ounces) apricot nectar
½ lemon, sliced
2 cinnamon sticks
15 whole cloves
8 whole allspice

Mix all ingredients in heavy saucepan; heat to boiling. Reduce heat; simmer gently 5 minutes. Remove from heat. Cover tightly; allow to stand 30 minutes. Strain. Reheat before serving.

12 servings (½ cup each).

SPARKLING ORANGE JUICE

For each serving, fill glass with 2 parts orange juice and 1 part chilled carbonated lemon beverage. Float a half-slice of orange or a fresh mint sprig in each glass.

TOMATO BOUILLON

¾ cup tomato juice
¼ cup water
1 teaspoon instant beef bouillon

Heat all ingredients to boiling over medium-high heat, stirring occasionally. Serve hot or cold.

2 servings.

HERBED CREAM OF CHICKEN SOUP

1 can (10½ ounces) condensed
   cream of chicken soup
1 can (10½ ounces) condensed
   chicken with rice soup
½ cup milk
1 teaspoon tarragon leaves

Heat all ingredients over low heat, stirring occasionally. For an unusual garnish, top each serving with a spoonful of whipped cream and sprinkle with paprika.

3 servings (1 cup each).

MUSHROOM-CORN SOUP

2 slices bacon
1 medium onion, chopped
   (about ½ cup)
1 can (8 ounces) cream-style corn
1 can (10½ ounces) condensed
   cream of mushroom soup
1 soup can milk

In saucepan, fry bacon until crisp; remove bacon and drain. Add onion to bacon fat in saucepan; cook and stir until onion is tender. Stir in corn, soup and milk; heat through, stirring occasionally. Crumble bacon; sprinkle over each serving.

3 servings (1 cup each).

OYSTER STEW

¼ cup butter or margarine
1 pint fresh oysters
2 cups milk
½ cup light cream (20%)
1 teaspoon salt
   Dash pepper

Melt butter in small saucepan. Add oysters (with liquor); cook and stir over low heat just until edges curl. Heat milk and cream in another saucepan. Stir in salt, pepper and oysters.

4 servings (1 cup each).

COCOA-CEREAL MILK SHAKE

1 cup milk
1 pint chocolate ice cream, slightly softened
2 cups Cocoa Puffs
1 tablespoon malted milk powder, if desired

Measure all ingredients into blender. Cover; blend at high speed about 30 seconds.

Complete this breakfast with Honey Bee Ambrosia (page 115).

2 servings.

BLENDER BREAKFAST COMBOS

Blend any of the following combinations 5 to 10 seconds at high speed:

1 cup milk
1 envelope (1.22 ounces) strawberry-
flavored instant breakfast drink
¼ cup crushed pineapple

1 cup milk
1 envelope (1.22 ounces) vanilla-
flavored instant breakfast drink
1 jar (4¾ ounces) pureed fruits (baby food) or 6 canned apricot halves

1 cup milk
1 envelope (1.22 ounces) chocolate-flavored instant breakfast drink
1 small banana, cut up

1 serving.

ORANGE EGGNOG

1 can (6 ounces) frozen orange juice
   concentrate (thawed)
2 cups milk
2 cups eggnog

Beat orange juice and milk with rotary beater or in blender. Stir in eggnog. A sprinkling of colored sugar or nutmeg makes a pretty topping.

4 servings.

Pictured at left:
Strawberry Blender Breakfast, Cocoa-Cereal Milk Shake, Banana Orange Frost and Orange Eggnog— have your breakfast in a glass.

BANANA ORANGE FROST

1 ripe banana
½ cup orange juice
½ cup cold milk
½ pint (1 cup) orange sherbet

Mash banana with fork; stir in orange juice. Beat with rotary beater or in blender. Add milk and orange sherbet; beat until smooth. Serve on scoops of orange sherbet. An orange slice makes a pretty decoration.

2 or 3 servings.

FLAVORED MILKS

For each serving, add one of the following to a tall glass:

   2 tablespoons caramel syrup

   1 maraschino cherry and 2 tablespoons maraschino cherry juice

   1 tablespoon chocolate syrup and 1 tablespoon chunky peanut butter

   1 to 2 tablespoons chocolate syrup, cocoa mix or ice-cream topping

   1 tablespoon honey, 1 tablespoon grape juice, orange juice or lemonade or limeade concentrate

Fill glass with milk and stir thoroughly. Serve immediately.

SUNNY SIPPER

¼ cup honey
½ cup orange juice
   Juice of 1 lemon
1 can (6 ounces) evaporated milk
   (undiluted)
1 can (12 ounces) apricot nectar

Blend honey, orange juice and lemon juice. Add evaporated milk and apricot nectar; beat until foamy. Chill. Just before serving, beat again. Serve in small cups.

4 servings.

CHOCOLATE MILK SHAKE

Measure ¼ cup Chocolate Fudge Sauce (below) and ¾ cup milk into blender. Cover; blend 2 seconds. Add 3 scoops vanilla ice cream; blend at low speed 5 seconds. (Or, beat all ingredients with rotary beater.)

1 serving.

CHOCOLATE FUDGE SAUCE

 1 package of our chocolate fudge
 frosting mix
 2 tablespoons light corn syrup
 3 tablespoons butter or margarine
 ⅔ cup milk

Mix frosting mix (dry), corn syrup, butter and milk in saucepan. Cook, stirring frequently, until mixture boils. Boil 1 minute.

Substitution

 For Chocolate Fudge Sauce: ¼ cup chocolate ice-cream topping.

VARIATIONS

■ *Chocolate Mint Shake:* Add ⅛ teaspoon peppermint extract.

■ *Chocolate Mocha Shake:* Add ½ teaspoon powdered instant coffee.

COCOA-FLAVORED COFFEE

For each serving, stir ½ teaspoon cocoa into 1 cup hot coffee.

PINEAPPLE MILK SHAKE

Measure ¼ cup pineapple ice-cream topping and ¾ cup milk into blender. Cover; blend 2 seconds. Add 3 scoops vanilla ice cream; blend at low speed 5 seconds. (Or, use rotary beater.)

1 serving.

VARIATIONS

■ *Cherry Milk Shake:* Substitute cherry ice-cream topping for the pineapple ice-cream topping.

■ *Strawberry Milk Shake:* Substitute strawberry ice-cream topping for the pineapple ice-cream topping.

CONTINENTAL COCOA

 2 cups milk
 ⅓ cup Chocolate Fudge Sauce (left)
 ¼ teaspoon cinnamon
 3 or 4 large marshmallows

Mix milk, Chocolate Fudge Sauce and cinnamon in saucepan. Heat through, stirring occasionally, but do not boil. Drop a marshmallow into each cup and pour hot cocoa over it.

3 or 4 servings (½ to ⅔ cup each).

HOT CHOCOLATE MILK

Heat 1 quart chocolate-flavored milk over medium-low heat until small bubbles form around edge of pan. Beat with rotary beater until foamy.

6 servings (⅔ cup each).

Pictured at right:

TOP
 Beef Stew Lunch
 Tomato Shortcake
 Chef's Salad

CENTER
 Hash and Cheese Grill
 Individual Submarine Sandwich
 Shrimp Bisque

BOTTOM
 Fish Sticks with Cucumber Sauce
 Fruity Cereal Squares
 Mexican Dip

Lunches and Munches

Soups

VEGETABLE CHEESE CHOWDER

1 package (10 ounces) frozen
  mixed vegetables
1 can (10½ ounces) condensed
  cream of chicken soup
1 soup can milk
1 cup shredded Cheddar cheese (4 ounces)

Cook vegetables as directed on package; drain.
Return to saucepan. Stir in soup and milk. Heat
through, stirring occasionally. Sprinkle cheese on
each serving.

4 servings (about 1 cup each).

CREAM OF CORN SOUP

1 can (10½ ounces) condensed
  cream of chicken soup
1½ cups milk
½ cup mayonnaise
1 can (16 ounces) whole kernel corn
  Chopped pimiento
  Snipped parsley

Heat soup, milk, mayonnaise and corn, stirring
occasionally. Garnish with pimiento and parsley.

5 servings (1 cup each).

SHRIMP BISQUE

Pictured on page 133.

1 can (10¾ ounces) condensed
  tomato soup
1 can of our Newburg sauce (1 cup)
2 cups milk
1 can (4½ ounces) broken shrimp,
  rinsed and drained

Heat tomato soup, Newburg sauce and milk, stirring occasionally. Stir in shrimp; heat through.

4 servings (1 cup each).

HERBED SOUPS

For a new flavor in soup, heat one of the following combinations:

1 can (10½ ounces) condensed chicken
  noodle soup
1 can (10½ ounces) condensed chicken with
  rice soup
1 soup can water
½ teaspoon marjoram

1 can (10¾ ounces) condensed tomato soup
1 soup can milk
¼ teaspoon cloves

1 can (10½ ounces) condensed cream of
  chicken soup
1 soup can water
¼ teaspoon curry powder

1 can (10½ ounces) frozen condensed
  green pea soup
1 soup can water or milk
¼ teaspoon chili powder

3 servings (about ¾ cup each).

QUICK SOUP COMBOS

Create a new soup treat by combining and heating old favorites, for example:

1 can (10½ ounces) condensed beef noodle
  soup
1 can (10¾ ounces) condensed tomato soup
1 soup can water
1 soup can milk

1 can (10¾ ounces) condensed Cheddar
  cheese soup
1 can (10¾ ounces) condensed tomato soup
1 soup can water
1 soup can milk

1 envelope (1¾ ounces) chicken noodle
  soup mix, prepared
1 envelope (about 1½ ounces) onion soup
  mix, prepared

1 can (10¾ ounces) condensed vegetable
  soup
1 can (11½ ounces) bean with bacon soup
2 soup cans water

5 servings (1 cup each).

CLAM AND TOMATO BISQUE

1 can (7 to 8 ounces) minced clams
1 can (10¾ ounces) condensed
  tomato soup
1 soup can water
1 teaspoon salt
⅛ teaspoon pepper
1 teaspoon lemon juice

Heat clams (with liquor) and remaining ingredients to boiling. Reduce heat; simmer 5 minutes.

4 servings (about ¾ cup each).

CLAM-POTATO CHOWDER

1 package of our scalloped potatoes
1 can (7 to 8 ounces) minced clams,
  drained (reserve liquor)
2½ cups milk
1 tablespoon butter or margarine

In large saucepan, heat potato slices, sauce mix, amounts of water and milk called for on package and clam liquor to boiling, stirring occasionally. Reduce heat.

Cover tightly; simmer about 25 minutes or until potatoes are tender, stirring occasionally. Stir in clams, 2½ cups milk and the butter; heat through.

6 servings (about 1 cup each).

VARIATIONS

■ *Clam-Corn Chowder:* Stir in 1 can (8 ounces) whole kernel corn, drained, with the clams.

■ *Lobster Chowder:* Omit clams and liquor; stir in 1 can (5 ounces) lobster, drained and broken into small pieces, with the milk and butter.

SHERRIED MADRILENE

2 cans (13 ounces each) clear madrilene
2 cans (13 ounces each) red madrilene
½ cup sherry

Heat madrilenes to boiling. Remove from heat; stir in wine. Serve immediately.

5 servings (about ¾ cup each).

CREAMY POTATO SOUP

2 tablespoons butter or margarine
2 tablespoons finely chopped onion
1½ teaspoons salt
¼ teaspoon celery salt
⅛ teaspoon pepper
3½ cups milk
1⅓ cups Potato Buds
  Paprika
  Snipped parsley

In medium saucepan, heat butter, onion, salt, celery salt, pepper and milk *just* to boiling. Stir in Potato Buds (dry); continue cooking until smooth, stirring constantly. Garnish with paprika and parsley.

4 servings (1 cup each).

Substitution

For fresh onion: 1 tablespoon instant minced onion.

SOUTH-OF-THE-BORDER BEAN SOUP

1 can (11½ ounces) condensed bean and
  bacon soup
1 can (10¾ ounces) condensed
  tomato soup
1 can (10½ ounces) chili without beans
1 soup can water
⅛ to ¼ teaspoon garlic powder
  Corn chips

Heat all ingredients except corn chips to boiling. Garnish soup with corn chips.

5 servings (1 cup each).

Sandwiches

MEAT ROLL SANDWICHES

4 frankfurter buns
  Soft butter or margarine
2 hard-cooked eggs, chopped
2 tablespoons chopped ripe olives
2 teaspoons pickle relish, drained
2 teaspoons prepared mustard
8 slices large bologna

Spread buns with butter. Mix eggs, olives, pickle relish and mustard. Arrange bologna in stacks of two slices each. Spoon ¼ of the egg mixture down center of each stack; roll up. Place meat rolls in buns. Secure with wooden picks.

4 sandwiches.

INDIVIDUAL SUBMARINE SANDWICHES

Pictured on page 133.

4 loaves French bread, each 6 inches long
  Soft butter or margarine
4 lettuce leaves
2 to 3 tablespoons Italian salad dressing
4 slices salami
4 slices American cheese
4 slices boiled ham
4 slices Provolone cheese
4 to 8 slices tomato
  Thin slices onion
4 endive leaves

Cut loaves in half horizontally. Spread cut sides with butter. Dip lettuce leaves into salad dressing. On bottom halves of loaves, layer lettuce, salami, American cheese, ham, Provolone cheese, tomato and onion slices.

Dip endive into remaining salad dressing; place on onion slices and top with remaining halves of loaves. Secure with wooden picks.

4 sandwiches.

SANDWICH FILLING CHART (for 5 or 6 sandwiches)

Make your own combinations of ingredients from the chart below, being careful not to choose too many. Stir together and chill if necessary. Remember to serve fillings on a variety of breads. Try any one of the many available sliced breads, but don't forget biscuits, corn muffins, hard rolls and buns.

Basic Ingredient (Choose one to total 2 cups)	Add Interest with . . . (Choose one or combine to total ½ to ¾ cup)	Spread with . . . (Use one or combine to total ½ cup)	If Desired, Season with	Garnish with
Chopped, ground or minced cooked meat (veal, ham, pork, lamb, beef, corned beef, chicken or frankfurter)	Chopped or minced vegetables (celery, onion, radishes, cucumber, carrot or green pepper)	Mayonnaise or salad dressing	Salt	Lettuce
		Thousand Island dressing	Pepper	Spinach
	Chopped fruits (apples, avocado, oranges or pineapple)		Garlic salt	Watercress
Shrimp, rinsed and drained		Dairy sour cream	Onion salt	Endive
Crabmeat, drained and cartilage removed		French dressing (for only partial amount)	Onion juice	Bermuda onion slices
Tuna, drained	Pickle relish, drained, or chopped dill or sweet pickles		Lemon juice	Orange slices
Salmon, drained and boned			Worcestershire sauce	Radish slices
6 hard-cooked eggs, chopped			Tabasco	Tomato slices
American or Cheddar cheese, shredded	Chopped olives (green, ripe or pimiento-stuffed)		Prepared mustard	Pear slices
			Horseradish	Pineapple slices or spears
Creamed cottage cheese, drained	Bac*Os chips or crumbled crisply fried bacon		Dill weed	Green pepper slices
	Chopped nuts		Chili powder	Paprika
Baked beans, drained			Ground cloves	

CONEY ISLAND HOT DOGS

1 can (15 ounces) chili with beans
1 can (6 ounces) tomato paste
¼ cup chopped green pepper
¼ cup chopped onion
1 teaspoon prepared mustard
½ teaspoon salt
½ teaspoon chili powder
8 to 10 frankfurters
8 to 10 frankfurter buns, buttered

In saucepan, mix all ingredients except frankfurters and buns. Heat to boiling. Reduce heat; simmer uncovered 10 minutes.

Drop frankfurters into boiling water; reduce heat. Cover tightly; simmer 5 to 8 minutes.

Toast buns. Serve frankfurters in buns; top frankfurters with chili mixture.

8 to 10 sandwiches.

GRILLED REUBEN SANDWICHES

⅓ cup mayonnaise or salad dressing
1 tablespoon chili sauce
12 slices rye bread, buttered
½ pound sliced Swiss cheese
½ pound sliced corned beef
1 can (16 ounces) sauerkraut, drained
   Soft butter or margarine

Mix mayonnaise and chili sauce; spread on 6 bread slices. Top with cheese slices, corned beef, sauerkraut and remaining bread slices.

Butter outsides of sandwiches. Grill in skillet over low to moderate heat 5 to 7 minutes on each side or brown in sandwich grill 5 to 7 minutes.

6 sandwiches.

VARIATION

■ *Rachel Sandwiches:* Substitute 1½ cups coleslaw for the sauerkraut.

CHEESE CLUB SANDWICH

Set oven control at broil and/or 550°. Toast bread slice 5 inches from heat until golden brown on one side; toast lightly on second side. Butter second side; top with tomato slice. Place 2 or 3 slices crisply fried bacon on tomato and top with cheese slice. Broil until cheese melts.

1 sandwich.

GRILLED HAM AND SWISS SANDWICHES

1 package (3 ounces) sliced ready-to-serve
   smoked ham
4 slices Swiss cheese
8 slices bread
½ cup soft butter or margarine

Place ham and cheese slices on 4 slices of bread; top with remaining bread slices. Butter outsides of sandwiches. Grill in skillet over low to moderate heat 5 to 7 minutes on each side or brown in sandwich grill 5 to 7 minutes.

4 sandwiches.

Substitution

For smoked ham: 4 to 8 thin slices fully cooked ham.

HASH AND CHEESE GRILL

Pictured on page 133.

1 can (16 ounces) roast beef hash
⅓ cup catsup
¾ teaspoon oregano
1 teaspoon parsley flakes
2 teaspoons instant minced onion
4 English muffins, split and buttered
8 slices American cheese, cut into strips

Mix hash, catsup, oregano, parsley flakes and onion; spread evenly on muffin halves. Top with cheese strips. Set oven control at broil and/or 550°. Broil 8 to 10 inches from heat until cheese melts and hash mixture is bubbly and hot.

8 sandwiches.

Substitutions

For parsley flakes: 1 tablespoon snipped parsley.
For instant onion: 2 tablespoons minced onion.

HAMBURGERS

1 pound ground beef
1 tablespoon instant minced onion
½ teaspoon salt
¼ teaspoon pepper
4 hamburger buns, split

Mix ground beef, onion, salt and pepper. Shape mixture into four 4½-inch patties. Set oven control at broil and/or 550°. Broil hamburgers 3 inches from heat 2 minutes on each side for rare, 3 to 4 minutes on each side for medium. Serve in buns.

4 sandwiches.

To Charcoal-grill: Add ¼ cup water to ground beef mixture; shape into 5 patties. Place on grill 4 to 6 inches from hot coals; cook 12 minutes or until done, turning once.

Substitution

For instant onion: 3 tablespoons minced onion.

VARIATIONS

■ *California Hamburgers:* Top each with lettuce, onion slice, tomato slice and a dab of mayonnaise.

■ *Cheeseburgers:* About 1 minute before hamburgers are done, top each with cheese slice. Continue cooking until cheese melts.

■ *Panfried Hamburgers:* Turning frequently, fry patties in medium skillet in ½ teaspoon hot shortening over medium heat, about 7 minutes.

FREEZER BURGERS

1 pound ground beef
1 envelope (about 1½ ounces) onion
  soup mix
½ cup finely crushed cracker crumbs
8 hamburger buns, split

Mix ground beef, onion soup mix and cracker crumbs. Shape mixture into eight 4½-inch patties. Wrap each patty in single thickness aluminum foil; freeze. (Keep no longer than 3 months.) Wrap each bun in aluminum foil; freeze.

Heat frozen hamburgers and buns (in foil wrappings) in 425° oven 10 minutes.

8 sandwiches.

SLOPPY JOES

1 pound ground beef
¾ cup chopped onion
1 can (10½ ounces) condensed
  chicken gumbo soup
3 tablespoons catsup
3 tablespoons prepared mustard
6 hamburger buns, split and toasted

Cook and stir ground beef and onion until meat is brown. Drain off fat. Stir in soup, catsup and mustard. Simmer uncovered 15 minutes, stirring occasionally. Serve in buns.

6 sandwiches.

Substitution

For chicken gumbo soup and catsup: 1 can (10¾ ounces) condensed tomato soup; decrease prepared mustard to 1 tablespoon.

SPREAD-A-BURGER

1 can (10¾ ounces) condensed
  tomato soup
½ cup shredded Cheddar or
  American cheese
¼ cup chopped onion
2 teaspoons salt
1 teaspoon dry mustard
¼ teaspoon pepper
1 pound ground beef
8 hamburger buns, split and toasted
16 thin green pepper rings
  Pimiento-stuffed olives, sliced

Heat oven to 350°. Mix soup, cheese, onion, salt, mustard and pepper. Stir in ground beef; spread evenly on bun halves, being careful to bring mixture to the edges.

Place eight of the bun halves on ungreased baking sheet. Bake 15 to 20 minutes or until meat is done. Set oven control at broil and/or 550°. Broil 6 to 8 inches from heat about 3 minutes or until brown. Repeat with remaining bun halves. Garnish with pepper rings and olive slices.

16 sandwiches.

BARBECUED HAMBURGER MAKE-AHEAD MIX

4 pounds ground beef
2 medium onions, chopped (about 1 cup)
1 bottle (14 ounces) catsup
1 cup water
½ cup chopped celery
¼ cup lemon juice
2 tablespoons brown sugar
1 tablespoon Worcestershire sauce
1 tablespoon salt
2 teaspoons vinegar
½ teaspoon dry mustard

In Dutch oven, cook and stir ground beef and onion until meat is brown and onion is tender. Drain off fat. Stir in remaining ingredients; heat to boiling, stirring frequently.

Reduce heat. Cover tightly; simmer 30 minutes. Cool; divide among pint-freezer containers and freeze for future use. Or, use portion of hot mixture for variations below; freeze remainder.

5 pints.

Note: To thaw frozen Make-ahead Mix, heat slowly in saucepan or thaw in refrigerator.

VARIATIONS

■ *Baked Frank Rolls:* If desired, stir 1 cup shredded American cheese (about 4 ounces) into 1 pint Make-ahead Mix. Split 8 to 10 frankfurter buns; scoop part of bread from center of each. Spoon mixture into buns, wrap individually in aluminum foil. Heat in 350° oven 30 to 35 minutes.

■ *Barbecued Burger Buns:* Fill each buttered hamburger bun with about ¼ cup hot Make-ahead Mix. The entire recipe will fill 30 to 40 hamburger buns.

■ *Easy Chili:* Stir 1 can (15½ ounces) kidney beans (with liquid), ½ to 1 cup tomato juice and 2 to 3 teaspoons chili powder into 1 pint Make-ahead Mix; heat through. *4 servings.*

■ *Mock Pizza:* Split 6 to 8 hamburger buns; toast. Place on rack in broiler pan. Spoon 1 pint Make-ahead Mix on halves; sprinkle with shredded American cheese and dash oregano. Set oven control at broil and/or 550°. Broil 3 to 4 inches from heat just until cheese is bubbly.

Barbecued Burger Buns

Mock Pizza

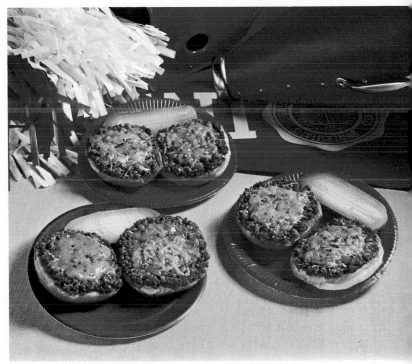

TOMATO SHORTCAKES

Pictured on page 133.

2⅓ cups Bisquick
 3 tablespoons butter, melted and cooled
   slightly
 ½ cup milk
 6 slices bacon
 1 can of our cheese sauce (1 cup)
   Soft butter
 3 medium tomatoes, sliced

Heat oven to 450°. Mix Bisquick, 3 tablespoons butter and the milk with fork until a soft dough forms. Knead 8 to 10 times on lightly floured cloth-covered board. Roll dough ½ inch thick. Cut with floured 3-inch cutter. Bake on ungreased baking sheet about 10 minutes.

Fry bacon until crisp; remove bacon and drain. Heat cheese sauce over low heat, stirring occasionally. Split warm shortcakes crosswise; spread with butter. Place tomato slices between layers and on top of each shortcake. Spoon hot cheese sauce onto shortcakes; garnish with bacon.

6 sandwiches.

Substitution

For melted butter and milk: ⅔ cup light cream.

DENVER SANDWICHES

 ¼ cup minced onion
 ¼ cup minced green pepper
 2 tablespoons shortening (half butter)
 4 eggs
 ½ cup minced cooked ham
 ¼ teaspoon salt
 ⅛ teaspoon pepper
 8 slices bread or toast, buttered

In 10-inch skillet, cook and stir onion and green pepper in hot shortening until onion is tender. Beat eggs slightly; stir in ham, salt and pepper. Pour egg mixture into skillet. Cook over low heat *just* until set. Cut into 4 wedges; turn. Brown slightly. Serve between bread slices.

4 sandwiches.

Substitution

For ham: 1 can (2¼ ounces) deviled ham and ¼ teaspoon Worcestershire sauce.

HAM-BROCCOLI SANDWICHES

1 package (10 ounces) frozen
  broccoli spears
1 can of our cheese sauce (1 cup)
4 slices toast, buttered
4 slices cooked ham

Cook broccoli as directed on package; drain. Heat cheese sauce just to boiling, stirring frequently. Top each toast slice with ham slice, broccoli spears and about ¼ cup cheese sauce.

4 open-face sandwiches.

SHRIMP TOWERS

 2 hamburger buns, split and toasted
   Soft butter or margarine
 1 tomato, sliced
16 cleaned cooked shrimp
   Bac*Os chips
 4 slices process Cheddar cheese

Spread cut sides of buns with butter. Top each bun half with tomato slice, shrimp, Bac*Os chips and cheese slice.

Set oven control at broil and/or 550°. Broil 5 or 6 inches from heat 2 to 3 minutes or until cheese melts and bubbles.

4 open-face sandwiches.

TUNA BURGERS

1 can (6½ ounces) tuna, drained
1 cup chopped celery
½ cup diced American cheese
1 tablespoon instant minced onion
¼ teaspoon salt
⅛ teaspoon pepper
¼ cup mayonnaise or salad dressing
6 hamburger buns, split and buttered

Heat oven to 350°. Mix all ingredients except buns. Fill buns with tuna mixture. Place each sandwich on square of aluminum foil; fold foil over sandwich and seal securely. Place on baking sheet. Bake 20 minutes or until heated through.

6 sandwiches.

Substitution

For instant onion: 3 tablespoons minced onion.

Lunch Main Dishes

BEEF STEW LUNCH

Pictured on page 133.

1 can (16 ounces) sliced carrots
1 can (8 ounces) whole potatoes
1 can (8 ounces) cut green beans
¼ cup Gold Medal Flour
1 envelope (about 1½ ounces) onion soup
  mix
3 cups cut-up cooked beef

Drain vegetables, reserving liquid. Combine flour and soup mix in large skillet. Add enough water to reserved vegetable liquid to measure 3 cups; stir into mixture in skillet. Heat to boiling, stirring constantly. Boil and stir 1 minute.

Stir in vegetables and beef. Cover tightly; cook over low heat about 10 minutes or until heated through.

4 servings (about 1½ cups each).

CHILI CASSEROLE

1 can (15½ ounces) chili without beans
1 tablespoon instant minced onion
1 can (12 ounces) vacuum-pack whole kernel
  corn with sweet peppers, drained
½ cup shredded Cheddar cheese

Heat oven to 350°. Pour chili into greased baking dish, 8×8×2 or 9×9×2 inches. Top with onion and corn; sprinkle with cheese. Bake uncovered 20 to 25 minutes or until cheese is bubbly.

Plan a Mexicali menu with shredded lettuce, fried tortillas (they come frozen, you know) and Pears au Chocolat (page 82).

4 to 6 servings.

Substitutions

For instant onion: 3 tablespoons minced onion.
For Cheddar cheese: ½ cup shredded Swiss cheese.

CHOW MEIN CASSEROLE

1¼ cups boiling water
½ cup uncooked converted rice
½ teaspoon salt
1 pound ground beef
¾ cup chopped celery
3 tablespoons instant minced onion
1 can (10½ ounces) condensed chicken
  with rice soup
1 can (4 ounces) mushroom stems and
  pieces, drained
2 tablespoons soy sauce
1 tablespoon brown sugar
1 teaspoon butter or margarine

Heat oven to 350°. Mix water, rice and salt; cover. Cook and stir ground beef, celery and onion until meat is brown. Drain off fat.

Mix all ingredients. Pour into greased 2-quart casserole. Cover tightly; bake 30 minutes. Uncover and stir; bake 30 minutes longer.

4 or 5 servings.

Substitution

For instant onion: ½ cup minced onion.

SIRLOIN STROGANOFF

1-pound sirloin steak, 1 inch thick
1 tablespoon butter or margarine
⅛ teaspoon garlic salt
⅛ teaspoon pepper
1 package of our noodles stroganoff
1⅔ cups milk
⅓ cup red Burgundy, if desired
1 tablespoon soft butter or margarine
1 teaspoon poppy seed

Cut meat across the grain into ½-inch strips, about 1½ inches long. Melt 1 tablespoon butter in large skillet; cook meat until light brown. Season with garlic salt and pepper.

Mix in sauce mix (from noodles stroganoff) and milk; heat to boiling, stirring constantly. Reduce heat; stir in wine. Cover tightly; simmer 20 minutes, stirring occasionally.

Cook noodles as directed on package; drain. Return to saucepan. Stir in 1 tablespoon butter and the poppy seed. Serve sauce on noodles.

4 servings.

BEEF AND MUSHROOM SALAD

1½-pound sirloin steak, 1½ inches thick
 1 jar (4½ ounces) sliced mushrooms, drained
 1 medium green pepper, sliced into thin rings
 ⅓ cup red wine vinegar
 ¼ cup salad oil
 1 teaspoon salt
 ½ teaspoon onion salt
 ½ teaspoon Worcestershire sauce
 ¼ teaspoon pepper
 ¼ teaspoon tarragon leaves
 2 cloves garlic, crushed
   Lettuce cups
   Cherry tomatoes

Set oven control at broil and/or 550°. Place top of steak 3 to 4 inches from heat. Broil until medium, about 15 minutes on each side; cool.

Cut steak into ⅜-inch strips; arrange in baking dish, 13½×9×2 inches. Top meat with mushrooms and pepper rings. Mix vinegar, oil and seasonings; pour on meat and vegetables. Cover; refrigerate at least 3 hours, spooning marinade over vegetables occasionally.

With a slotted spoon, remove vegetables to lettuce cups. Arrange strips of meat beside vegetables; garnish with tomatoes.

Chocolate cake for dessert makes this a man-designed lunch.

4 servings.

HAM AND NOODLE COOLER

 1 package (5.5 ounces) of our noodles Romanoff
 ½ teaspoon grated onion
 2 teaspoons lemon juice
 1½ cups seedless green grapes
 1½ cups cubed cooked ham

Prepare noodles Romanoff as directed on package; cool slightly. Stir in remaining ingredients; chill.

6 servings.

Substitution

For ham: 1 can (12 ounces) pork luncheon meat, cubed.

HAM 'N HASH

 1 package of our hash browns with onions
 1 cup cubed cooked ham
 2 tablespoons chopped green pepper

Prepare hash browns as directed on package except—decrease salt to ½ teaspoon and stir in ham and green pepper before cooking.

Start the lunch with Tomato Bouillon (page 129) and finish with Dried Fruit Compote (page 116).

4 servings.

SPANISH RICE

 6 slices bacon
 ¼ cup chopped onion
 ¼ cup chopped green pepper
 3 cups cooked rice
 1 can (16 ounces) tomatoes
 1½ teaspoons salt
 ⅛ teaspoon pepper

Fry bacon in large skillet until crisp; remove bacon and drain. Drain off all but 2 tablespoons fat. Stir in onion and green pepper; cook and stir until onion is tender.

Crumble bacon; stir in with remaining ingredients. Cook uncovered over low heat about 15 minutes.

4 to 6 servings.

Note: To bake casserole in oven, heat oven to 400°; pour mixture into greased 1½-quart casserole and bake uncovered 25 to 30 minutes.

VARIATION

■ *Spanish Rice with Sausage:* Omit bacon and substitute 7 to 8 pork sausage links, cut into ¾-inch pieces (2 cups); cook sausages until brown.

Nobody Lunches at Home?

Your husband works in the city; the kids eat at school. And maybe you're tied to a desk all day too. Then keep these hearty recipes in mind for other things...for sending off something hot in the lunch-box thermos or for the day when it's your turn to entertain the girls. And nothing says you can't take any one of them to the table later and call it dinner.

FRANKFURTER CHOWDER

1 tablespoon butter or margarine
6 frankfurters, cut into ½-inch pieces
¼ cup chopped green pepper
2 tablespoons chopped onion
1 can (16 ounces) cream-style corn
3 dashes Tabasco

Melt butter in large skillet; cook and stir frankfurters, green pepper and onion over medium heat until brown. Stir in corn and Tabasco; heat through.

4 to 6 servings.

CHEF'S SALAD

Pictured on page 133.

1 head lettuce, washed and chilled
1 small bunch romaine or endive,
   washed and chilled
1 cup julienne strips cooked meat
   (beef, ham, tongue)
1 cup julienne strips cooked chicken or
   turkey
1 cup julienne strips Swiss cheese
½ cup chopped green onions
½ cup sliced celery
1 can (2 ounces) anchovy fillets, if desired
2 tomatoes, cut into wedges
½ cup mayonnaise or salad dressing
¼ cup French dressing
   Ripe olives
1 hard-cooked egg, sliced

Into large salad bowl, tear lettuce and romaine into bite-size pieces (about 12 cups). Reserve few strips of meat and cheese. Toss remaining meat and cheese strips, the onion, celery, anchovies and tomatoes with the salad greens.

Blend mayonnaise and French dressing; pour on salad and toss. (If you prefer a clear dressing, use the traditional oil and vinegar.) Garnish with reserved meat and cheese strips, the olives and egg slices.

4 servings.

HOT CHICKEN SALAD

2 cups cubed cooked chicken
2 cups thinly sliced celery
1 cup toasted bread cubes
1 cup mayonnaise
½ cup chopped or slivered almonds, toasted
2 tablespoons lemon juice
2 teaspoons instant minced onion
½ teaspoon salt
½ cup shredded cheese
1 cup toasted bread cubes or crushed
   potato chips

Heat oven to 450°. Mix all ingredients except cheese and 1 cup toasted bread cubes. Pile lightly into ungreased 1-cup baking dishes. Sprinkle with cheese and remaining bread cubes. Bake 10 to 15 minutes or until bubbly.

6 servings.

Substitution

For instant onion: 2 tablespoons minced onion.

VARIATIONS

■ *Hot Tuna, Turkey or Veal Salad:* Substitute 2 cans (6½ ounces each) tuna or 2 cups cubed cooked turkey or veal for the chicken.

CHICKEN À LA KING

1 can (10½ ounces) condensed cream of
   of celery soup
1 cup cut-up cooked chicken
1 tablespoon chopped pimiento
1 teaspoon parsley flakes
1 can (4 ounces) mushroom stems and
   pieces, drained
   Chow mein noodles or hot rice

Heat soup. Stir in chicken, pimiento, parsley flakes and mushrooms; heat through. Serve on chow mein noodles.

3 or 4 servings.

Substitution

For parsley flakes: 1 tablespoon snipped parsley.

VARIATION

■ *Turkey à la King:* Substitute cut-up cooked turkey for the chicken.

Chicken and Macaroni Salad

Speedy Chicken and Shrimp with Asparagus

CHICKEN AND MACARONI SALAD

  1 cup uncooked elbow macaroni
  1 cup diced cucumber
1½ cups cut-up cooked chicken
  1 tablespoon grated onion
  1 tablespoon snipped parsley
  ½ cup mayonnaise or salad dressing
  ½ teaspoon salt
  ¼ teaspoon pepper
  4 cups bite-size pieces lettuce

Cook macaroni as directed on package; drain and rinse in cold water. Mix all ingredients except lettuce. Cover and refrigerate.

Just before serving, toss with lettuce. Garnish with parsleyed tomato wedges.

4 to 6 servings.

Substitutions

  For fresh onion: 1 teaspoon instant minced onion.

  For fresh parsley: 1 teaspoon parsley flakes.

VARIATIONS

■ *Tuna or Turkey and Macaroni Salad:* Substitute 1 can (9¾ ounces) tuna, flaked, or 1½ cups cut-up cooked turkey for the chicken.

SPEEDY CHICKEN AND SHRIMP

1 medium onion, chopped
1 can (8½ ounces) pineapple tidbits, drained
3 to 4 tablespoons butter or margarine
2 cans (10½ ounces each) chicken à la king
1 can (4½ ounces) shrimp, rinsed and drained
2 tablespoons lemon juice
3 to 4 cups hot cooked rice
  Bac*Os chips

In large skillet, cook and stir onion and pineapple tidbits in butter until onion is tender. Stir in chicken à la king, shrimp and lemon juice; heat through. Serve on rice; sprinkle with Bac°Os chips.

4 to 6 servings.

Substitution

  For pineapple tidbits: 1 medium apple, pared and diced; omit Bac°Os chips and add 2 to 3 teaspoons curry powder with the lemon juice.

TUNA ON A SHOESTRING

1 can (6½ ounces) tuna, drained
1 cup shredded carrots
1 cup diced celery
¼ cup minced onion
¾ to 1 cup salad dressing or mayonnaise
1 can (4 ounces) shoestring potatoes

In large bowl, separate tuna into chunks. Add carrots, celery, onion and salad dressing; toss until tuna is well coated with dressing. Cover and chill.

Just before serving, fold in potatoes. Add a bright touch with parsley and carrot curls.

4 to 6 servings.

TUNA-POTATO SCALLOP

1 package of our scalloped potatoes
1 can (9¼ ounces) tuna, drained
1 can (10½ ounces) condensed
   cream of celery soup
2 tablespoons chopped pimiento

Heat oven to 400°. Empty potato slices into ungreased 2-quart casserole; sprinkle with packet of sauce mix. Stir in amount of boiling water as directed on package, the tuna, soup and pimiento. Bake uncovered 35 to 40 minutes.

Chilled Asparagus (page 61) makes an interesting vegetable salad.

4 to 6 servings.

SWISS TUNA ROMANOFF

1 package (5.5 ounces) of our noodles
   Romanoff
1 can (6½ ounces) tuna, drained
1 cup shredded Swiss cheese (about 4
   ounces)
1 tablespoon snipped chives

Heat oven to 350°. Prepare noodles Romanoff as directed on package except—increase milk to ½ cup. In ungreased 1½-quart casserole, layer half the noodles, all the tuna and cheese and remaining noodles. Sprinkle with chives. Cover tightly; bake 15 to 20 minutes.

Add a pretty and colorful garnish of green grapes.

4 servings.

Tuna on a Shoestring

Swiss Tuna Romanoff

CRAB LOUIS

2 cans (7½ ounces each) crabmeat
  Louis Dressing (below)
4 tomatoes, quartered
4 hard-cooked eggs, quartered
  Ripe or green olives
4 cups bite-size pieces salad greens, chilled

Drain crabmeat and remove cartilage; chill. Prepare Louis Dressing. Arrange crabmeat, tomatoes, eggs and olives on greens. Pour Louis Dressing on salad.

4 servings.

LOUIS DRESSING

¾ cup chili sauce
½ cup mayonnaise or salad dressing
1 teaspoon instant minced onion
½ teaspoon sugar
¼ teaspoon Worcestershire sauce
  Salt to taste

Mix all ingredients. Cover; chill 30 minutes.

Substitution

For canned crabmeat: 2 packages (6 ounces each) frozen cooked crabmeat, thawed.

FISH STICKS WITH CUCUMBER SAUCE

Pictured on page 133.

1 package (16 ounces) frozen fish sticks
¼ medium cucumber
1 teaspoon salt
½ teaspoon lemon pepper
1 cup unflavored yogurt

Cook fish sticks as directed on package. Cut unpared cucumber into 1-inch pieces. Chop in blender, watching carefully; drain thoroughly. (Or cucumber can be finely chopped by hand.) Stir cucumber and seasonings into yogurt. Serve sauce with fish.

3 servings.

SEAFOOD NEWBURG

3 cups cooked seafood* (large pieces)
¼ cup butter or margarine
2 tablespoons lemon juice
2 cans of our Newburg sauce (2 cups)
3 cups cooked rice
¼ cup buttered bread crumbs

Cook and stir seafood in butter until heated through. Stir in lemon juice and Newburg sauce; heat through, stirring frequently. Serve on rice; sprinkle with bread crumbs.

Cucumber Relish Mold (page 57) is a nice accompaniment.

4 or 5 servings.

Use crab, shrimp, lobster or a combination.

WELSH RAREBIT

1 can of our cheese sauce (1 cup)
¼ teaspoon dry mustard
¼ teaspoon Worcestershire sauce
  Dash pepper
4 slices toast, buttered

Heat sauce as directed on can except—stir in dry mustard, Worcestershire sauce and pepper. Pour about ¼ cup sauce on each slice of toast.

2 servings.

CHEESE SOUFFLÉED PEPPER SHELLS

3 large green peppers
1 package (12 ounces) frozen cheese
  soufflé, thawed

Heat oven to 325°. Cut peppers lengthwise in half; remove seeds. Arrange pepper shells in ungreased baking pan, 13×9×2 inches. Pour soufflé into shells. Bake uncovered 1 hour or until knife inserted in center comes out clean.

Nice with Best Tossed Salad (page 55) and Corn Bread (page 80).

3 servings.

VARIATION

■ *Ham-Cheese Souffléed Pepper Shells:* Before baking, sprinkle ½ cup finely diced cooked ham on cheese soufflé in pepper shells.

Snacks

FRUITY CEREAL SQUARES

Pictured on page 133.

1 package (3 ounces) fruit-flavored gelatin
⅓ cup light corn syrup
2 tablespoons butter or margarine
4 cups cereal (Cheerios, Kix, Trix)

Butter baking pan or dish, 9×9×2 inches. In large saucepan, mix gelatin (dry), corn syrup and butter. Heat to boiling over medium heat, stirring constantly. Remove from heat; stir in cereal until evenly coated.

With buttered back of spoon, spread mixture in buttered pan. Cover; chill until set, about 30 minutes. Cut into squares.

3 dozen squares.

Note: Chill the candy to set it, but store at room temperature.

PEANUTTY SQUARES

¼ cup butter or margarine
3 cups miniature marshmallows
½ cup peanut butter
4 cups Cheerios
1 cup salted peanuts

Butter baking pan, 9×9×2 inches. In large saucepan, melt butter, marshmallows and peanut butter over low heat, stirring until smooth. Remove from heat; mix in cereal and peanuts until evenly coated.

Spread mixture quickly in buttered pan. Cool; cut into squares.

16 squares.

Substitution

For miniature marshmallows: 32 large marshmallows, quartered.

CHOCOLATE-O BARS

½ cup light corn syrup
1 package (6 ounces) semisweet chocolate pieces
1 teaspoon vanilla
4 cups Cheerios

Butter baking pan, 9×9×2 inches. In medium saucepan, heat syrup to boiling. Remove from heat; add chocolate pieces and vanilla, stirring until chocolate is melted. Mix in cereal until coated.

With buttered back of spoon, spread mixture in buttered pan. Cool 1 hour; cut into bars.

3 dozen bars.

Substitution

For Cheerios: 4 cups Cocoa Puffs or Frosty O's.

CARAMEL CRUNCH

28 vanilla caramels
2 tablespoons milk
2 cups Cheerios
1 cup Spanish peanuts

Melt caramels with milk, stirring constantly until smooth. Mix cereal and peanuts in large bowl. Pour melted caramels on cereal mixture; stir until evenly coated.

With buttered hands, shape mixture into 1-inch balls. Cool on waxed paper.

About 2 dozen candies.

OVEN CARAMEL CORN

3¾ quarts (15 cups) popped corn
1 cup brown sugar (packed)
½ cup margarine or butter
¼ cup light corn syrup
½ teaspoon salt
½ teaspoon soda

Heat oven to 200°. Divide popped corn between 2 ungreased baking pans, 13×9×2 inches. Heat sugar, margarine, corn syrup and salt, stirring occasionally, until bubbly around edges. Continue cooking over medium heat 5 minutes.

Remove from heat; stir in soda until foamy. Pour on popped corn, stirring until corn is well coated. Bake 1 hour, stirring every 15 minutes.

MEATBALLS BORDELAISE

1 pound ground beef
1 egg
½ cup dry bread crumbs
¼ cup milk
2 tablespoons instant minced onion
1 teaspoon salt
⅛ teaspoon pepper
1 can of our Bordelaise sauce (1 cup)

Mix all ingredients except sauce. Shape mixture into 1-inch balls; place in ungreased jelly roll pan, 15½×10½×1 inch. Bake uncovered in 400° oven 8 to 10 minutes or until brown.

While meatballs bake, heat Bordelaise sauce in large skillet. Stir in meatballs until all are coated.

35 meatballs.

Substitution

For instant onion: ⅓ cup minced onion.

VARIATION

■ *Mushroom Meatballs:* Substitute 1 can of our mushroom sauce for the Bordelaise sauce.

"TARTARE STEAK" APPETIZERS

½ pound ground sirloin
1 egg
1 green onion, finely chopped
½ teaspoon salt
2 dashes Tabasco
   Soft butter or margarine
5 slices bread

Mix meat, egg, onion, salt and Tabasco. Set oven control at broil and/or 550°. Butter one side of each bread slice. Broil 3 inches from heat until bread is toasted. Turn; cover unbuttered side with meat mixture. Broil 1 to 2 minutes for rare, 2 to 3 minutes for medium. Cut each bread slice into 9 bite-size pieces.

45 appetizers.

To Charcoal-grill: Cover unbuttered side of bread with meat mixture. Carefully spread butter on meat mixture. Place bread side down 2 inches from medium coals; cook about 1½ minutes or until bread is toasted. Turn; cook 1½ minutes longer.

LONDON BROIL APPETIZER

Pictured at right.

1-pound flank steak, scored
1 cup rosé
1 teaspoon salt
½ teaspoon rosemary leaves
¼ teaspoon pepper

Place steak in shallow glass dish. Combine remaining ingredients; pour on meat. Cover; refrigerate several hours, turning meat occasionally.

Set oven control at broil and/or 550°. Remove steak from marinade. Broil 2 to 3 inches from heat 4 minutes. Turn; broil 3 to 4 minutes longer.

Cut meat at an angle across grain into thin slices. If desired, salt before serving. Serve on thin rounds of rye or French bread.

6 to 8 servings.

Substitution

For rosé: 1 cup cranberry cocktail.

MARINATED SHRIMP

Pictured at right.

1½ teaspoons salt
1 package (12 ounces) frozen cleaned
   raw shrimp
1 cup oil and vinegar salad dressing
1 bay leaf, crushed

Heat 2 cups water and the salt to boiling. Add shrimp; heat to boiling. Cook 1 to 2 minutes or until shrimp are tender; rinse quickly under running cold water to cool.

Mix shrimp, salad dressing and bay leaf in glass bowl. Cover; refrigerate at least 2 hours.

Substitution

For frozen shrimp: 2 cans (4½ ounces each) medium shrimp, rinsed and drained.

Pictured at right:
Snack time is any time. Clockwise from top right: Guacamole Dip with Tacos, Marinated Shrimp, Salami Wedges, London Broil Appetizer, Fresh Vegetable Relishes.

FRESH VEGETABLE RELISHES

Pictured on page 149.

Prepare a variety of the vegetable relishes below. Keep crisp in ice and water in refrigerator until serving time. Arrange in a large bowl filled with crushed ice. Delicious with a cheese dip.

Broccoli Buds and Cauliflowerets: Break head of broccoli or cauliflower into bite-size flowerets.

Carrot Curls: With vegetable parer, cut carrot lengthwise into paper-thin slices. Roll up and fasten with picks. (Remove picks before serving.)

Cucumber Petals: Run tines of fork down length of unpared cucumber. Cut crosswise into very thin slices.

Green Onions: Remove any loose layers of skin. Trim, leaving about 3 inches of green.

Radish Fans: Remove stem and root ends from large radishes. Make thin crosswise cuts almost through radishes.

MEXICAN DIP

Pictured on page 133.

1 can of our cheese sauce (1 cup)
½ cup finely chopped tomato
3 tablespoons finely chopped green chili peppers
2 green onions, finely chopped
⅛ teaspoon garlic salt

Heat all ingredients over low heat about 15 minutes, stirring occasionally.

1 cup.

HOT CURRIED CRAB DIP

2 packages (8 ounces each) cream cheese, softened
2 teaspoons curry powder
1 can (7½ ounces) crabmeat, drained and cartilage removed

Heat oven to 375°. In small mixer bowl, beat cream cheese and curry powder. Stir in crabmeat. Turn into ungreased baking dish. Bake about 20 minutes.

3 cups.

SHRIMP DIP

2 tablespoons milk
1 teaspoon lemon juice
1 teaspoon Worcestershire sauce
½ teaspoon garlic salt
¼ teaspoon dill weed
1 cup creamed cottage cheese
1 can (4½ ounces) broken shrimp, rinsed and drained

Place all ingredients except shrimp in blender. Blend on high speed until smooth and creamy, about 2 minutes. Pour into small bowl. Stir in shrimp. Cover; refrigerate at least 1 hour.

About 1½ cups.

VARIATION

■ *Yogurt-Shrimp Dip:* Substitute 1 cup unflavored yogurt for the milk and cottage cheese; stir together all ingredients.

VEGETABLE DIPPERS WITH HOLLANDAISE

1 pound fresh asparagus
¼ pint cherry tomatoes (about 10)
1 or 2 small zucchini
1 can of our hollandaise sauce (1 cup)

Chill asparagus, tomatoes and zucchini. Cut unpared zucchini into strips. Serve sauce as a dip.

4 servings.

Substitution

For asparagus: 1 can (16 ounces) vertical-pack whole green beans, drained.

GUACAMOLE DIP WITH TACOS

Pictured on page 149.

1 can (7¾ ounces) frozen guacamole dip, thawed
¼ teaspoon cumin
4 drops Tabasco
1 package (5½ ounces) frozen cocktail tacos

Blend guacamole dip, cumin and Tabasco. Heat tacos as directed on package; serve with dip.

4 or 5 servings.

DEVILED HAM ROLL

1 can (4½ ounces) deviled ham
3 tablespoons finely chopped pimiento-
    stuffed olives
1 package (3 ounces) cream cheese,
    softened
1 teaspoon prepared mustard

Mix deviled ham and olives; chill until firm. Shape mixture into a roll. Blend cream cheese and mustard; spread over ham roll. Cover; chill at least 2 hours. Serve with crackers.

4 to 6 servings.

SALAMI WEDGES

Pictured on page 149.

Soften 1 package (3 ounces) cream cheese; spread cheese on 9 large salami slices. Stack spread slices and top with a plain slice of salami. Cover and chill. To serve, cut into 12 wedges. If desired, garnish each wedge with a pimiento-stuffed olive, pearl onion or cherry tomato on a wooden pick.

12 appetizers.

VARIATION

■ *Bologna Wedges:* Add 1 tablespoon prepared mustard to the cream cheese; use only 5 slices large bologna.

LIVERWURST TIDBITS

½ pound liverwurst, softened
1 clove garlic, crushed
½ teaspoon basil leaves

Mash liverwurst with fork; mix in garlic and basil. Shape by teaspoonfuls into balls; chill.

36 tidbits.

CRABMEAT SPREAD

1 can (7½ ounces) crabmeat, drained
    and cartilage removed
½ cup mayonnaise or salad dressing
2 tablespoons celery flakes
1 tablespoon lemon juice
2 teaspoons instant minced onion
¼ teaspoon salt
    Dash paprika

Mix all ingredients. Cover; refrigerate at least 2 hours. Serve with crackers.

1½ cups.

Substitution

For instant onion: 2 tablespoons minced onion.

CHEESEY-O'S

⅓ cup butter or margarine
⅓ cup grated Parmesan cheese
5 cups Cheerios

Heat oven to 300°. In oven, melt butter in baking pan, 13×9×2 inches. Stir in cheese. Mix in Cheerios. Bake 10 minutes.

5 cups.

PARMESAN SNACKS

2 tablespoons butter or margarine
½ teaspoon onion salt
½ teaspoon dry mustard
4 cups Kix
2 tablespoons grated Parmesan cheese

Heat oven to 300°. In oven, melt butter in baking pan, 13×9×2 inches. Stir in onion salt and mustard. Gently mix in Kix until butter is absorbed. Sprinkle with cheese. Bake 10 minutes. Stir; bake 10 minutes longer.

4 cups.

PLANNING YOUR MEALS—

When you stop to think about it, every meal you serve says a good deal about you. It reflects your cooking know-how, of course. It also shows off your ability to manage money, your knowledge of nutrition, your imagination, your own good taste and that very special feeling you have for your family. To make sure that reflection is a pretty picture, take this little refresher course.

PLANNING AHEAD

...or how to coordinate three meals a day with ease and expertise. The first thing to do is organize, your thoughts and your menus.

Begin with the Basic Four. You're concerned about your family's health, of course; so safeguard it. Get the Basic Four Food Groups down pat, and plan your meals around them. Here's what you need, every day, for your full share of good nutrition.

Meats: 2 or more servings
   (This group includes poultry, fish, eggs, dried beans or peas and peanut butter.)

Vegetables and Fruits: 4 or more servings
   (Plan on serving one dark green or yellow vegetable every other day, one citrus fruit each day.)

Milk: 2 or more cups for adults;
   3 or more for children and teenagers.
   (This group also includes cheese and ice cream.)

Breads and Cereals: 4 or more servings
   (Make sure they're whole-grain, enriched, restored or fortified.)

Note: Don't forget fats, sweets and extra servings—they provide additional food energy and other food values.

You can be flexible though. For example, those two servings of meat per day can be scheduled any way you like. If your family goes for hamburgers at breakfast—why not? If they won't drink fruit juice in the morning but they will buy it as a dinner appetizer—then switch. What matters most is that they get their quota of the Basic Four Foods each and every day.

Think Through the Menus. Plan them by the day or by the week, whichever is easier. Either way, try putting things down on paper. Then you can see at a glance how breakfast, lunch, dinner and in-between snacks balance out.

If you start your thinking with the main-meal meat, the high-powered protein food, the rest of the plan will fall right into line. Besides, you'll know better where you stand with the budget. And stop and think. Can you double up on the meat and plan for a repeat performance?

Then consider your side-dish strategy. Round out the meal with a vitamin-rich salad and/or colorful vegetables. Think about potatoes, noodles, homey breads. And keep things pretty—mix colors, contrast textures, vary shapes and sizes.

Give the same careful attention to your other meals. When it comes to breakfast, plan to do something different. For lunches that travel, be sure to tuck in some sweets—that's one way you can try to control the amounts. For snacktime, push the fruit and vegetable munches.

Point of emphasis: variety is the secret of success in the care and feeding of a family. Keep an eye out for the latest convenience foods. Use our recipes and suggestions to introduce new ideas, but experiment on your own, too.

Now take a look at the total picture. Did you get in enough meat? Enough milk? Do all the servings add up according to the Basic Four Food Groups? Good planning! Easy, too.

EXERCISING ECONOMY

... or how to stretch your minutes *and* your food dollars.

☐ Keep a running shopping list. Jot down items as you run low, or as they come to mind. When you're tempted to buy on impulse, ask yourself: "Do I really need it? Will my family eat it?" Remember, food that doesn't get eaten is money *and* nutrition down the drain.

THE GOOD AND EASY WAY

☐ Check the food pages in your newspaper and shop for bargains. But if the bargain takes you across town, be aware that it costs you money to get there. On days when you plan to stock the freezer, it may be well worth the trip. Other days, convenience may count more.

☐ Follow a shopping route, in the order of your menu plot. Buy meat first, depending on the day's best buy. Then match up vegetables and salad items. Move on to desserts and snacks. See how well-plotted shopping aids well-balanced eating.

☐ Brush up on your arithmetic. Check out package sizes and the cost-per-serving; buy the one that's best for your needs—small, regular, even extra large. This is true for meat, too. The lower-priced bone-in cut may well end up costing more than the seemingly higher-priced boneless cut, which allows an extra serving.

☐ Follow the seasons for fruits and vegetables. You can tell when they're in season by the lower prices and the plentiful supply.

☐ Read and heed package directions. The manufacturers of convenience foods have tested their products exhaustively; they *know* which procedures will yield the best results. Look for new recipe ideas on the packages, too.

☐ Remember that time is money, and convenience foods may well save you both.

SERVING WITH STYLE

. . . or how to set the stage to double the pleasure of family meals.

Revamp the Routine. Everybody likes change—even in serving patterns. Sometimes serve from the kitchen, other times go family style. Or give Dad the honors with the head-of-the-table treatment. Buffet service lets youngsters learn to serve themselves—and it gives them a good excuse for not sitting still.

And here's a cagey way to make sure hot foods get eaten while they're still hot. Call the gang together for a just-before-dinner appetizer. Something simple will do—like tomato juice with carrot and celery sticks, or hot bouillon with crisp crackers.

Be Dashing with Dishes. Mix and match colors and textures. Red pottery plates with white china cups and saucers are fun. Match up one shade of green dishes with another. Or set out plates in a rainbow of colors. Soups and cereals can be served in mugs as well as bowls. Fruits and puddings look elegant in wine glasses.

Try a New Cut of Cloth. Switch from place mats to trays to a table runner to a conventional cloth in a gay color or splashy print. Think about a roll of gift-wrap paper, the narrow size, for slashing off a special-treat runner. Or use contact fabric for cutting out place mats in a pattern. Brighten the scene with colorful napkins—those great big paper ones as well as the fabrics.

Show Off with Work-savers. Serve from attractive triple-treat casseroles that go right from freezer to oven to table. Let everyone share in the cooking with do-it-at-the-table helpers such as electric skillets, chafing dishes and fondue pots. And remember those backstage aids that can mean so much to your good and easy plans: electric blenders, knives and can openers; nonstick finishes on anything and everything. Indeed, good equipment is a good investment.

Spruce Up with a Centerpiece. Pile shiny red apples in a pretty bowl. Pop limes into an apothecary jar. Tuck a bunch of parsley in a demitasse cup, or tiny cherry tomatoes in a straw basket. And for goodness' sake, show off that prized piece of kindergarten art right alongside.

Now you take it from here. Use these ideas as starters, then dream up new ones of your own. You'll find dozens of ways to make do with what you have on hand and come up with imaginative, and very personal, treats for the family table. And that's what we call adding a dash of love to good and easy cooking.

FACTS ABOUT FREEZING—

	MEATS AND POULTRY	FISH AND SEAFOOD	STEWS, SAUCES AND CREAMED DISHES	EGGS (UNCOOKED)
MAXIMUM STORAGE TIME	Red Meat: 4 months Corned Beef, Sausage: 2 weeks Poultry and Game: 2-3 months	3-4 months	3-4 months	9 months
FREEZING TIPS	Uncooked: Trim off excess fat (to conserve space, remove bones). Do not salt before wrapping. Cooked: Leftover roasts and Swiss steak freeze satisfactorily for a short time.	Clean; wash, drain and wrap. For small fish, cover with water in leakproof container.	Do not overcook; cool quickly. (Fats tend to separate but will usually recombine.) Leave headspace in freezer container.	Stir eggs and egg yolk with a fork. Add 1 tablespoon sugar or corn syrup or 1/2 teaspoon salt per cup before freezing. For yolks, add 2 times the salt or sweetener recommended for whole eggs.
THAWING AND REHEATING TIPS	Thaw wrapped uncooked or cooked meats in refrigerator. Uncooked meats may stand at room temperature *just* until defrosted and then be cooked immediately.	Thaw under running cold water in original wrap. Cook while still chilled. If only partially thawed, cook a little longer at a lower temperature.	Partially thaw at room temperature to prevent scorching. Heat in double boiler 30 to 40 minutes. Add liquid if necessary; keep stirring to a minimum.	Thaw in refrigerator. Or let stand at room temperature *just* until defrosted and then use immediately.
NOTES	Freeze as soon as possible. Just about all meats freeze well. Do not freeze picnic hams, canned hams or other canned meats. Do not freeze fried foods.	Cooked shrimp can be frozen; shrimp cocktail and shrimp creole can also be frozen but no longer than 6 weeks.	Cool quickly by partially submerging the saucepan in large pan of ice and water. Potatoes do not freeze well; add when thawing. Keep spice level low.	Whites need no additions—put through a sieve for uniform texture.

If you're interested in streamlining your cooking and serving chores without short-cutting flavor and variety, learn to use your freezer—or the freezer compartment of your refrigerator—to its full capacity. Cooking for the freezer is simply a matter of habit, and a very good habit at that. It can save you time. It can save you money. It can save you wear and tear. And these days, that's a lot of savings.

We've given you some specific freezing recommendations in the chart above, but here are some general guidelines for your freezer "savings bank":

1. Start with top-quality foods. Freezing will never make them any fresher or better than they were to begin with.

2. Remember that superior packaging and wrapping materials go a long way toward insuring a top-drawer product. Best materials include heavy-duty aluminum foil, heavy-weight plastic wrap and freezer bags or containers. These are all good because freezer wraps and containers should be airtight, moisture- and vapor-proof. They should also be convenient to use and occupy as little space as possible.

3. Wrap food securely in an airtight package—unless recipe directions indicate otherwise.

..HE GOOD AND EASY WAY

RICE, BAKED BEANS AND PASTA DISHES	BREADS	CAKES AND CUPCAKES	COOKIES	PIE AND PASTRY
3 months	Quick Breads (biscuits, muffins, nut breads, waffles): 2-3 months Yeast Breads: 9 months	2-3 months	9-12 months	Baked Shells: 4 months Baked Pies: 4-6 months Unbaked Pies: 2-3 months Chiffon Pies: 1 month
Cook only partially; cool quickly. Freeze in casserole or in freezer container.	Bake before freezing. (Unbaked dough and batters lose some rising capacity.) Stack waffles but separate with wrap.	Bake and cool cakes before wrapping. Confectioners' sugar and fudge frostings freeze best. Boiled are difficult to store—freeze before wrapping. Or insert wooden picks in frosting to prevent wrapping from touching.	Arrange baked cookies in a sturdy box lined with plastic wrap or aluminum foil. Separate each layer with wrap or foil; seal. Package dough for drop cookies in an airtight container, aluminum foil or plastic wrap.	Baked Pies: Cool quickly; freeze, then wrap. Do not freeze custard, cream or meringue-topped pies.
Heat frozen food in covered saucepan (with small amount of butter in bottom) over medium heat. Or place frozen casserole in 350° oven until center is bubbly, about 45 minutes. (Add small amount of liquid if food seems dry.)	Quick Breads: Thaw in wrap at room temperature or warm in 325 to 350° oven.\n\nYeast Breads: Thaw in wrap at room temperature. Or heat in 350° oven 20 to 25 minutes.	Thaw frosted cakes, loosely covered, in the refrigerator. Thaw unfrosted cakes in original wrap at room temperature 2 to 3 hours. Or place in 250 to 300° oven a short time, but watch closely.	Thaw baked cookies at room temperature for about 10 minutes. Thaw cookie dough until just soft enough to spoon or slice onto baking sheet.	Baked Pies: Thaw unwrapped at room temperature 2 to 4 hours. Or unwrap and let stand a short time, then place on lower shelf in 350° oven; heat just until warm. If using lightweight aluminum pie pans, place on baking sheet.
Casseroles of this type vary considerably and some loss of flavor may occur.	Heat frozen waffles in toaster. Overwrap bakery bread if it is to be stored longer than 3 months. A 1-pound loaf of bread thaws in about 3 hours.	Some frostings and fillings do not freeze well. The frostings change texture; fillings make the cake soggy.	Both cookie dough and baked cookies can be frozen.	Best to freeze baked pies—the bottom crust of an unbaked pie may absorb juices from filling and become soggy.

4. Before freezing cooked food, cool quickly.

5. Don't refreeze thawed foods.

6. Freeze in family-size packages or individual portions.

7. Clearly label each package (freezer tape and magic marker are good for this) with the contents, number of servings and expiration date. Rotate packages so the nearest-to-expiration-date foods are near the front.

8. Store food at 0° or lower (unless directions specify otherwise); the temperature will affect the quality of the food. In fact, it's a good idea to keep a freezer thermometer in the compartment to be sure the temperature's low enough.

Following are some estimated maximum storage times for other freezer-ready foods:

Food	Storage Time
Butter	6 months
Canapés	1 month
Candies	1 year
Cheese (small amounts)	6 months
Ice Cream	3 weeks
Vegetables	1 year

CARVING—THE GOOD AND EASY WAY

Beef Standing Rib Roast

■ Start with large side down. (If necessary, remove wedge-shaped slice from large end so roast will stand firmly.)

■ Insert fork firmly below first rib; cut horizontal slices from the outside of roast toward the rib side.

■ Cut several thin slices or one or two thick slices, if you prefer. Then cut down along inner side of rib bone. (Cut as close to the bone as possible.) As each slice is released, slide knife under it and lift to plate.

Whole Ham

■ Start with the fat side up and shank facing right; cut a few slices from the thin side. (The thin side will face carver if ham is a left leg and away from carver if ham is a right leg.)

■ Turn ham to rest on cut side, where slices were removed. Make vertical slices down to bone. Then run knife horizontally along bone to release slices.

■ Or make only the first and last vertical slice and run knife along bone to release the section intact; then slice.

Beef Blade Pot-roast

■ Cut between muscles and around bones (bones are easily removed). Remove one section of pot-roast at a time.

■ Turn section so grain runs parallel to platter; carve across the grain. (Slices should be about 1/4 inch thick.)

Leg of Lamb

■ With shank bone to carver's right, cut a few length-wise slices from thin side.

■ Turn to rest on cut side. Make slices down to bone.

■ Cut horizontally along bone to release slices (as for a whole ham, see above).

Porterhouse Steak

■ Start with bone at carver's right. Cut closely around bone and remove.

■ Carve 1-inch-wide slices across the full width of steak. Carve thick steaks on the diagonal.

Turkey or Chicken

■ Start with legs at carver's right. Gently pull leg away from body and cut through joint between leg and body. Remove leg to another platter or board. Cut through leg between drumstick and thigh; slice meat parallel to the bone.

■ Make a deep horizontal cut into breast, just above wing. Insert fork firmly in top of breast; starting halfway up breast, carve thin slices down to the cut, working upward.

Pork Loin Roast

■ First remove backbone by cutting between rib ends and backbone.

■ With rib side toward carver, cut slices on each side of rib bones. (Every other slice will have a bone.)